Northern
Windows

For Mary Lappin

Maybe, if I look back, I shall find that my life
is not just mine, that it mirrors the lives of the
others — or shall I say the Life of the Other?
Louis MacNeice

The past is not disposed of, as we might have
expected; it is, in a very special way, still
there and still alive. It has entered into
the Now; so that it never becomes old,
however thickly the grass grows over it.
Karl Heim

Northern Windows

An anthology of Ulster autobiography

edited by
Frank Ormsby

THE
BLACKSTAFF
PRESS
BELFAST AND WOLFEBORO, NEW HAMPSHIRE

First published in 1987 by
The Blackstaff Press
3 Galway Park, Dundonald, Belfast BT16 0AN, Northern Ireland
and
27 South Main Street, Wolfeboro, New Hampshire 03894 USA
with the assistance of
The Arts Council of Northern Ireland

Printed in Northern Ireland by
The Universities Press Limited

British Library Cataloguing in Publication Data
Northern windows: an anthology of Ulster
autobiography.
1. Northern Ireland — Biography
I. Ormsby, Frank
920'.0416   CT803

Library of Congress Cataloging-in-Publication Data
Northern windows.
Bibliography: p.
1. English prose literature—Irish authors.
2. Autobiographies. 3. Ulster (Northern Ireland and
Ireland)—Biography. 4. Authors, Irish—Ulster
(Northern Ireland and Ireland)—Biography. 5. Ulster
(Northern Ireland and Ireland)—Intellectual life.
6. Ulster (Northern Ireland and Ireland)—Social life
and customs. I. Ormsby, Frank, 1947–
PR8874.A96N67   1987   820'.9'9416   87–5201

ISBN 0 85640 375 X

CONTENTS

FOREWORD

The first autobiography I can recall reading was *The Autobiography of a Super-tramp* by W.H. Davies, an account of life among the doss-houses and down-and-outs of England and America. It was peopled with characters – Wee Shorty, New Haven Baldy, Philadelphia Slim – at once exotic and menacing and though we had all seen drunkenness and men fighting and tramps on the country roads, it portrayed a world that seemed far removed from the Co. Fermanagh we knew. Clearly, autobiography was written by people whose lives were full of incident and who lived elsewhere. Robert Harbinson had not then published *Song of Erne*, which opened in Ballinamallard, a few miles up the road; Patrick Shea had not recorded, in *Voices and the Sound of Drums*, his time as a civil servant in Enniskillen; we had not heard of Shan F. Bullock's *After Sixty Years*, set near Newtownbutler; and we certainly did not regard our essays on how we had spent the Christmas holidays or on the most exciting day of our lives as embryonic autobiography.

A few years ago, while writing poems about American GIs in Ulster during World War II and about small ethnic groups in Belfast, such as the Jewish, Italian and Chinese communities, my sense of the 'local' and its ramifications was renewed to the extent that I began thinking again about public and private, familiar and unfamiliar, individual and communal experience as reflected in Ulster autobiography. I found that much of what I had read since my schooldays was still vividly present in memory and imagination. Again I was savouring William Carleton's unexceptionably vain, engagingly ingenuous sense of himself: 'I remember well that when nineteen years of age, my appearance in fair or market caused crowds to follow the young fellow who stood unrivalled at every athletic sport which could be named.' Again I was remembering Shan F. Bullock's account of the almost self-contained English colony on the Earl of Erne's estate, and how his response to the 'barefooted, ragged Catholic, with his hair through his cap' and to Mary Roche with her raven black hair and Rose Healy with her freckles was qualified by an honest recognition that he was being somewhat sentimental. And there too was Patrick Kavanagh submitting his early verses to a local newspaper, or buying the *Irish Statesman* on his way to the market in Dundalk:

> 'Any stir on the paper?' a fellow asked me.
> 'Plenty,' I replied. 'Gertrude Stein is after writing a new book.'

It was the recollection of such moments that prompted this anthology.

Reading the other autobiographies represented here, I have often had a feeling akin to standing at a window looking in: at the rectory worlds of Louis MacNeice and George Buchanan, for example, or at Protestant working-class life as portrayed by Robert Harbinson. I did not belong in these worlds, but would suddenly find myself inside them in stirring, poignant, liberating ways – as when Harbinson writes about the death of his father or when MacNeice and Buchanan register public events on the periphery of their childhood, and also in the moments when all these writers perceive themselves as apart from their background or are themselves curious or even hostile observers of what is beyond their immediate experience.

At other times, of course, the feeling was of being inside a familiar house, cheerfully at home or, sensing what was claustrophobic and potentially crippling there, wanting out and wondering to what extent one ever succeeds in escaping. I think of Tomás Ó Canainn's hilarious portrait of himself (in modest third-person disguise) as an altar boy mangling the Latin responses in the Mass, Bernadette Devlin's account of some of her formative influences and Polly Devlin's intense re-creation of what she found nourishing and blighting in the ritual and symbolism of the Catholic church. Indeed, one of the challenges of reading Ulster autobiography, for Ulster readers especially, is that it can force them to examine the range of attitudes they bring to, and take away from, particular accounts.

This selection is presented in the conviction that a region (especially one in which the urge to stereotype and polarise is so strong) should have a sense of its plurality, that a body of autobiography is one significant expression of such plurality, that varieties of human experience are always interesting and an awareness of them at least potentially illuminating. The writers included here seem to me both to preserve the singular nature of the familiar as experienced by different people and to provide access to the unfamiliar. Their work is not of the kind 'thickly studded with capital I's' that made the American critic Irwin S. Cobb think of 'a picket-fence around a vacant lot'; vigorous, restrained, passionate, humorous, self-effacing, they speak without arrogance as themselves.

The publication dates given at the end of each extract and in the Bibliography are those of the editions used in the anthology.

Frank Ormsby, 1987

WILLIAM CARLETON
1794–1869

COUNTY TYRONE, EARLY NINETEENTH CENTURY

It is unnecessary to say that for some years after the Rebellion of
'98 a bitter political resentment subsisted between Protestants
and Catholics. Well do I remember it. The party fights at that time
were frequent and in many instances fatal. This, indeed, was the
period which I selected for my 'Party Fight and Funeral'. In this
instance the political rancour became dramatic. The plays of *The
Siege of Londonderry*, and *The Battle of Aughrim* were acted
in barns and waste houses night after night, and were attended by
multitudes, both Catholic and Protestant. *The Battle of Aughrim*, however, was the favourite, and the acting play. I heard that
The Siege of Londonderry had been also acted, but I never saw
it. This feeling of political enthusiasm directed my attention to the
plays, which in their printed shape were schoolbooks at the time.
In fact I had *The Battle of Aughrim* off by heart, from beginning
to ending. This came to be known, and the consequence was that,
though not more than ten years of age, I became stage director and
prompter both to the Catholic and Protestant amateurs. In the
mornings and in the evenings such of them – and there were not a
few on both sides – as could not read, spent hours with me in
attempting to make themselves perfect in their parts. It is
astonishing, however, what force and impetus such an enthusiastic desire to learn and recollect bestows upon the memory. I
had here an opportunity of witnessing this, for the quickness and
accuracy with which they prepared themselves was astonishing.

 The play selected for action on this occasion was, of course,
The Battle of Aughrim, and the theatre the. . . barn belonging to
Jack Stuart. . . The crowds that flocked to it, both Catholics and
Protestants, would, if admitted, have overcrowded the largest

theatre in Europe. One element of their great curiosity, independently of the political feeling, was simply the novelty of seeing a play. On the right-hand side of the lofted floor which constituted the barn, and under which. . . were the cowhouse and stable, was a range of chairs and forms for the audience to sit upon; on the left was a range of sacks filled with barley, the heaviest grain that grows; on these the other portion of the spectators were placed. It was summer, and the heat was suffocating. I was on the left side, standing behind those who sat upon the sacks, and with my feet upon them. In order to keep myself at ease and steady, I held by a wattle in the roof above me, and in that position enjoyed the play. When it had reached the scene in which the ghost makes its appearance, or rather a little before it, I felt something like a descent of that part of the floor on which the sacks had been stretched. In about a quarter of a minute there was another descent of the sacks, and I shouted out, 'The floor is going to fall.' Such, however, was the attention of the audience, that my warning had no effect. The ghost came forward, when a tremendous crash took place, and the last thing I saw was his heels in the air, as he and that portion of the audience with whom I stood, sacks and all, went down together. Fortunately, there was a large beam which ran longitudinally through the barn – by which I mean from end to end. The barn was an old one, and its timbers, as was found afterwards, quite decayed with age. The weight of the sacks, and the crowded audience on the left-hand side, was more than the rotten rafters could bear, and the consequence was that one half the barn floor with its weighty burthen was precipitated into the cowhouse and stable. I dropped down upon those who fell, and scrambled over their heads towards those who were on the safe side, by whom I was pulled up without having received any injury. . .

These senseless exhibitions inflamed political feeling very much. In the town of Augher, this stupid play was acted by Catholics and Protestants, each party of course sustaining their own principles. The consequence was, that when they came to the conflict with which the play is made to close, armed as they were on both sides with real swords, political and religious resentment could not be restrained, and they would have hacked each other's souls out had not the audience interfered and prevented them. As it was, some of them were severely if not dangerously wounded.

During the period of which I now write, the country was in a state sufficient, in the mind of every liberal and thinking man, to fling back disgrace and infamy upon the successive administrations which permitted it. This was the period of Protestant, or rather of Orange, ascendancy. There were at that time regular corps of yeomen, who were drilled and exercised on the usual stated occasions. There were also corps of cavalry who were subjected to the same discipline. Now all this was right and proper, and I remember when a review day was looked forward to as we used to look for Christmas or Easter. On those occasions there were thousands of spectators, and it would have been well if matters had ended there. Every yeoman with his red coat on was an Orangeman. Every cavalryman mounted upon his own horse and dressed in blue was an Orangeman; and to do both foot and cavalry justice, I do not think that a finer body of men could be found in Europe. Roman Catholics were not admitted into either service. I think I may say that I knew almost every yeoman in the parish, but I never knew of a Roman Catholic to be admitted into either force, with one exception – his name was William Kelly, a cousin of my own.

Merciful God! In what a frightful condition was the country at that time. I speak now of the north of Ireland. It was then, indeed, the seat of Orange ascendancy and irresponsible power. To find a justice of the peace *not* an Orangeman would have been an impossibility. The grand jury room was little less than an Orange lodge. There was then no law *against* an Orangeman, and no law *for* a Papist. I am now writing not only that which is well known to be historical truth, but that which I have witnessed with my own eyes.

These yeomen were in the habit – especially when primed with whiskey, or on their way from an Orange lodge – of putting on their uniform, getting their guns and bayonets, and going out at night to pay domiciliary visits to Catholic families under the pretence of searching for firearms; and it is painful to reflect upon, or even to recollect, the violence and outrage with which these illegal excursions were conducted. Take an instance.

I have mentioned Sam Nelson as one of Pat Frayne's scholars and of course the schoolfellow of myself and my brother; and I have said, I think, that his father's house was next to ours – in fact it was not ten yards from us; in truth we were in daily intercourse of the most neighbourly and friendly character. We were perpetually in each other's houses, lending and borrowing, and discharging all those duties towards each other which constitute friendly neighbouring. Sam Nelson was what is termed a humorous or droll kind of good-natured 'slob', and evidently fond of me and my brother. On one occasion he made us a present of a little tin gun or cannon about four or five inches in length, of which we were naturally very proud. Before I proceed farther in this reminiscence I think it necessary to say that my father was one of the quietest and most highly respected men in the parish, considering his position in life. Neither he nor any of his family were ever known to give utterance to an offensive word. They took no part whatsoever in politics, neither did they ever engage in those senseless party or faction fights which were so disgraceful to the country, or give expression to any political opinion that could be construed into offence. Having made these observations, I now proceed with my reminiscence.

One night, about two or three o'clock, in the middle of winter, a violent bellowing took place at our door, and loud voices were heard outside. My father got up, alarmed, and asked who was there.

'Open the door, you rebellious old dog, or we will smash it in.'

'Give me time to get on my clothes,' replied my father.

'Not a minute, you old rebel; you want to hide your arms – open or we smash the door,' and the door was struck violently with the butts of guns. My father, having hurried on his small clothes and lit a candle, opened the door, when in an instant the house was filled with armed yeomen in their uniform.

'Come, you traitorous old scoundrel, deliver up your d—d rebelly gun.'

4

'My good friends,' replied my father, 'I have no gun.'

'It's a lie, you rebel, it's well known you have a gun. Produce it, or I put the contents of this through you.' And as he spoke the man cocked and deliberately aimed the gun at my father. (I forgot to state that the men appeared with screwed bayonets.) When my mother saw my father covered by the ruffian's gun, she placed herself, with a shawl about her, between them, and corroborated what my father said, that we had no gun. She was called a liar; it was notorious we had a gun. In the meantime, some others of them began to institute a search. Two of them went into my sister's bedroom, a third man holding the candle.

'Who is this?' said one scoundrel.

'It's my daughter,' replied my mother, trembling and in tears.

'Well,' he returned, 'let her get up until we have a look at her; it's likely she has the gun in the bed; at all events we'll rouse her a bit –' and as he spoke, he put the point of the bayonet to her side, which he pressed until she screamed with pain. At this moment his companion pulled him back with something of indignant violence, exclaiming:

'D—n your soul, you cowardly scoundrel, why do you do that?'

At this moment my mother, with the ready collection and presence of mind of her sex, exclaimed:

'I think it likely that all this trouble has come from the little tin gun that Sam Nelson gave the children – here it is,' she proceeded, 'here is the only gun that ever was under this roof. If it's treason to keep *that*, we are rebels' – and as she spoke she handed them the gun. They looked at it, and after some ruffianly grumbling they retired. My sister was slightly wounded in the side. My readers will be surprised to learn that one of Sam Nelson's brothers was among this scoundrelly gang, and never once interfered on our behalf. No man knew better than he did that my father had no gun. No man knew better than he that this midnight and drunken visit was a mere pretence, deliberately founded upon the history of the tin gun which his brother Sam had given to me and my brother John. My readers may form an opinion of the state of society, when they hear that there was not an individual present that night in this gross and lawless outrage with whom we were not acquainted, nor a man among them who did not know every one of us intimately.

Such was the outrageous and licentious conduct of the Orangemen of that day, and of many a day long before and afterwards. As a public writer, guided by a sense of truth and justice, I could not allow such a system as that which Orangeism then was to remain without exposure, and I did not. It is to that midnight visit that they owe *Valentine McClutchy*. Little they dreamt that there was a boy present, not more than ten years of age, who would live to punish them with a terrible but truthful retaliation. . .

The time was now approaching. . . when I was to feel the exquisite charm of 'first love' in all its power. The 'festivals' were then expected and enjoyed with spirit and zest which have long passed away. Preparations were then made for Christmas and Easter of which we now know little or nothing. Easter was within ten days of us, and I felt the more anxious for its arrival because I had got a full suit of new clothes, by far the most respectable I had ever worn. I felt that I was quite a young gentleman; and as I was then fifteen years of age, I began to have vague notions of something that I did not well understand. In the 'Forth', which was our place of worship, I felt somehow exceedingly anxious to show myself off on the next Sunday, which was Easter Day. The 'Forth'. . . was a circular green about one hundred yards in diameter. It was surrounded by a grassy ditch, apparently as ancient as the 'Forth' itself. On this ditch were verdant seats; and upon these seats, to the right hand as you turned up towards the altar, sat the young men, opposite to whom on the other sat the young women. They were thus separated, and never, under any circumstances, joined or spoke to each other until after they had left the 'Forth'. Notwithstanding this devotional sense of decorum, I am bound to say that the eyes on each side were not idle, and that many a long and loving look passed between the youngsters of both sexes.

At length, the Easter Sunday came, and a glorious one it was. I went abroad in my new suit for the first time in public, and certainly, if the spectators did not entertain a favourable opinion of my whole appearance, I know one who did. Until the priest came, the men chatted to each other, and so did the women; but the moment he entered the 'Forth', all the congregation assumed the best places they could, and dropped on their knees, prepared to join the devotions of the day.

There was at that time a vocal choir of young men and women in the parish, who, in virtue of their office, were obliged to kneel around the altar, where they sang some very beautiful music. Among the females was one tall, elegant, and lady-like girl, whose voice was perfectly entrancing. Her name was Anne Duffy, daughter of George Duffy, the miller of Augher Mill. She knelt that Sunday, and, in fact, every Sunday, on the left-hand side of the priest, next the altar; while I, more by accident than anything else, placed myself in the same position on the other side, so that we were right opposite to each other. Whether it was the opportunity of having her before me, or her beauty, I cannot decide – probably it was both together – but I said no prayers that day. My eyes were never off her – they were riveted on her. I felt a new sensation, one of the most novel and overwhelming delight. After Mass I followed her as far as the cross-roads at Ned McKeown's. Ned's was a corner house, with two doors of entrance – one to the kitchen, and the other into a small grocery shop, kept by a man named Billy Fulton. It was a great convenience to the neighbourhood, especially to those who lived in the mountain districts, or what was termed the 'Mountain Bar'. Before Mass, a great number of both sexes, but principally men, lingered about these cross-roads, engaged in chat upon the usual topics of the day: the most important, and that in which they felt the deepest interest, was the progress of the Peninsular War. Bonaparte was their favourite, and their hopes were not only that he would subdue England, but ultimately become monarch of Ireland. From what source they derived the incredible variety of personal anecdotes respecting him it is impossible to conjecture. One of the most remarkable, and which was narrated and heard with the most sincere belief in its truth was the fact of his being invulnerable. It mattered nothing whether he went into the thickest part of the battle or not, the bullets hopped harmlessly off him like hailstones from a window.

Now Anne Duffy's father was a great politician, and sometimes spent half an hour at the cross-roads, both before and after Mass, and Anne herself occasionally stopped a short time there, but very rarely. At all events I saw her there again, and our looks met. She appeared to be amused by my attention, which she seemed to receive agreeably, and with pleasure. Well, I went home a changed man – of fifteen years of age – wrapped up from the world and all external nature; the general powers of my mind concentrated into one thought, and fixed upon one image, Anne Duffy.

There has been much controversy upon the subject of love at first sight. I, however, am a proof of its truth. The appearance of the sun in the firmament is not more true. I went home, elated, entranced – like a man who had discovered a rich but hidden treasure. My existence became important. I had an interest in life – I was no longer a cipher. I had something to live for. I felt myself a portion of society and the world. How I spent the remainder of the day I scarcely remember, especially as to assocation with my companions on this festive occasion. All I know is, that Anne Duffy was never for a single moment out of my head, and when I was asleep that night she appeared as distinctly before me as she did during the day; but with this difference, that her beauty was more exquisitely angelic and ideal, and seemed to bear a diviner stamp.

For nearly five years after this my passion for her increased with my age, although I thought when I first fell in love with her that nothing could have added a deeper power to it. For upwards of four years I knelt opposite her at the altar; for upwards of four years my eyes were never off her, and for upwards of four years I never once, while at Mass, offered up a single prayer to heaven.

As I grew up, she seemed to feel a deeper interest in me. The language of her eyes could not be misunderstood. Through the medium of that language, I felt that our hearts were intimately acquainted, precisely as if they had held many a loving and ecstatic communion. During the period of this extraordinary passion, I indulged in solitude a thousand times in order to brood over the image of her whom I loved. On returning home from Mass of a summer Sunday, I uniformly withdrew to the bottom of the glen behind our house and there, surrendered myself to the entrancing influence of what I felt. There in the solitude of that glen I felt a charm added to my existence which cannot be described. I knew – I felt – that she loved me. This habit of mine was so well known by my family that, when dinner was ready and they found that I was absent, they knew perfectly well where to call for me. After the first six months I could not rest satisfied with parting from her at the 'Forth'; so, for three years and a half, I walked after her, and never turned back until I left her at the town of Augher, at the turn which led by a side street to her father's mill; and this during the severity of winter and the heat of summer.

Now this I am describing was my silent – my inner life; but the reader is not to imagine that it prevented me from entering into the sports and diversions of the day. I devoted myself to athletic exercises until I was without a rival – until, in fact, I had a local fame which spread far beyond the limits of my native parish. I was resolved to make myself talked of – to be distinguished by my excellence in these feats – and the ambition which I then felt owed its origin to my love for Anne Duffy. I remember well that when nineteen years of age, my appearance in fair or market caused crowds to follow the young fellow who stood unrivalled at every athletic sport which could be named. This fact is well known and remembered by some of the oldest inhabitants of my native parish to the present day.

The reader will consider it strange that during this long period of devoted and enthusiastic attachment, I never spoke to Anne or declared my passion. It is, however, a fact, that during the period I allude to, a single syllable of spoken language never passed between us. This, however, is easily accounted for. My father died in the early course of my passion, and the family began to feel with some bitterness the consequences of decline. Had I spoken to Anne, and gained her consent to marry me, I had no means of supporting her, and I could not bear the terrible idea of bringing her to distress and poverty, both of which she must have endured had she become my wife.

I was sitting before our kitchen fire one evening (in autumn, I think), thinking of her as usual, when my eldest brother came in, and after having taken a seat, communicated the following intelligence:

'Did you hear the news?' said he.

'No,' replied my mother, 'what is it?'

'Why, that the miller's daughter,' (by this appellation she was generally known, and not by her Christian name), '. . .was married this morning to M.M., of Ballyscally.'

The sensation I felt was as if something had paralysed my brain or my heart. I was instantly seized with a violent dizziness, and an utter prostration of bodily strength; an indescribable confusion seized upon me – thought for a moment abandoned me – and I laboured under the impression that some terrible calamity had befallen me. So long as she remained unmarried, I still entertained a vague and almost hopeless hope that some event might occur which, by one of the extraordinary turnings of life, might put it in our power to marry. Even this faint hope was gone – my doom was irrevocably sealed, and the drapery of death hung between her and me. I rose from my chair with difficulty – I staggered out, and went into the barn, where I wept bitterly. My life had now lost its charm, and nothing but a cold cheerless gloom lay upon it and my hopes. During three or four months this miserable state of feeling lasted. I was, however, in the heyday of youth – just in that period of existence when sorrow seldom lasts long. The sensation gradually wore away, and after a lengthened interval I recovered my usual spirits.

A short but interesting anecdote will now close this extraordinary history of my first love. I think it was in the year 1847 that I resolved to pay a visit to my native place. When I left it, many years before, it was with a fixed resolution never to write a letter home, or to return to my friends, unless I had achieved some distinction which might reflect honour upon my name. Fortunately I was able to accomplish this strange determination; and what is, after all, not strange, I do assure my readers that Anne Duffy, though the wife of another, was a strong stimulus to my pursuit of fame, and in the early period of my literary life a powerful element in my ambition. She would hear of the distinction I had acquired, she would probably even read of the honourable position I had reached, by universal consent, in the literature of my country.

On paying this visit to the City of the Stone of Gold, I went first to Lisburn, where my friend John Birney, the solicitor, resided. With him I stayed for a few days, when we started for Clogher, his native town; and it was rather singular that the very inn we stopped at had been during my boyhood the residence of his father, who was a most respectable magistrate, and a man deservedly loved by the people of all creeds and classes. It was to John Birney that I dedicated the first series of my *Traits and Stories of the Irish Peasantry*. He had a good property about Clogher, and on this occasion, as he was going there to collect his rents, we went together. I stayed at the inn, which had formerly been his father's house, and so did he. One day, after I had been about a week there, I received an invitation to breakfast with a gentleman who lived in a pretty, secluded spot, formerly called 'The Grange', but changed by its present proprietor into 'Ashfield', if I remember correctly. After breakfast, he proposed – or I proposed, I forget which – to take a walk up to what was once Ballyscally, but which was now a scene of perfect desolation. Out of seventy or eighty comfortable cottages the gentleman in question had not left one standing. Every unfortunate tenant had been evicted, driven out, to find a shelter for himself where he could. Ballyscally had, I think, been the property of the See of Clogher, but how it came into this person's possession I know not. Upon second thoughts, it must have been I who proposed the walk in that direction, and for this reason: there was but one house left standing in Ballyscally – certainly the best that ever was in the town – but that house, as I knew for many a long year, was the residence of the husband of Anne Duffy. We went up by Ballyscally, which had consisted of houses scattered over the top and side of an elevated hill, that commanded a distant view of a beautiful country to an extent of not less than fifty miles. The long depression of the land before you to the west and north under the hill constitutes that portion of the county known in ancient Irish history as the 'Valley of the

11

Black Pig'. My companion brought me up to see an obelisk which he was building, on the top of a much higher hill than Ballyscally. It was nearly finished, but we reached the top with some difficulty, and after all saw very little more than we could see from its base. Like many other similar and useless structures it was called 'B—'s Folly'.

As we returned, I proposed that we should pay a visit to *her* husband's house, then, as I said, the only one in all Ballyscally. Up to this moment, she and I had never exchanged a word. What she might have expressed, had she known I was on my way to visit her, I do not know, but, notwithstanding every attempt to keep cool, I felt my heart palpitate as it had not done for years. We shook hands, and had some commonplace conversation, when after a few minutes her husband came in; and as he and I had known each other long before his marriage, we also shook hands as old acquaintances.

After a little I looked at her, and then turning to him, 'Michael,' said I, 'there stands the only woman I ever loved beyond the power of language to express. She had my first affection, and I loved her beyond any woman that ever breathed, and strange to say, until this occasion we never exchanged a syllable.'

'Well,' she replied, 'I can say on my part – and I am not ashamed to say it – that I never loved man as I loved you; but there was one thing clear, that it wasn't our fate ever to become man and wife. Had you married me it's not likely the world would have ever heard of you. As it is, I am very happily married, and lead a happy life with as good and as kind a husband as ever lived.'

Michael laughed, and appeared rather pleased and gratified than otherwise. We then shook hands again, I took my leave, and that was my first and last interview with her whose image made the pleasure of my whole youth for nearly five years.

The Autobiography of William Carleton, 1968

CHARLES McGLINCHEY
1861–1954

Down to my young days there was nothing spoken in this parish at fair or chapel or gathering of any kind but Irish. A lot of the people in my father's time had some English and a few of them could read it. The English language came in greatly in my own time and in the one generation Irish went away like the snow off the ditches. But with the old people it was all Irish you would hear spoken. . .

At the time of the Ordnance Survey in 1835, two of the sappers stopped in our house when they were mapping this part of the parish. My father went chaining with them whenever they would want him. They gave him some sketch of measuring land but he couldn't carry it out for he didn't know the rule of figures that was needed. The sappers were telling him their pay came to half-a-crown a day, and that was thought to be a great pay entirely, for working men at that time were paid 6d. a day, or 10d. for a day in the moss [bog].

One day the sappers were out on the face of Bulaba somewhere about Currachbeag, and they lay down to rest and take a smoke. When they went to look again, their whole kit was stolen, with papers and records of their work and instruments that were valued for £50 that could not be got nearer than Dublin. With the way of travelling that time, it would take three weeks to get them replaced. They came home and told my father. He questioned them if they had seen anyone about the place and they said they noticed a young fellow about the rocks before they sat down. From the description, my father knew it to be a fellow from that part who had a bad name. So my father went out to his home and

13

asked him if he had noticed any men in Currachbeag that day and he said not. Then my father asked if he had seen a kit of tools belonging to them, and from the way he blushed he gave himself away, and my father knew he had him. So my father told him the sappers knew about him and were going to get a warrant for his arrest, but if the fellow handed the kit and papers over to him that he would stand between him and any other bother. The mother then told the lad who had taken them to give them up. So he took my father over to the rock where he had the lot hidden.

When my father came home with the kit, the sappers were delighted because they said the loss of the kit would likely cost them their jobs. They sent for a bottle of whiskey – that cost a shilling at the time – and they had a big drink. It took my father all his time to keep them from getting the young man arrested. He told them he had undertaken there would be no more bother and when they had got the kit to leave him to somebody else. . .

I often heard my father telling about a night some men came to lift a woman from the Glen. Long ago women were often seized like that and taken away to marry some man. There was a mentioned girl named Betty Barr and one night a band of horsemen came for her. She had a sister, Katie, that wasn't so good looking. The men looked in the window and saw Betty cloving lint on a stool in the corner and Katie at the spinning wheel. The men moved in then but the girls happened to change places and they took Katie down the road where they had a horse with saddle and pillion ready for her. They discovered their mistake there and let her go. But they didn't get back for Betty for the Glen was alarmed by that time.

Seizing women that time was called *fuadach* [abduction/rape] by the old people. In my grandfather's time or before it there was a girl from the lower end of this parish seized and taken up about Kinnagoe or Buncrana. One Sunday afterwards her father saddled his horse and went up to see her. The people of the place were away at Mass about the hills somewhere and he found his daughter in the house. She warned him he would be in great danger if

14

they came on him about the place. She made a scone for him called a *toirtín bog* [sponge cake] and hurried him away. They overtook him at the brook in the Glen that divides the two parishes. As soon as he got across and into his own parish, he turned to face them and put his trust in God and the *tearmann* [monastic sanctuary] of Clúan Máine [Clonmany] and fell to them with a cudgel of a stick he had and killed them as they came forward to him. The people that were killed were buried at that spot and it was always called Sruthán na gCorp [the Stream of the Corpses]. Many a time I fished that brook when I was a boy. . .

In my father's early days there was only one shop in the whole parish. It belonged to James Shiels and was the only house in the Cross at the time. The wallsteads are there yet. He was married to a daughter of Neal Roe Doherty. Shiels went to Derry once a week or so with an imitation of a cart with black wheels for whatever groceries would be wanted, soap or sugar, or salt or tea. Before that, up to about 1820 or so, the only commodities coming into the parish were iron and leather. Big Pádraig Doherty of Tirhoran and Andy Porter of Gaddyduff (now Clonmany) and carters from Ballyliffin and Urris went to Derry regularly with cart loads of butter in butts and the only goods they had back was a supply of leather. It would be cut in soles and uppers and tied in bundles for different shoemakers that sent the orders with them.

Later on women went along with the carts to Derry and took back baskets of goods and went round selling the goods from house to house with their baskets on their arm. You could buy tea and sugar, or soap, or needles or pins from them. Anne Bhán MacCearáin went round the Glen and took one side going up and another side coming down. In my mother's time a man went round Urris buying eggs at 3d. a dozen. As he bought them he packed them in a creel and carried them on his back to James Shiels's shop at the Cross. . .

In those days the roads in the winter-time would take a cart to the axle, for there was no regulation on them such as now. In my father's time Jimmy Butler was overseer for roads in these parts. He was the same Butlers as the Butlers of Grouse Hall and it was likely through their influence he got the job. Jimmy was married to a woman called Máire Muirgheasan. One day Máire was down along the road somewhere and she was attacked by a dunty cow, and nearly killed, till some Clonmany man was passing and drove the cow off. When Máire reached home and told all that happened the ones in the house said: "*Sé Dia féin a shábháil thú* ['Twas God Himself that saved you].' But Máire said: '*M'anam féin, nabh b'é ach gur fear as Clúan Máine é* [Indeed it wasn't but a Clonmany man].' The people in times ago were innocent. . .

In my father's time and before it, people went in greatly for bleeding cattle in the summer-time. They boiled the blood with oaten meal and it was very nourishing. For drawing the blood they used a thing called a pair of flames. It had three blades with a spur at the back of each. The blades were of different sizes, the small one for young cattle and the others for older ones, two-year-olds or four-year-olds. They used to keep bullocks till they'd be five or six-year-old. A rope was tied round the animal's neck and a vein would swell till it would be as thick as a man's thumb. The spur was put on top of the vein and the man gave it a knock with a stick. The blood came out and was capped in a piggin. They took a quart or so of blood at a time. The two sides of the cut were then squeezed together and a pin pushed through and sweeled [wrapped] round with a thread. After a day or two the cut was healed and the pin was taken out. The old people said the stirk wouldn't start to thrive till it was bled. In the summer-time, when the cattle were all outliers in the hills, people had to sit up at night and watch or their cattle would be bled to death. My father was a good hand at bleeding cattle but it was done away with since my time. . .

The best spinner I heard of was Annara Dhiarmada of Effishmore. She was my father's time. She used to card and spin a lot during the night when the house was quiet and would work on till the small hours many a night. One Saturday night there was a priest staying with her who was on his banishment. He was on one side of the fire and Annara on the other side, spinning. She had some hens clocking at the side of the kitchen. Sometime in the middle of the night a rooster jumped up on a creel in the middle of the floor and started to crow. The priest said to Annara if she'd take his advice she'd stop working after twelve o'clock on a Saturday night any more. A rooster crowing at any time during the night was a sort of a sign and people never liked it.

In Paddy Mór Roddy's house there was a roost for the hens down at the door, and one night at bedtime the rooster began crowing and flapping his wings till he frightened them. The old man was lying in the kitchen bed, and he asked the young people what direction was the rooster facing. They told him he was facing in his direction. Then he told them to feel the rooster's feet, were they cold or warm. They told him they were warm, so Paddy said the thing would go past without a death. That same night a son of Paddy's nearly died with a colic but he pulled out of it next day and got all right.

My father was weaving a web of cloth for Annara one time and he sent her word he'd need a couple of hanks to finish the web. Annara's brother, Neall, took a grey wether in from the side of Bulaba next morning and clipped him, and the women spun the yarn and took it to my father and had the web home with them that night. The old people used to tell of a man who clipped the sheep in the morning and had the suit made with the tailor that same night for a wedding he was going to.

I learned the weaving trade from my father and it came naturally to my hand. Many a night I spent at the loom and many a half-crown I made when other young fellows of my age were away at dances or ceilidhing. I could make a yard of blanket cloth in the hour, and that was the wide breadth. *Drogat* gave more bother in the weaving. The women gave me the yarn to weave in hanks, and I set it up in the loom. There were four treadle feet in the loom to get the different patterns. I could weave herring-bone patterns, or dice patterns, some with eight threads to the dice and some with

17

sixteen. Phil Devlin of Ballinabo was a good weaver and so was Michael Harkin, Micheál Figheadóir [Michael the Weaver] he was called. Phil was supposed to weave a hare and a hound into a web of cloth, but that couldn't be done on the looms we worked with.

The shuttle was made of apple-wood or holly, and had two wire runners on the bottom to make it run over the threads. The reed was made of cane wood and had to be made by a reed-maker. There was a good reed-maker in Donagh by the name of Doherty. A reed cost 7s. 6d. They were of different closenesses. For wool they had fourteen splits to the beer, and for linen or ticking maybe twenty-two or twenty-five a beer. That was the finest I ever used but you could get ones finer than that. At a lint cloving or gathering like that, some people could take right music out of a reed by putting a piece of paper on it and blowing on the paper. Children do it yet with a coarse comb. As a piece would be woven, I rolled it up on a beam. A weaver always kept a pot or vessel like that with water in it for wetting the work. That kept the yarn from breaking. But the yarn would break many a time and had to be tied with a weaver's knot. No other knot would pass through the reed.

If the cloth was woven fancy for men's wear, it was taken to the cloth-mill to be thickened and dressed and pressed. The cloth was put into troughs and soft soap was spread over it. Then it was dried and pressed. The blue cloth would be rubbed with a stiff brush and then gone over with a pair of scissors and clipped.

I didn't do any weaving this long and many a year. The loom went to wreck on me. I don't think there's a loom in the whole of Inishowen at the present day. . .

Colonel McNeill was a bad man who lived at Binnion. He was a Scotsman. He died in 1709. He likely got Binnion after the Reformation or after the Battle of the Boyne. I heard my father saying it was people by the name of Toland who were driven out of Binnion when it was taken over by McNeill. My father was at Carn fair one cold day in winter, and there was an old Malin fisherman taking shelter from a shower beside him. So my father remarked to him that this was a day for a topcoat. The old man said if his people had their rights, it wasn't one but two or three topcoats he could have, for it was his people who owned Binnion in the old days. He was the name of Toland from Ardmalin.

This Colonel McNeill had a very bad name and always kept a band of henchmen or yeomen about him, who helped him to evict tenants and seize girls and persecute the people. Some of them were from Crossconnell, and some from Binnion.

There was an old woman called Máiread Dhubh who lived in a sod house in Bunacrick moss with her four children. She caught salmon during the summer-time to make a living and always went into the river and caught them with her hands. One day she was in the river down at Clochwan when McNeill and his men came on her, and with their swords and bayonets they kept her in the water till she was drowned. A Tanderagee man was going home from the Keelogs mill with a load of meal, and Máiread Dhubh called on him to save her but he drove on, and they say that Máiread cursed him and said the day would come when there wouldn't be one of his name in Tanderagee.

I heard that story told another way, where a man called Dochartach Mór na dTulcha was said to have killed Máiread Dhubh and that it wasn't McNeill at all.

Another time there was a funeral of some young woman who hadn't pleased Colonel McNeill. When they were carrying the coffin round Teampall Deas, McNeill and his men held up the funeral and took the lid off the coffin and put their swords through her. There was a girl about Crossconnell, too, and one night McNeill's men came to seize her, but she got out of bed and made up the side of Rachtan and got away on them.

Some of the women who had children to him got a rood of ground for their support. There was one of these roods in Gortnahinson, and some about Ballyliffin and different parts of the parish. The Ballyliffin Hotel is built on one of McNeill's roods. Some of his descendants were known in my young days, but I think they are all died out by now.

It was a common thing for women from the lower side of the

parish to gather on the Binnion and Annagh hills and curse McNeill.

McNeill used to attend the fair of Pollan with his henchmen and pick out the best looking girl at the fair and carry her off to Binnion. One June fair they were taking a girl over the hill to Binnion, and when they were crossing behind Ardagh, Séimí Airis McCole heard her screaming and calling for help. Séimí was a mentioned man with the stick. He was hanging on a pot of potatoes at the time, so he called: '*Cá bhfuil mo bhataigín* [Where is my baton]?' and grabbed his stick and made out and jumped hedges and ditches till he overtook them about Mullach and fell to them with the stick till the girl got away.

Another fair of Pollan, a fine looking girl from Urris came in with her three brothers over through Annagh. When McNeill and his men went to seize the girl, she blew a birler, a kind of a whistle she carried, and it was heard all over the green. The brothers knew their sister's whistle and came to the rescue in time to save her. I heard, too, of a girl from Meentiagh Glen who went there for the first time. McNeill got his eye on her and arranged with her to meet him at six o'clock and that he'd leave her home on horseback. Some friends of hers warned her about the sort of a man he was and advised her to leave the fair at once and get home as hard as she could. She cut up through Tornabratly and over the side of Crockaughrim and got away home that way.

Things got so bad at the finish-up that some of the Ardagh men attacked McNeill one night at a place called Gallach in Annagh Hill, and felled him with a stone on the head, and Eoin Airis McCole castrated him with an old hook. His henchmen carried him home, and he lay for days before he died. The doctor maintained he would have recovered only for the blow on the head. I heard that the night he died he tore the side wall out of the house when the devil took him. The old people always said he was buried in the house at Binnion standing up, and that the corner where he is buried is built up. But there is a tombstone in the old churchyard at the corner facing Binnion with his name on it. . .

When Father Corr came here as parish priest in the year 1784, the persecutions must have been past, for at that time Mass was said for the whole parish at a place above Andy Porters called the Scallan. Near it is a height called Ard na hEaglaise – the Chapel Height. The corner stones of the Scallan are there yet. It was a kind of a shelter, for I always heard there was a big sheet of cloth put up on whatever side the wind was coming from, to give shelter to the altar. People came to the Scallan from all ends of the parish, and all the men took their *camáns* [hurley sticks], and when Mass was over someone threw out the *cnag* [ball] and one side of the parish played the other, the Isle of Doagh side against the Urris side. Each side tried to take the *cnag* home, and they played through fields and everything, and the side that took home the *cnag* had the game won. There was no prize or anything. *Camán* was the whole game before this. It was the common game till about forty or fifty years ago. . .

Father Shiels took over Termain and built the big house that is there yet about the year 1820 or so. In order to make up the farm seven families had to be evicted. He helped at the evictions himself, too. I heard that he evicted one family after he had said Mass and before he took his breakfast; and he even carried out a cradle with an infant in it and left it on the street. The old people didn't want to talk about it. The place afterwards fell to a niece of his who married Owen Doherty, a son of Niall Seán's. Termain was a place that nobody ever thrived in. There was always a writ or a subpoena hanging over it. . .

The Waterloo priest, Father O Donnell, came home from the wars the same time as my grandfather got out of the navy. He had two brothers priests but they were ordained and dead before he was ordained in 1818. The three brothers are buried in the one grave at Cock Hill.

The Waterloo priest was a fine upstanding man and a great horseman. He had a big chestnut horse home with him from the battle of Waterloo and he called him Paddy Whack. He lived at

Crossconnell and later on at the Cross. One day one of the redcoats was passing and struck Father O Donnell's dog with his whip. When the housekeeper gave off to him about it, the soldier said he'd do the same to the dog's master. When she told Father O Donnell, he put on his uniform and jumped on Paddy Whack and overtook the redcoat at the Carry Hole near Buncrana and made him go down on his knees on the roadside and apologise.

There was a mark of a wound on the horse's hip and the story was that during the wars they ran short of food and cut a piece off the horse to eat.

Father O Donnell spent a quarter in Lifford jail one time for not paying tithes. When he was released, the whole parish turned out to meet him out of face. It was the Glen House people who put him to jail. So he made a speech to the crowd out there and said the day would come when there would not be one of the Glen House breed in this parish. . .

In my father's time and before it there was always some kind of a school kept going in Meentiagh Glen. It would be held in a barn or some *cró* of a house with stones round the wall for seats. The last of the old teachers was a man by the name of Graham. He was a well educated man and a poet but he was greatly given to the drink. I don't know where Graham went to or what happened to him. He was a good teacher and turned out better scholars than what's going now.

Everybody attending Graham's school spoke Irish and knew nothing else. But he taught English and figuring. When they were learning the English letters they picked them up from the names of things that had the same shape as the letters:

A – *cúpla toighe*, B – *spéaclóirí*, C – *déanamh na gealaighe*, D – *bogha is saighead*, E – *áit toighe*, F – *cos speile*, G – *crudh gearrain*, H – *geafta*, I – *bata*, J – *camán*, K – *eochair an dorais*, L – *súiste*, M – *scoil oidhche*, N – *lena chois sin*, O – *gealach*, P – *cor shúgán*, Q – *réalt an rubaill*, R – *ruball an mhadaidh*, S – *an t-eascon*, T – *cos spáid*, U – *crudh asail*, V

– compáis, W *– gearran gorm,* X *– an Croch cheasta,* Y *– cos an raca,* Z *– crúca.*

[A – the couple of a house, B – spectacles, C – the shape of the moon, D – a bow and arrow, E – the foundation of a house, F – the handle of a scythe, G – a horseshoe, H – a gate, I – a stick, J – a caman, K – the key of a door, L – a flail, M – night-school, N – beside it, O – the moon, P – a throw-hook, Q – a comet, R – dog's tail, S – the eel, T – a spade-handle, U – a donkey shoe, V – a compass, W – a dark grey horse, X – the Crucifix, Y – the handle of a rake, Z – a crook.]

It was all slates they used till they got on a distance and then they wrote with quill pens. The teacher would have a bunch of feathers and trimmed them himself as they were needed. They made some sort of ink, as far as I remember hearing, from the seeds of the elder tree. . .

I am the only one of the name that is left now. I never got married myself for I never had a rid house or a way of marrying till it was past my time. I got a long life and have a lot to be thankful for. I often noticed, when one member of a family is left after the others die early or in middle age, that that person generally takes a long life.

In my time I have seen six or seven generations of people, and lots of things I see happening today are not to be wondered at, for there are things that run in breeds of people and come out somewhere in nearly every generation. A weakness for drink follows certain families, and stealing and dishonesty can be traced in breeds of people as far back as memory goes. The old people called that a *dúchas.* But the old people always said that drink was a thing no man had to hang his head for. Insanity, too, follows people, but it is not as common as it was, for in times ago there were more sib marriages than now. Men wouldn't leave their own townland when looking for a wife, till they would be all related through other. By-children [illegitimate children], too, follow certain breeds, and

23

there are some that leave nothing at all behind.

But it ill becomes any of us to be too uncharitable. There was an old saying common long ago that would apply to most people: '*Sa choill is feárr, gheobhaidh tú oiread brosna is a dhoghfas chun talaimh í* [In the cleanest forest that ever grew, you will find as much twigs as will burn it to the ground].'

With all the changes I have seen in the world in my time, I have come to the stage where I would be surprised at nothing. I often wondered what Eibhlin Roddy or the Daisy – that was her mother – would think if they could come back for a Sunday afternoon along the Glen road and see the buses and cars and the silk stockings and the style that's going now. I think a while of an hour would do them. They would wonder what the world was coming to.

I had a long life and I must be thankful for I always had the best of health. I never had an hour's sickness in my life and I don't know what toothache is. I was ninety-two last Christmas and I have every tooth in my head yet. There is no doctor ever got a penny of my money. I was attended by the priest once, but that was one evening a few years ago that I took a weak turn on the roadside, and the neighbours got the priest without getting my permission. I apologised for putting the journey on him and explained how it happened. I told him, when I was able to do without sending for a priest for over four score years, that it was hardly worth my while starting. He was a Dr Collins who was afterwards made parish priest of Gortin. I said the *Confiteor* for him in Latin and in Irish, to let him see I wasn't as far through as the people made out. I learned the Latin from listening to the clerks at Mass on a Sunday.

But my time on this world must be getting short. The people I knew and grew up along with are nearly all gone before me. Over our grave there was always an old quarry flag, but it was getting sunk in the ground with grass growing over it. So ten or twelve years ago I gave an order for a new one to Owen Roddy. The making of it cost £5, but I was out the best part of £6 to get it erected, with the price of drink and all. A pound doesn't go far on drink these times.

So, whenever I die, they will know where to bury me. And after my day the grave will not be opened again, for I'm the last of the name. And when I do go and fall in with Paddy Mór Roddy and the Ogaster and Eibhlin and Eoin O Kerrigan and all the rest, sure I'll be no stranger to them.

The Last of the Name, 1986

SHAN F. BULLOCK
1865–1935

Often. . . when I ought to have been at home, sweeping our lawn and walks, splitting the week's supply of firewood, giving the latest born a ride in the perambulator, and so on, I might be found in the woods watching Mr Bean, the forester, and his men at their work of felling and clearing. I loved trees and their ways, but not to the sentimental extreme of not being thrilled when the last stroke of the axe went home and another giant crashed to his death. The work, too, was clean, open, skilled, often dangerous, varied with the changes of season and weather, had associations of pleasant glimpses and sounds and smells that perhaps I took in; besides, Mr Bean was a character in his way, and his men all came of the peasant stock I knew least and liked the best.

Mr Bean was a stocky, hard-faced Scot, humorous in his dry way, woefully fond of whisky and sugar, gifted with a broad Doric that not even Father could quite mimic. He always carried a small bill-hook under his arm, sign at once of office and authority. His silver watch matched Sheridan's for size and power. He smoked a clay pipe, filled from black twist, and lighted by means of flint and tinder. I loved to hear him talk, his eyes glinting wickedly, his face all puckers, his theme some memory of boyish adventure long syne in bonnie Scotland, perhaps a story against himself or another, or happen the way he had outwitted the wife when she keepit the sugar basin from him.

Mrs Bean was a tall grim woman. Usually she wore a frilled night-cap all the day. Her sober face and ways and thin high-pitched voice used to make me think of the witches and scolds that in Father's boyhood were punished at the ducking-stool in the river below Bunn. For all, she was a kindly good woman. On Saturdays she baked a supply of delicious white bannocks, placing each to cool on a tread of the newly scrubbed stairs, and ceasing only when the stairs were full.

At times, the bells would tell out one o'clock to some part remote from Mr Bean's home on the Derryvad side; then he would take a bannock and perhaps a bit of bacon from the side pocket of his rough tweed coat, draw away a dignified distance from the men, sit on a stump and munch his dinner. If there was a wee drappie in a naggin bottle in his breast pocket, so much the merrier his tongue would wag should I chance to share the bannock.

Once Father bought a very small calf, and for safety shut it in a poultry shed, the door of which had an opening just sufficient to let the fowls pass in and out. In course of the day Mr Bean strolled into Father's office and in his pawkiest manner explained that, with intent to keep yon beastie from escaping, he had closed the opening with a brick.

When I was twelve or thereabouts and able to look in upon myself, it happened that Mr Bean and his men were working in the Curleck woods behind our school. Knowing that a great ash tree was being felled, I made some excuse to the master and slipped away to see the death. Four woodmen with long-headed axes were felling. Behind, facing the line of fall, stood Mr Bean, smoking, his bill-hook under his arm. He looked at me as I came up, his eye reproving, but he said nothing. Soon the tree shivered, tottered fell some way, caught its upper branches in two other trees and hung there. 'Clear away,' shouted Mr Bean; then caught me by the arm and swung me violently aside. I was still stumbling backwards when the butt cracked from the stump and the whole tree shot back over the spot where, seconds ago, I had been standing. A minute perhaps I lay, with Mr Bean looking down at me and the tree almost touching my feet; then quietly he pointed his bill-hook towards the school, and I rose and went. Many times, in those wild days, death must have passed me by as near; that passing I felt, and often since the memory of it has fretted sleep.

What religion Mr Bean and his family observed I cannot say.

27

None of them went to church. Perhaps they were Methodys, as we called them; if so their nearest place of worship was five miles off. Occasionally, it is true, the preacher, as we called him, held a service in some farm parlour of a Sunday evening; but the Beans, I fear, hardly valued their souls to the extent of journeying far over field and wood and lake to give them nurture. Mr Bean himself seemed an unbeliever, judging by his talk; a pagan perhaps, or possibly that awful thing – an atheist. He used to speak as though he himself and not the Almighty made the sap rise and fall, the ferns come curling up at their due season; and when he made fun of Mr Logan, the chaplain, one looked for she-bears to come up out of the wood and devour him.

Out of their hearing, too, he would gird bitterly at his men for losing good pay at the bidding of priests who made them keep perhaps a whole month of holy days in course of the year. The men were all Roman Catholics, excepting Mr Bean's own son Andra, who worked sometimes as a sort of foreman, and he, of course, may have been a lesser atheist.

There were good reasons in those days, however it may be now, why the men of one particular creed should work together, Catholics with Mr Bean, Protestants with Terry, the gardener, and with Father also. Protestants as a body stood for something tangible and not necessarily religious; Roman Catholics as a body stood for something else that perhaps was more religious, but almost of necessity was no less smirched with worldliness. Naturally, therefore, each sect looked a little askance at the other, and could at times come to bitter and bloody strife over very little.

I never heard of any serious ructions between the parties in our territory, but precautions, you see, were taken, and quite obviously it would have been a foolish thing for Mr Bean's Roman Catholics to make trouble, say, with Terry's Protestants. For one thing, they would have been in the minority and, according to the higher powers, assuredly would have been in the wrong; for a second thing, any presumption on their part could be punished effectively by dismissal.

In our homes the True-Blue colours were never flaunted; indeed, one of my vivid recollections brings Father's protesting voice at sound of the drums rolling forth their challenge outside Orange lodges, far away among the hills. The noise disturbed our island peace; in his view it kept alive feuds and passions that needed rest. What did the Others think of the hubbub? When these processions, with flags and drums and flaring sashes, went past their homes? When the gallant Castle infantry marched to church, in red and white, carrying their muskets and bayonets and wearing on their shakos the device *Croppies Lie Down*? How could there ever be peace and fellowship in face of such folly? Was not one man, in the sight of heaven, as good as another, even though one had everything and the other only rags and a crust?

I was old enough to be impressed by such views; they seemed right, in line with the teaching Father read from the Bible every morning, and given to us authoritatively by the chaplain on Sundays. Indeed, it came easily to have sympathy with the Others, as Father called them, because I found them so likeable.

Our school in Curleck, like that in Leemore and elsewhere beyond the land of Gorteen, was an estate school, for general use, but so controlled that primarily it was adapted to the small educational and religious needs of little Protestants. Before I went to Thalma the great change to Nationalisation had come, but even then the atmosphere was Protestant, and not many more little Catholics came for secular instruction than in the days when old deans taught the church catechism and little else, enforcing it with a stout cane and without much respect of creed or pupil.

We little Protestants were, I suppose, always better clad and fed, certainly we had the rightful air of superiority becoming an ascendant class; this nothwithstanding, it would be always the barefooted, ragged Catholic, with his hair through his cap and only a bit of oaten bread in his pocket, that I was drawn to for play or company. He was of another breed than ours, had softer ways and speech, better manners somehow, knew more about the country and its life and the things that mattered; and, supposing him to have a sister – generally he had five or six – there could be small question about it. Mary Roche with her raven black hair and wide soft eyes; Rose Healy with her freckles and hair the colour of honey, and the smile she had and the quiet chuckling laugh. . .

Enough of that. Raven hair and freckles are good enough for sentimental reverie; they trouble little the emotions of a healthy young savage, even though they may catch his impressionable eye. Besides, had not the savage sisters of his own, and a mother who had dowered them with obvious beauty?

As it happened with the children, so it was with their fathers and brothers who worked for Mr Bean in the woods, or elsewhere in the demesne. As mere humans they might be the inferiors of Sandy the smith, Mr Greig the carpenter, Tom the keeper, old John who ferried us to church and school, of all Terry's Protestant workers, and of our own fortunate selves even – inferior in point of strength, appearance, education, and the rest; yet I preferred their company, and others also did. Why I did is hard to say or why the impulse of preference continued, so that later on any attempt to portray them or their like in a book would come easier and with kindlier effect than would the attempt at picturing their dominant fellows.

They seemed more picturesque and homely and lovable, were less worldly and aggressive, had a sense of humour all their own and a habit of kindness, too; they had more stories and told them better, knew little yet had great old knowledge, were very poor and somehow rich. Perhaps, in a word, they charmed because they were real Irish. Much as I liked them it was plain, even to young eyes, that ourselves and the Others were people apart, different types, different ideals; perhaps they understood us, certainly a deal in them was outside our knowing.

As I sat now and then with the woodmen round their midday fire, listening to their stories and jests, eating a piece of their soda bread perhaps, or showing the man I was by taking a draw from some black doodeen, I had the feeling often that so far I might go with them, but never an inch further.

After Sixty Years, 1931

FORREST REID
1875–1947

The primary impulse of the artist springs, I fancy, from discontent, and his art is a kind of crying for Elysium. In this single respect, perhaps, there is no difference between good and bad art. For in the most clumsy and bungled work (if it has been born of the desire for beauty) we should doubtless find, could we but pierce through the dead husk of it to the hidden conception, that same divine homesickness, that same longing for an Eden from which each one of us is exiled. Strangely different these paradisian visions. For me it may be the Islands of the Blest 'not shaken by winds nor ever wet with rain... where the clear air spreads without a cloud', for you the jewelled splendour of the New Jerusalem. Only in no case, I think, is it our own free creation. It is a country whose image was stamped upon our soul before we opened our eyes on earth, and all our life is little more than a trying to get back there, our art than a mapping of its mountains and streams.

I am speaking, of course, of a particular kind of art, for I know there are artists whose work bears witness to a complete acquiescence in the world and in life as it is. *'Fuir! là-bas fuir!'* – it would be difficult to discover an echo of such a cry in any line written by Thackeray or Jane Austen. Take it, then, as a point of view suggested because it helps to explain my own writings, because the general impression remaining with me of the origin of these experiments and strivings is that they were for the most part prompted by just such a feeling of exile – exile from a world of which I did have a later glimpse from rare time to time. No matter how objective, how impersonal I tried to be, this subconscious lyrical emotion before long crept in, perhaps merely in a des-

31

criptive passage, in the dwelling upon this or that aspect or mood of nature, which had somehow opened a door into my secret world. . .

My waking world. . . was gradually expanding, though it still remained the very small world of a provincial town – a rather hard, unromantic town too – devoted exclusively to money-making; yet a town, for all that, somehow likeable, and surrounded by as beautiful a country as one could desire. The Belfast of my childhood differed considerably from the Belfast of today. It was, I think, spiritually closer to that surrounding country. Then, as now, perhaps, it was not particularly well educated, it possessed no cultured and no leisured class (the sons of even the wealthiest families leaving school at fifteen or sixteen to enter their fathers' offices); but it did not, as I remember it at any rate, bear nearly so marked a resemblance to the larger English manufacturing towns.

The change I seem to see has, of course, brought it closer to its own ideal. For some not very intelligible reason, a hankering after things English – even what is believed to be an English accent – and a distrust of things Irish, have always characterised the more well-to-do citizens of Belfast. But in the days of my childhood this was not so apparent, while the whole town was more homely, more unpretentious. A breath of rusticity still sweetened its air; the few horse trams, their destinations indicated by the colour of their curtains, did little to disturb the quiet of the streets; the Malone Road was still an almost rural walk; Molly Ward's cottage, not a vulcanite factory, guarded the approach to the river; and there were no brick works, no mill chimneys, no King's Bridge to make ugly blots on the green landscape of the Lagan Valley. The town itself, as I have said, was more attractive, with plenty of open spaces, to which the names of certain districts – the Plains, the Bog Meadows – bear witness. Queen's University was not a mere mass of unrelated, shapeless buildings; the Technical Institute did not sprawl in unsightly fashion across half the grounds of my old school. Gone is the Linen Hall, that was once the very heart of the town in its hours of ease. A brand new City Hall, all marble staircases and inlaid floors, garnished with statues and portraits of Lord Mayors and town councillors, and fronted with wooden benches on which rows of our less successful citizens doze and scratch the languid hours away, flaunts its expensive dullness where that old mellow ivy-creepered building once stood, with its low, arched entrance, its line of trees that shut out the town bustle and dust. The Linen Hall Library, transported to another building, still exists, but, as with the city, expansion has robbed it of its individuality. The old Linen Hall Library, with the sparrows flying in and out of the ivy all day long, fluttering and squabbling, was a charming place. It was very like a club. Its membership was comparatively small; its tone was old-fashioned; it belonged to the era of the two and three-volume novel; it had about it an atmosphere of quiet and leisure.

Does anybody nowadays read the romances of Jessie Fothergill, of Helen Mathers, of Mrs Alexander? These were the books adored by my sisters, the books I saw lying about the house – *Healey, Probation, Cherry Ripe, Her Dearest Foe, The Wooing O't*. And Rita. I have never read a line by Rita. Yet *Dame Durden* I knew was the most beautiful novel ever written. My eldest sister mentioned this casually one day at dinner, and it never occurred to me to question the statement, so I need not question it now.

In the Linen Hall Library, curled up in a low deep window seat, I would sit gazing out between the trees and right up Donegall Place, which on summer afternoons was a fashionable promenade, where one was almost sure to meet everybody one knew. Here, hidden in a box below the counter, Mr Gourley (then Johnnie) kept the latest novels for his favourite subscribers. Here when, at the request of my eldest sister, I asked one day for Miss Florence Warden's *House on the Marsh*, that same Mr Gourley, knowing the library did not possess a copy, utterly abashed me by suggesting with great severity that perhaps it 'was not a nice book'. I blushed, for I was sophisticated enough to associate 'not niceness' with the improper, even while, for the sake of the family, I asserted indignantly that it *was* nice. And here, one summer

33

afternoon, just outside the tall iron gates, I beheld my first celebrity. Not that I knew him to be celebrated, but I could see for myself his appearance was remarkable. I had been taught that it was rude to stare, but on this occasion, though I was with my mother, I could not help staring, and even feeling I was intended to do so. He was, my mother told me, a Mr Oscar Wilde; and she added, by way of explanation I suppose, that he was aesthetic, like Bunthorne, in *Patience*.

It was years before I heard his name again, years before I came upon the short stories dedicated to Margaret, Lady Brooke; to Mrs William H. Grenfell, of Taplow Court; to HSH Alice, Princess of Monaco. At the time I saw him, he was the guest of a Mrs Thompson of College Gardens [and her] two bouncing daughters. . . Flaxen haired and voluble, with their mother they got into the carriage now, while the aesthete climbed up on to the box seat beside the coachman. . .

O, what land is the Land of Dreams?
What are its mountains, and what are its streams?

I do not know, but I can map out one little corner of that land, which had begun to acquire for me a strange reality. 'Look with thy soul. For while it sleeps, the mind is lit with eyes. . .' So counselled the ghost of Clytemnestra, and I looked, but looked exactly as I looked with my bodily eyes when I was awake. There were two worlds, and it never occurred to me to ask myself whether one were less real than the other. It did not seem to me that either was unreal, that either was my own creation. I lived in both, and the fact that I should open my eyes night after night in precisely the same spot in dreamland was no more surprising than that I should open them morning after morning in my bedroom at home.

Of course, there were foolish dreams, dreams that travestied the ordinary things of one's waking life, and dull dreams that merely echoed them, and terrifying dreams which, as I have said, I had learned to elude. But *this* particular dreaming was pure happiness; and always the setting was the same, the time the same, the season the same; for it was always summer, always a little after noon, and always the sun was shining.

The place was a kind of garden. There were no flower-beds, there was no wall to shut it in; but there were flowering shrubs, and glades, and lawns, that looked as if they had been tended by human hands. Always when I first awakened I was in broad sunlight, on a low grassy hill that was no more than a gentle incline sloping down to the shore. A summer sea stretched out below me, blue and calm. No white sail ever drifted across the horizon; no footsteps ever marked the unbroken crescent of the sandy beach. And inland, no trail of smoke ever rose into the coloured air. I saw no house or building, no sign of human habitation. But I did not feel lonely. I knew there were people there, and that I could find them if I went in search of them – older people, I mean, than the playmates I had so often met here in the past – men and women whom one day I should know. Meanwhile, I sat still, facing the wide blue glittering sea, and waited. I could hear a droning of bees, mingled with the splashing of the waves; I could follow the wavering, curving flight of a butterfly; I could hear birds calling softly from the woodland near.

I was waiting for someone who had never failed me – my friend in this place, who was infinitely dearer to me than any friend I had on earth. And presently, out from the leafy shadow he bounded into the sunlight. I saw him standing for a moment, his naked body the colour of pale amber against the dark background – a boy of about my own age, with eager parted lips and bright eyes. But he was more beautiful than anything else in the whole world, or in my imagination.

Afterwards the dream might wander hither and thither; we might bathe in the sea or in one of the pools, or play upon the shore, or plunge into the woodland; we might be alone, or others might join us in a game; only the beginning was always the same, or very nearly the same.

And from the moment I found myself on that hill-side I was happy. All my waking life, indeed, was blotted out. I had a sense of security, as if no doubt or trouble or fear could ever again reach me. It was as if I had come home; as if I were, after a long absence among strangers, once more among my own people. But the deepest well of happiness sprang from a sense of perfect communion with another being. It was this I looked forward to, this that I still longed for when I awoke. Having tasted it, no earthly love could ever fill its place, and the memory of it was in my waking hours like a *Fata Morgana*, leading me hither and thither, wherever some faint reflection of it seemed for a moment to shine. . .

Two of my brothers were in the linen business, but the linen business they considered to be overcrowded; another was in a bank, but there seemed to be little in favour of banking; so it was decided that I should be apprenticed to the tea trade. Nobody knew anything about the tea trade, and it was apparently on this singular ground that it was held to be suitable for me. I was taken by my brother-in-law to interview Henry Musgrave, the head of the firm, and on the following Monday morning started work at a salary of fifty pounds for five years.

As the Musgraves were among the wealthiest merchants in Belfast, these terms did not strike me as brilliant, nor was I surprised by the derision with which my eldest sister regarded my entrance into commercial life. Still, though generosity was not a Musgrave characteristic, I liked Henry: towards his brother, Edgar, when I watched him saving the backs of envelopes and lifting up little bits of string from the floor, my feeling was more one of curiosity. But things might have been worse. There were three other apprentices besides myself, two of whom I had known at school; and I liked the place; it was old-fashioned and very easy-going; not even a telephone had been installed.

My duties at first kept me a good deal in the open air, particularly round and about the docks, while during the mid-day interval, under the coaching of the manager, I learned the game of billiards. This, for some reason, did not meet with the approval of the boss of my own department, Robert Alexander (Mr Robert, as he was always called); but since he knew very well in whose company I had been, nothing much could be said. And if they did little else for me, these new activities dissipated the cloud in which I had been living: my troubles disappeared; both physically and mentally I recovered my balance.

But of course I had been taken from school too soon – another year would have made all the difference. Perhaps my development had been slow; at any rate, now, when it was too late, there awoke in me an eagerness for learning which I had given no sign of possessing before, and I began to work at Greek, and also to make a systematic study of the Greek philosophers, aided by the monumental volumes of Zeller. In one of the upper lofts, in a recess near a dusty window, I rigged up a little den surrounded by a wall of tea chests, and to this solitude, shared only by an occasional mouse, I would vanish when opportunity arose. Here I kept my books, and here, when I was not wanted, I was allowed to read more or less in peace. Now and again Mr Robert would pop his head round the corner and stand watching me and pulling his beard. 'Sonny, this is supposed to be a business establishment,' he would presently drawl. But he would end by taking up one of my books and turning its pages contemplatively, or by discussing for a few minutes *The Return of the Native,* which I had lent him, and which, though he was deeply interested in it, it took him a month to read.

I had not been in business very long before the manager advised me to turn my studies to a practical end. He assured me he was perfectly satisfied with the way I did my work; it was only that in case I *should* happen to have thought of another career he might as well tell me that the prospects in the tea trade were limited, and that unless one 'went on the road', or out to India, there were very few decently paid jobs, and he did not think I should be either happy or successful as a commercial traveller.

Not a word of this did I breathe at home. I knew there was no use talking about it, because to the tea trade I had been put, and to the tea trade I must stick – at all events for the present. If I reported what I had been told it would merely be regarded as a further proof of my unpracticality, and of the worry I seemed destined to create at every step. So I continued as before, neither shirking my work nor, on the whole, disliking it. But in the tea trade itself I had no interest, because, apart from the money to be made out of it, it possessed none. To pretend that it took five years to learn it was simply a way of securing cheap labour. All there was to be learned could be learned in six months. The rest was a matter of office routine, and for this, too, a six months' training would have sufficed.

The chief life of the place centred in the mixing-room. It was in the charge of the senior apprentice, and here – though the dry, dusty air was too solid for comfortable breathing – on the counter that ran under the windows I would sometimes sit watching the tea being tramped down into chests and half-chests, to an accompaniment of tales and songs. There was also now and then a game of cards, always of the simplest description. On these occasions a heap of empty packages, with their loose lids and hoops, would be propped against the door for the benefit of Mr Robert. At a touch the whole pile would come tumbling down with a terrific clatter, at the same time effectually blocking up the entrance, so that before he could force his way in, and long before he had recovered his temper, the cards would have disappeared and work be in full swing. This particular alarm signal (which never actually could be proved to be one) was the invention of James Quigley, who had been longer in the place than anybody else – except perhaps Mr Robert himself – and who miraculously retained a reputation for an industry and handiness he may have possessed twenty or thirty years earlier. When I knew him he was as arrant and thirsty an old loafer as ever existed: nevertheless, he became my guide, philosopher, and friend.

Quigley was fond of conversation, was fond of young people, and was fond of giving me the benefit of his experience. My acquaintance with life seemed to him incomplete, though my curiosity was not unpromising; and he adopted the role of Mentor, being distinctly pleased, I fancy, to discover a Telemachus. Two of the other apprentices he described as 'mugs'; the third had outgrown the period of pupilage. So it was with Quigley I had my first drink – I mean, in the proper way, standing at the counter of a 'pub' – two drinks there were, because he was never a sponger: but from the backing of horses, his own favourite hobby, he warned me to keep clear. Quigley was completely unmoral, and completely without vice. He detested what he called 'meanness and greediness', but I never heard him condemn anything else. He unveiled certain of the pitfalls youth is apt to tumble into, taking it for granted I was of the kind that does tumble in (otherwise, I suppose, I should have been one of the 'mugs'); but his philosophy really was as ancient as the earth, and, though it was not expressed poetically, could all have been found in Herrick's poetry:

> That Age is best, which is the first,
> When Youth and Blood are warmer. . .
>
> Then be not coy, but use your time. . .

Such was its burden. It was the examples, however, rather than the precept, which interested me, for he liked to dwell upon the days when he himself had used his time. And I wronged him when I said he had no poetry, since there was surely poetry, of a kind, in those careless memories of opportunity grasped, those adventures of a light-hearted and very unspiritual lover. Perhaps it was because the adventures had all happened in mellow, golden years long before I was born; because the other persons involved were now either grandmothers or, it may be, but a little heap of silvery bones in some quiet old churchyard; or because of their rural setting (for as a youth he had lived in the country), that they appealed to me. At all events, those tales of summer lanes, and leafy copses, and shadowy barns with the corn piled high, created in my mind pictures that were like the pictures of a rougher and homelier Theocritus: 'Ah, once again may I plant the great fan on her corn-heap, while she stands smiling by, with sheaves and poppies in her hands. . .'

When I knew Quigley he was an old white-haired, white-bearded man, bordering on seventy; but so perfect had been his physique that he was still powerful and good to look at, without a trace either of the feebleness or grossness of age. He was a pagan who had never heard of paganism: his mind was simple and earthy, entirely unspiritual, and entirely free from corruption.

39

> Gather ye Rose-buds while ye may,

for

> Golden lads and girls all must,
> As chimney-sweepers, come to dust.

That was the wisdom he tried to teach me, with many details concerning the gathering, and many descriptions of the roses. His own songs you will find neither in the pages of Herrick nor of Shakespeare, but they were entirely free from that taint of music-hall vulgarity which characterised the songs of the younger men. And he frequently sang while I sat and watched him at work, hooping the chests with their slender willow bands, hammering in one nail, perhaps, between every other verse. I can remember the tunes of these songs perfectly, but only fragments of their words. Here is the beginning of one of them:

> Patsy McGann, you must marry my daughter,
> Patsy McGann, my child you must wed;
> Five golden sovereigns, Patsy, I'll give you,
> And the brass warming-pan, and the old feather-bed.

And this, which was sung with a great flourishing of the hammer:

> O, I'm ninety-five, I'm ninety-five,
> And to live single I'll contrive.

In a less defiant key were the verses of:

> When I was a wee thin'
> I lived with my granny,
> And many's the caution
> The ould woman give me;
> She bid me be wise
> And take care of the boys
> And not let my dimity
> Over my knee.

But again the gayer note was struck by a very long song, which, from both tune and words, was evidently designed to be sung in a tavern, and to a company well supplied with beer and tobacco:

> O, there was three flies
> Upon a time
> Resolved to travel
> And to change their clime;
> The one was green
> And the one was blue
> And the other one was
> A yeller one too:
> So off they flew
> With a merry merry hum
> And they told their mammas
> For to. . .

The rest, I suppose, would be considered coarse, though neither in it nor the others was there a hint of nastiness. Nor was I myself of a squeamish habit of mind, so that one and all they bring back to me principally the summer afternoons when I so often heard them sung, with the sun slanting through the open windows across the dusty floor, the throb of the old gas-engine that worked the hoist faint in the distance, the venturesome mouse (which I thought of as a lady mouse) who would peep out at us with bright black little eyes, and then delicately approach and daintily drink up two or three of the tobacco spittles she found so delicious in this dusty waterless world.

When one thinks of the incalculable difference a little leisure makes in life, it seems strange that anybody should wish to adopt American habits of 'hustle' and 'rush'. The time of which I write is not after all so very long ago, and yet I am sure that today you could not find a business house conducted as this one was. And it was prosperous. Things, doubtless, were not squeezed quite so dry as they might have been; but when one's life, or the greater part of it, is passed in certain fixed conditions, is not the pleasantness of those conditions more important than the distinction of paying a super-tax? If I had been chained all day long to a desk I should have been unhappy; as it was, I was happy, my mental growth was not checked; on the contrary, my mind ex-

41

panded more rapidly and freely than it had ever done before; I did not acquire elderly and methodical habits; the spirit of boyhood was left untouched. I had been brought into contact with ordinary rough-and-tumble life, but I had not been caught in the wheels of a machine. . .

I had been at work for only a very few months when a new apprentice came. It was my business to teach him his duties, and on a cold bright winter morning, when the ground was white with frost and a thin powder of snow, we set off for the docks. In the still, grey water the boats, looking strangely naked and black, were reflected as in a glass. Gulls wheeled restlessly about the masts and funnels; the wintry sun shone on frozen ropes and slippery decks; the ground rang with a hard metallic sound. Crates and bales, boxes and sacks were being piled on the wharves; iron trucks were busy, for the dock-labourers were working hard to keep themselves warm, their faces, ears, and hands scarlet, their breath turning to vapour the moment it passed their lips.

I had always found this scene attractive, and, though it was by now familiar enough, and I knew these boats were, with one or two rare exceptions, merely cross-channel steamers and coasters, it still continued to suggest romance, the great unexplored world that lay beyond my experience, glimmering with a mysterious fascination. Today there was added to this the pleasure of acting as guide to my companion, of showing him *our* boats, *our* sheds, of telling him what he must do, of introducing him to the different shipping clerks. And through it all I was becoming more and more conscious of something pleasanter still, of an uplifting of the spirit that turned everything to beauty and filled my mind with sunlight. I knew this sunlight well, because it was the sunlight of my dream world. A long time had gone by since it had last shone for me, but with its first rays it burned up the intervening period like a thin sheet of paper, and filled me with a peculiar exultation. I seemed to be approaching a point; we both seemed, actually, physically, with every step we took, to be drawing nearer to a point where the wide sea flowing between my two worlds was narrowed to a stream

42

one might pass dry-shod: my conduct of the business we were engaged on grew more and more mechanical.

Meanwhile, the new boy walked beside me, rather shy, and with a simple, unconscious charm about him that I had felt from the moment (an hour or two back) when he had been introduced to me by his father. I prolonged our walk unnecessarily: I did not want to go back at all. . .

And thus began a friendship which as the days passed, and then the weeks and the months, grew ever closer and deeper, till at last it seemed to draw into itself the two divergent streams of my life, so that for the first time, in dreaming and waking, they found a single channel. Somehow, somewhere, I felt that a shadow had been lifted. It was as if in my spirit a new day were breaking, transforming everything in the world around me, because I saw everything now in its fresh clear light.

When I was with this boy I was happy, and I could conceive of no greater happiness than to be with him always. He was an odd enough youngster in his ways, not a bit like any other boy I had known; but he was extraordinarily lovable. Sometimes, indeed, the sunshine, filled with little dancing golden dust specks, touching his hair or his cheek, would set me dreaming of him as a kind of angel who had strayed into this world by chance, or perhaps not quite by chance. The pleasantness of his manner, of his temper; his kindness, his intelligence, a sort of childish quality there was in his gaiety – all helped to deepen the affection I had for him. The future lay before us like a wide green plain. There were plans and daydreams – plans that involved leaving our present employment and going to a university. Life in this humdrum old warehouse, amid its simple daily tasks, amid its comings and goings, its working hours and hours of leisure, became a wonderful voyage of discovery to be undertaken no longer alone.

Both here, and at home after the day's work was finished, we were constantly together. I showed him my writings, I got him to read poetry, to listen to music; I poured out all my enthusiasms, and in return became absorbed in his. That they took me into the unfamiliar paths of scientific theory and experiment did not matter. I read books on astronomy, and geology, and physics; he tried to interest me in mathematics, and of all our studies this was the only one I was obliged to abandon. But if I could make no headway here, we splashed happily enough in the shallows of philosophy, and it was while we were reading Caird's *Evolution of Religion* that between his father and mother a momentous discussion took place (of which I heard nothing until years later) as to whether this friendship should be discouraged or allowed to continue. They had been extremely kind to me, asking me frequently to the house; but they were very strict in their attitude to religion, and it was because of the Caird book and of Spencer's *First Principles,* which were supposed to have been my choice, that the discussion arose. In the end (I cannot help thinking it was his mother's counsel that prevailed) they decided not to interfere, but to let things take their course. . .

I have wandered too far into the future in all this – farther than the scheme of these pages really carries me. For I see them, somehow, as embracing a definite period, which began in dreamland and ended with the winter morning of this chapter's opening. Or perhaps I should say that it ends on an evening some five or six months later.

I had never spoken of the affection which now filled my life: I had never alluded to it, though I had often longed to do so, though I had even once or twice tried to do so, though I knew it must for ever remain incomplete unless I did do so. Incomplete, that is, for me: for the rest I did not, could not know. And thus it went on, until I thought of a way by which I might surmount my shyness, or at least circumvent it – a way which would at any rate be easier than speech.

For some months back I had been keeping a diary, or journal, writing in it not regularly, but still fairly frequently. I wrote just before going to bed, and I poured out everything I felt, for I intended to destroy it (and did do so) when the book should be filled. What I wrote was not meant to be read. I wrote as the servant of King Midas whispered into the hollow earth. Yet now I wanted him to read it. I knew it contained pages he might find bewildering, extravagant, and perhaps distasteful: but I also knew that if I looked back over it with a view to tearing out such pages I should never show it at all.

And the desire to take him completely into my confidence had begun to haunt me. It was what filled my mind as we walked home together one day some five or six months after our first meeting, and what kept me silent when, later on, we went out for a ramble through the fields and woods by the Lagan. Yet, though I was silent, I was intensely excited, for I had made up my mind to conquer my cowardice. Already I had had an opportunity to do so, and had put it off by coming out here. I would put it off no longer.

'There is something I have at home which I want to show you – something I have written. Do you mind turning back?'

Without questioning me he did what I asked.

And when once more we had reached the house in Mount Charles I took him upstairs to the room I now used as a study, and where I knew we should not be disturbed. It was growing dusk, but I welcomed the minutes I could employ on busying myself with the lamp, and fumbled longer than was necessary as I unlocked the desk where was my manuscript book. I gave him the book, moved the lamp over near to an arm-chair, and myself sat down at the table, some distance off, and facing the window. For the first time I had admitted someone to my secret world, to my innermost thoughts. . .

Already he must have crossed the threshold. In the quiet of the room I could hear no sound but now and then the rustle of a page when he turned it. For an instant I glanced at him. His face was a little flushed, his dark hair tumbled down over his forehead. But I turned away quickly and did not look back. I sat waiting, trying now to shut out every thought from my mind. . .

The time slowly drew on: half an hour, nearly an hour must have gone by. The window grew darker and darker, and presently I knew that in a little, a very little while, the reading must come to an end. Then the silence seemed all at once to grow so intense that I felt nothing could ever again break it.

Apostate, 1926

FLORENCE MARY McDOWELL
1888–1977

. . . on her one and only visit-by-favour to the Cogry Mill, Mary cared little for the processes that turned her father's flax into yarn for weaving. She looked at the people.

She was aghast at the great troughs of cold water from which the spinners had to lift the armfuls of big bobbins of dripping rove, pressed to thigh and breast; and the bare feet, red and blue with cold, that pattered up and down the length of the spinning-frame. The black or yellow glazed aprons, which the workers had to purchase from the mill owners, afforded by no means complete protection against the icy, sopping bobbins of rove, and clothes were often soaked through. Those who could afford boots kept them as near to the steam pipe as they could, to put on when going home. A few even brought black knitted stockings as well.

Near the steam pipe too sat the row of cup-lidded cans of once-hot tea. There was a half-hour lunch break, when the dwellers in Cogry Mill village ran home for a hurried meal, while those less fortunate, who lived at a distance, unwrapped their soda-bread pieces from the ever-present *Telegraph* and washed them down with tepid tea. In fine weather these workers sat in the shade of the wall opposite to the mill gate, under the ominous-looking chimneystack.

There was no break during morning or afternoon, but hungry workers who had left home between five and six o'clock in the morning could snatch a piece and a drink of still-warm tea while friends minded their machines. Then the like favour would be returned. Or they could eat and work at the same time.

During her tour of inspection Mary felt weary, for the mill was a big place. But to her dismay she found that it was impossible to sit down and rest for a few minutes. There was nowhere to sit. The workers were forbidden to sit down at any time so there was no necessity to provide seats. Any worker found resting for a moment on a bobbin-box or a rove-can was sacked on the spot as an example to the others, for workers were plentiful and any vacancy in the mill could be filled immediately. Often a working member of a family trysted the next vacancy for a younger one coming along, so that whole families worked for generations in the same mill, and anxious to get the work.

Mary had at first envied the half-timers who went to school only on alternate days and worked in the mill on the others. But her visit to the Cogry Mill made her realise how very hard it must be to work twelve hours one day and be expected to be a clear-brained academic the next. Even on schooldays the half-timers had to go to work as usual at six o'clock, do three hours' work, literally run along to school and return after the school-day to work until six again. It was a primitive form of day-release, and so fatiguing that it produced large numbers of anaemic, undersized, round-shouldered, tubercular children, who were exposed not only to the expected results of sweated labour, but also, like their parents, to incredible risks of injury among the flying belts and whirling machinery. Not light was the toll of disease and injury and death.

Twelve years was the official age for starting work as a half-timer. But, as a great favour, children of ten and eleven whose parents had 'influence' were allowed to begin a life of toil and hardship, and were whisked out of sight to be hidden if a factory inspector unexpectedly showed up. Their childhood was over so soon. It was very sad. But, then, they were paid two shillings a week, and that compensated for the loss of freedom and happiness, and the grinding labour helped to keep the family alive.

Mary ended her visit in the only pretty place in all the mill – the spotless engine-room, with its shining walls of coloured tiles and with every possible piece of brass glittering. There was the date, 1845, on the wall – the transition date between corn-milling and linen-spinning. Off went the steam hooter with a roar to signal the start of the afternoon's work. Already there was not a worker to be seen outside. They were all back in the building, for every second counted. Indeed the machinery was often allowed to run on 'accidentally' into lunch-time or after stopping-time so that the workers, who dare not leave the moving frames, were compelled to do unpaid overtime.

No, Mary was mistaken. There was one worker still on the road. A mother from the mill village, whom Mary knew by sight, was running desperately along outside the railings of the mill-yard, her once-weary bare feet flying, plaits bobbing on her breast. When, panting, she was three feet from the mill gate, the gatekeeper slammed it in her face. He grinned at her through the bars. 'No waste time here,' he said. 'That'll learn you to be in time the morrow.' Mary felt sick.

As the woman turned helplessly back towards the village, Mary knew that she would lose that afternoon's pay, no small matter, and that for another offence she would be workless. Mary stumbled the few yards from the engine-room door to the boiler-house, where the sweaty, coal-grimed men heaved the fuel into the hell-fires there. Even the glow of the open furnace-door was suddenly cheerless.

No weaving was done in Mary's neighbourhood now except by one old man called Harvey, who still spun his own yarn and wove it on the hand-loom in his back room.

Instead, all the bundled yarn from Cogry went off to various firms for turning into fabric. But much of it came back in hanks of yarn or in great webs of linen to be bleached at Springvale or beetled at Cogry Beetles, for Cogry Mill had its own beetling engines.

The days of bleaching on the grass were over, except in a few isolated cases. Springvale Bleachworks bleached yarn or cloth chemically and efficiently with the aid of the huge wickered glass flasks of 'vitrol' that Mary saw on the Springvale stiff-carts, but a little of the 'romance' had gone from the linen industry.

Not so, however, in the beetling engines. The beetles were giants with rows of blunt wooden teeth, rising and falling asymmetrically, pounding and flattening and almost polishing the big webs of cloth fed on to their rollers. It was the most utterly deafening place in the world. You could not hear yourself shriek.

All beetlers – there were always Boyds in every beetling engines in the district – became deaf and developed husky yet strident voices from their repeated attempts to overtop in volume the vast, thumping, vibrating beetles that roared and crashed and pounded with unbelievable din. In the centre of the building, and all the more frightening for being enclosed, the huge water-wheel turned menacingly in its abyss, where the foaming water would be seen dimly dozens of feet below in a horror of dark violence. Mary always shuddered at the great wheel, yet she loved the beetles. They were friendly giants.

As they were only a few hundred yards from her home, on the other side of the river, she visited them often. And got hot buttered soda-bread and buttermilk from kind Mrs Boyd to stem her ever-growing hunger. Mrs Boyd was kind to others too in a professional way, for numerous local women had an arrangement with her to bring all their sheets, pillowcases, bed valances, curtains, tablecloths and every such straightforward piece of washing to be beetled when there was no fabric on the rollers. And out came the laundry beautifully finished, smooth, creaseless, shining, to be carried home again in the big two-lugged baskets by the grateful housewives.

So much toil, so much hardship, so much endurance, so much discomfort, so much fear of poverty, illness, old age; too little money or clothes or food or comfort – and yet these were among the happiest people Mary ever knew, these toilers in the linen industry that made Ulster great and rich and famous. They were cheerful and industrious, proud and charitable, warm-hearted and often pious, coarse and witty – one of the great peoples of the world.

Small wonder that the flood-gates of Mary's compassion and affection were opened to them at an early age; and never, never closed again.

Other Days Around Me, 1972

December of 1905 brought its climax, in its usual way, to the school year. The official year might begin and end in summer, but the children's year followed that of the calendar. December was the end of the year. December was Christmas. December was the school swarry. Mary was ever to remember that particular year, for it was the first time she met the peculiar manifestation of hostility that can emanate from the Parent. The school swarry was, like Gaul, neatly divided into three parts. First, the children ate, drank and made quietly merry, for no raucous behaviour was possible until their later release into the cold night air. Next came the concert, provided by the pupils. Finally, the highlight of the evening arrived with the prize-giving of medals and books, provided by the mill-owner.

Adam McMeekin owned the Cogry Mill. He was a stocky, energetic little man with shrewd eyes, coarse features and a dark, scrubby moustache. He stood a good five feet tall in his shoes, and could arouse terror in the hearts of men and women a head taller than himself. Behind his back he was the 'Wee Buddy', this last being merely Ulster for 'man' and certainly *not* American for 'friend'. He was kind in his way. He saw that his school was always supplied, from the mill, with coal for heating and soft soap for cleansing. From small beginnings he had become a mill-owner, a land-owner and a cigar-smoking businessman, with a pleasant mill house in Ulster and a town house in London.

It seemed but a short time since he had arrived at the Cogry Mill for managerial training under the then owner, his brother William. He had been a small, slight youth, child of an Ulster farmer as Mary herself was. Sheer drive, ruthlessness, ambition and charm had placed him on that pinnacle of prosperity where Edwardian mill-owners, as *nouveaux arrivés,* were forgiven much because they had the money to buy much. William had acquired an accomplished English governess to bring up his children in the highest tone. Adam married her, and Miss Clements brought up not just his children but himself into reaches of English society he could scarcely have dreamt of as a youth. His children did not go to the school he heated with his coal and cleansed with his soft soap. They had, instead, not an English governess it is true, but a French Mademoiselle and a German

Fräulein. The Master was commanded to the schoolroom of the mill house to coach the mill-owner's children in the three Rs. Polish was acquired abroad. While girls left the mill school to finish their lives at the spinning frame, Adam's two daughters were finished with lessons in music and dancing. While Mary struggled with, even as she delighted in, her Goldsmith and Corneille, the 'Wee Buddy's' son went to acquire his veneer at Heidelberg, in those far-off days before Wilhelm of the withered hand had shown his other hand too clearly.

For the school swarry, all was bustle in the Mission Hall. Row after row of clean schoolchildren faced the little platform with its varnished front rails and steps. On the platform the concert and prize-giving would take place. In the meantime the tables and chairs were useful to hold the tin trays lined with thick, unbuttered slices of juicy currant-loaf and mugs painted with roosters and roses, filled with sweet, thick brown tea. Only the children would eat. Parents did not share in this part of the proceedings. The mill family would not share in it either, but would arrive in time to occupy the front seats at the concert, having dined in some splendour at home.

This year their gleaming barouche had been left in the coach house, and a strangely-named new building was a 'garage' for a horseless carriage. They would shortly arrive in this glittering monster driven by the former coachman, John Gibson, now a liveried chauffeur.

Miss Waide perspired in her usual ladylike way as she fluttered about in pink chiffon frills and lace-trimmed corsage of velvet roses. She was responsible for the concert, and the Paris Opéra could have held no more excitement and tension in its artists than Miss Waide had to manage in hers.

Mary knew her job to a nicety. She was the dogsbody. The tea was prepared in Mary Smith's house in the little Brookfield Row opposite to the Mission Hall. Mary was to supervise the senior girls carrying their brass kettles of tea from Smith's to the hall.

Outside in the dark, sparkling night, hopeful parents had arrived early. Beggs Robinson, one of the mill foremen, was the Keeper of the Door. Even though parents should not really come in until tea was over, early arrivals could count on a kind-hearted Beggsie to let them in from a bad winter's night. A rope, stretched across the aisle, separated the rows of children in front from the parents behind. Early parents sneaked silently into seats to which they were not entitled for another half-hour. They gazed at the walls in admiration. From end to end they were covered with examples of beautiful needlework pinned up by the girls. Sheets of paper in various colours had been tacked to the boards, and against the blue and pink and scarlet, the drawn-thread-work and crochet of the white linen cloths showed their perfection. From the finest handkerchief with its hem-stitching and edging of crocheted lace to the largest cloth flowered in most intricate embroidery, they were magnificent examples of needlecraft that would be heir-looms to the third and fourth generations.

More parents gathered outside the now firmly-closed door. The 'Wee Buddy' would arrive soon. Beggsie leaned against it confidently. They should not pass.

The favoured parents within waved as their children's faces turned to them, grinning mouths showing half-chewed currant loaf, moist with delicious tea. The press without became menacing, and Beggsie's door was threatened with assault and battery as snow-flurries appeared from nowhere. Mary wondered about her charges and their tea-kettles. The Master nodded towards the back door in the dressing-room. She took the hint, slid out by this door, ran across the road to Mary Smith's. Good! The last supplies of tea were almost ready. She warned the girls about the snow while urging them to hurry. As she crossed again to the hall she was aware of people. They were huddled in a dark, shapeless crowd at the main door, shawled heads covered from the winter's cold. Suddenly, one of the women spied her in the light from Smith's door.

'Look at her! Who does she think *she* is?' shouted the woman suddenly. She was fractious with frustration and with waiting in the cold darkness after a long day's work in the mill. She wanted to see her children. She longed for the exciting colour and entertainment. Here was a young brat of a girl, small and skinny, sailing in and out of doors as though she owned them. The others took up the cry.

'Look at *It*, going out and in.'

'It's *our* weans that's in there.'

'*She* gets in and we're shut out,' and much more in a worse vein until obscenity reared its ugly head.

The shouting and the sudden violent menace frightened Mary. She was very shaken. She almost believed that they would strike her, for she could not at the time understand the coldness of feet that had stood bare in even colder water all day at a spinning frame, nor the immense desire of all the women for the other-world of a concert, for an evening's pleasure. Trembling, she pushed herself in again at the dressing-room door. She had met the violence of a frustrated crowd and it had frightened her. That was all. Beggsie had seen all and said nothing.

Soon the tea was over. Every last mug was handed up, sticky with sugar. Some children ran to their parents in the back seats. Mothers spat on handkerchief corners and cleaned up rosy faces and rough little hands. The shining children raced back to their seats as the doorman let in the horde of potential Mesdames Defarge – but now they were quiet, tired, rather timid women, overawed by the glamour of a lighted hall and the exotic promises of excitement to come. Their voices were low and occasionally they giggled nervously or stared around with a false boldness.

The shining motorcar of the McMeekin family drew up at the door of the hall. The small group of lads and men coming to the concert had deliberately waited outside to see the monster close at hand, to have esoteric conversations with John Gibson, and to acquire expertise that would be displayed with pride and off-handedness at work. Horseless carriages were the most magical of news.

The family was greeted by the Master and a respectful silence. The former Miss Clements sailed regally to the front row. She, like her husband, was small of stature, but robust and rosy. She wore a black winter suit of fine barathea, the skirt touching her polished toes, with a three-quarter-length coat having an exaggeratedly-sprung waist and deep hem of astrakhan. On top of this stout, genteel little edifice was a very smart, very wide black silk hat with plumes of osprey. Her husband followed in black velvet-collared coat, high white collar and bow, his Homburg in his hand, wafting incense of Havana. Then came the two daughters, favoured by fortune, in pretty dresses. The Master brought up the rear. As they all edged themselves into comfortable positions, Beggsie tiptoed respectfully to whisper to the 'Wee Buddy'. The latter whipped round sharply and gazed for a moment at the offending women. He and Beggsie then looked across to Mary. The 'Wee Buddy' smiled reassuringly. Mary smiled back, unsure of what she was supposed to do or to have done. Miss Waide seated herself at the harmonium and the concert began. . .

Next morning came, the very last day of term, devoted to tidying up after the swarry, removing Christmas paper-garlands and controlling children ready to be off on holiday. Mary was surprised and a little disturbed to receive a message from the Big Room, ordering her to present herself at once before the Master.

She could read nothing from his expressionless face as she came in from her class in the Low Gallery. The Master quietly motioned, directing her gaze to a group of silent, shawled women assembled outside in the chill December air.

'Go out to them,' he said.

Mary hesitated and then went to the porch, closing the Big Room door behind her. She looked wide-eyed from one woman to another, seeking an explanation.

'Yes?' she queried, gently.

There was a heavy silence. One woman shuffled her bare feet uneasily on the cinders. Then another, braver then the rest, spoke up. Soon Mary knew all. She felt aghast. These were the harridans of the night before. Beggsie had let the 'Wee Buddy' know of their behaviour. They had every one been sacked on the spot.

But perhaps the Spirit of Christmas had been with the owner. He had offered them the possibility of being reconsidered for labour after they had apologised sufficiently, abjectly to the Monitress. They apologised. Mary flushed hot with shame. Tears stung behind her eyes. She felt a totally unreasonable guilt. As quickly as she could, she stammered an acceptance of the unwanted apologies and fled to safety in the Low Gallery.

She never again in all her life wished to see such an exercise of power. That incident stayed with her always.

Roses and Rainbows, 1972

DENIS IRELAND
1894–1974

BELFAST, EARLY TWENTIETH CENTURY

Walk on the Castlereagh Hills. A sunny day, the city, with its red tentacles of suburbs, sprawled below on the green floor of the Lagan Valley, with the dome of the City Hall and the gantries of the shipyards rearing themselves above the smoke haze. Behind all this rises the Cave Hill, evoking memories of Wolfe Tone and Napoleon, or perhaps, for twentieth-century inhabitants, only of Napoleon, since they prefer, for the most part, not to think of Tone. And yet Tone once walked those streets, as large as life – the same streets where the worthy citizens whose sons and grandsons were to become the pillars of Victorian commercialism in Ireland were carrying republicanism to the point of parading in uniforms fashioned on those of the French Republican Guard, and celebrating the downfall of the Bastille by the waving of tricolours and the firing of cannon. But all this happened in the last decades of the eighteenth century, and with the coming of the Union in 1800, Belfast's history was changed. Tone had come to a bloody end in the Provost's prison of Dublin barracks, and Ulster Presbyterianism, perhaps by force of example, had stopped fishing in the troubled waters of the French Revolution and had become respectable; the uniforms fashioned on those of the French Republican Guard disappeared from the wardrobes of prominent merchants, and no-one thought any more of firing off cannon to celebrate the fall of the Bastille – so much so that by the middle of the new century it had become impossible to tell where a Presbyterian left off and a Churchman began. At the same time steam began to replace water power in the spinning and weaving of cotton and linen, and the stage was set for the appearance of that Belfast of the nineties where I was born – a strange, tough, hybrid

56

town, with a forest of factory chimneys on both banks of the Lagan; a town which, paradoxically enough, regularly reared (and then promptly expelled) a host of writers, artists, and un-practical 'dreamers' of all kinds, spreading them with lavish generosity over the face of the earth and not being particularly kind to them when they made any attempt to return. . .

The thing to do with the world is to kick it in the pants, but my father would never have been, as he would have considered it, guilty of such a breach of good manners. All this sensitivity, however, did not prevent, and indeed was probably the cause of, his exploding in fits of violent rage – so violent and so explosive that the more timid of his work-people trod warily in his presence, though at the same time perfectly conscious of the goodness of his heart. Perfection was his motto, everything must be done perfectly; the linen must be the finest that was ever woven; it must be papered in paper as thick and lustrous as damask; the string must be the strongest (and, in consequence, was always the most expensive) that could be procured; even the tickets that were stuck on the tablecloths and the sheets and the pillowcases must be in themselves works of art, a tribute to the soundness of the workmanship they advertised. His weakness was that though he could not drive a nail himself, he must be present at the driving of nails, putting men who had spent a lifetime driving nails off their work; he could not delegate; he must be present, dancing about in a perfect fury of impatience, to watch a packing-case perfectly nailed up and labelled, when he should have been sitting at an empty desk planning the future of the business. He was, in fact, a good deal of an *artiste manqué*, and the lust for perfection that was in his blood gave him no rest in his lifetime – his only relaxations being music and short trips by coasting steamers to Bristol, Plymouth, or London, occasions when he could be out of reach of telephone or telegraph. The sea was his passion, and it has always seemed to me a major tragedy that this short-sighted man, condemned from boyhood by the early death of his father to an office stool, should have taken his pleasure in turning over the pages of Jane's *Fighting Ships* or in reading romances about the Navy. And since to every man it is granted according to his desire but never according to the letter of his desire, the sea brought him both his mountain of transfiguration and his Calvary. Vicariously, that is, in the life of my brother. From the first that life demonstrated the working-out at one remove of a destiny that had been denied an earlier generation. At eleven my brother would be a sailor and nothing else; at fourteen he entered the *Britannia*; at twenty-eight, as the youngest lieutenant-commander in the British Navy, after a career that had been one unbroken record of successes and golden opinions, he was washed overboard and drowned in the North Sea – as a reminder that life has no room for too radiantly golden lads and lasses on its stage. And it was here my father showed the stuff that was in him. We all knew, with the arrival of that telegram from the Admiralty on a January evening in wartime, just as he was sitting down under the chandelier in velvet coat and slippers to read the evening paper, that my father's life was laid in ruins. He might, and did, laugh and joke again, but something was gone that would never return. Yet after the first horror-stricken moment he gave no sign; next morning, to the scandal of his work-people, he was at his desk, outwardly as if nothing had happened. He had lived in the sun of my brother's career, seeing in it the fulfilment of all his inmost dreams, and now the light was gone. What he thought about it all, even those nearest to him never knew, for he never uttered a word on the subject, and the only change that the outer world could see was that he became a little less impatient with imperfection, less inclined to fly into a fury when things went wrong in the packing-room at the warehouse, a little more indulgent to a world with which he might well be indulgent because it was not to be very long before he had finished with it altogether.

From the Irish Shore, 1936

The family warehouse in Belfast had imposed itself upon the eighteenth-century orderliness of the streets behind the City Hall.

It was just an enormous square box of redbrick, with a towering redbrick smokestack to carry off the fumes of its boiler-house, and a succession of steeply-pitched glass roofs to give light in its machine-room. Inside, the red box was divided into almost water-tight compartments. On the top floor, under the glass roofs, were long benches of mechanically-driven sewing-machines at which rows of girls sat sewing and embroidering mats and doylies all day long, following their stencilled patterns with incredible speed and accuracy. Below them came the handkerchief department; the lapping-room, where the white linen coming in from the bleach works was examined for defects; the towel department; the fancy room; the damask room; the sales room, with its row of glass show-cases, its alleged Irish spinning-wheel, its dejected-looking samples of cultivated flax on the walls, its photographs of the New York and London offices, and its framed cases of medals and diplomas awarded at exhibitions. Then came the American department; and so on down to the packing-room and the pitch-pine and frosted-glass general office on the ground floor where type-writers and mechanical calculating machines clattered from morn-ing to night, making out invoices and customs declarations in duplicate, triplicate, and even quadruplicate. From the main en-trance a long passage, frosted glass on one side, pitch pine on the other, led past the general office to the private office, where my father sat at a large square table strewn with dusty papers. The view from the window of the private office was of a redbrick distillery, an iron water tank on the skyline, and distant factory chimneys.

Outside, in streets that once resounded to the music of the Irish harp and now re-echoed to the rattle of distillery drays, flowed the fierce life of the city, part product of the dark Satanic mills crowded between the mountains and the river, part of the myth-ical waters of the Boyne. Changes might appear here, decay there, but beneath the surface the fierce tides flowed unchecked. An eighteenth-century print shows a ship lying in the basin of the Farset river in High Street, her masts and yards silhouetted against the sky. Today no more masts or yards are silhouetted in High Street or any other street; instead squat-funnelled motor ships nightly reflect their floodlit upper works in the waters of the

Lagan; the area that was once slobland uncovered by the tide resounds to the clatter of automatic riveters in the shipyards; mail planes drone overhead to their aerodrome beside Lough Neagh; traffic lights wink red and green; business men dial one another on automatic telephones; and mill girls, whose mothers tramped through winter dawns to the sound of factory horns, barefooted and wearing shawls, dance at nights in cheap imported frocks and artificial silk stockings to the sound of saxophones and drums. Belfast, in other words, is learning the tricks of the twentieth century. As one mill girl remarked to another during the fashionable Saturday-night parade of North Street:

'You're stinkin' wi' perfume!'

To which the crushing retort was:

'Holy God, sure I'd be stinkin' if I wasn't.'

The Victorian Economic Men, frockcoated in stone, who surround the City Hall, might be excused if they held up their stone hands in horror at this new century with its cinemas, its dance halls, and its reckless consumption of tobacco. If they did, there would be a certain justification in their attitude. They may have ground the faces of the poor, but in their day the unemployed did not hang about the street corners, their hands in their pockets, congregated like shabby swallows on a wire. True the unemployed Belfast man can still exercise his fiercely ironical Belfast wit. He can still go to the football match and obliterate a myopic referee with 'Get thon mon a wee dog!', or attend a boxing tournament in the Chapel Fields and inquire plaintively during a rest period, while two heavyweights drape themselves affectionately round one another's necks, 'Mebbe the referee would favour us with a song?', or interrupt dramatically with 'Send for the polis; they're *murderin'* other!'. But he cannot feel himself a useful member of society in a community which under the influence of the bird-discredited statues round the City Hall still worships work as an end in itself; he has no philosophy of leisure, and no means of acquiring one; and the 'buroo' upon which he depends for his sixpences for the bookies, the pictures, or the dance hall, still hands him his money as if it were a charity; a draft upon a divinely-ordained banking system, and not his right as a man, a potential father of men, and the heir of all the processes and inventions that have themselves thrown him out of work. . .

Ten stories above the roaring canyon of Chestnut Street Johnny McDade was demonstrating to a packed audience the art of weaving linen on a hand-loom. Shaded electric lights suspended from the superstructure blazed down upon the web of brown cloth already woven, on the complicated Jacquard harness, on the shuttle that slid to and fro like a startled fish, on Johnny McDade's bald head where he sat like an organist wrapped in the mysteries of his art. Johnny, in fact, was in the spotlight, playing a new and outlandish form of Wurlitzer; the audience stood in shadow, pressing against the rope that encircled the demonstration area, while beyond them loomed the shadowy walls draped with faintly glowing flags, amongst which the Stars and Stripes and the green flag of Ireland, decorated with a gold harp but minus a crown, predominated. Against this vivid background stood a statue of Lafayette, faced by a bust of Daniel O'Connell – the sole statuary which I had been able to borrow from the art department of Messrs Klein & Seager. What Lafayette was doing in this galley I was not very sure, but I had read enough American history to know that, in spite of the Great War and the disillusionment that followed the American invasion of Paris, Lafayette was always a safe card to play, especially when united in the bonds of symbolical matrimony with *la belle* Kathleen Ni Houlihan. Effete but charming Europe was here seen demonstrating one of its ancient, complicated handicrafts in a setting of light and shade and colour that would have done credit to the late Mr Ziegfield himself; indeed with the creation of this tableau I felt that I had begun to deserve well of my country.

Johnny McDade, on the other hand, was not so sure. In the first place, as a technician, he objected to the battery of shaded lights with which I had flooded the show piece of my exhibition: the heat from the lamps snapped the yarn already rendered brittle by the dry, exciting American climate. In the second place, as an Orangeman, he objected to the bust of Daniel O'Connell.

'Mon,' he said, rubbing his chin at the sight of it, 'if yer father seen yon, he'd massacree ye!'

'Not he,' I said. 'Not if it helps to sell his linen.'

And as I was aware of aspects of my father's life and character of which Johnny remained respectfully ignorant; as, furthermore, I was Johnny's sole bulwark against the strange and frightening continent on which he found himself, Johnny was forced to hold his tongue. As Johnny was only too gratefully aware, it was I who, penetrating the mysteries of the American banking system, paid him his augmented wages every Saturday; I who had extricated him from the luxurious hotel in which we had stayed on our first arrival in Philadelphia; I who had found him lodgings with Ulster exiles from his own beloved county of Armagh. Johnny had hated the hotel, with its elevators, its thickly-carpeted corridors, its hot-house temperature, its obsequious bell-boys; in fact he had nearly died of thirst in one of its bedrooms rather than risk an encounter with its telephone system. Now everything was changed. Now Johnny went home in the evenings on a street-car to sit about in his shirt-sleeves in a sitting-room lit by bridge-lamps, to smoke his host's cigars, to spit in a cuspidor, and crack to his heart's content with exiles just as ready as himself to swop lies about the grand times they all had in Ireland. The only thing that worried him was the weather; it was now November and the tingling American frosts combined with the overheated atmosphere of Messrs Klein & Seager's store to keep him in continual trouble with the loom. The yarn kept snapping, and as the best 'weaver' in the County Armagh, a man with a reputation to maintain, he could not bring himself to accept my more adaptable and probably, from his point of view, more Jesuitical view of the situation.

'Just give her a bang now and again to keep the crowd round,' I would say. 'Sure they wouldn't know a loom from a sewing-machine. All we want is the crowd.'

But Johnny did not approve. Working away at the brittle warp with his long brushes and his evil-smelling concoctions, he would shake his head in doubt. I was becoming too much of a showman altogether. At afternoon sessions, when the swarms of fashion-ably-dressed women wandering through the apparently endless departments of Messrs Klein & Seager were at their thickest, I would arrive after a cup of coffee in Messrs Klein & Seager's sumptuous restaurant, or, as Johnny was beginning to suspect, after conversing with that decidedly Papish-looking young woman at the pencil counter on the ground floor, and talk, as Johnny expressed it, 'to bate the band'. Standing in the circle of light by the loom and searching the rows of ghostly white faces in the shadows between me and the flag-draped walls, I would deliver a series of short sermons on the history of the Irish linen industry, while Johnny, seated at his instrument like an organist waiting for his cue, his bald head shining under the shaded lights, would gaze at me with astonishment. So the loom was exactly the same in principle as that which had woven fine linen for the Pharaohs; barring the Jacquard machines that produced the pattern! Man, that just showed you what a fine thing education was when a young fella like myself who knew damn all about it could talk like that to the crowd. And cambric as fine as any that could be woven today had been found wrapped round the bodies of Egyptian princesses who died centuries before the dawn of the Christian era, had it! Boys, I could hear Johnny saying to himself every time he heard it, that was a powerful thought. He must remember to tell them about that when he got back to Annatravil. And so on down through the centuries to William III (at which point Johnny always sat up and took notice) and the arrival of the Huguenots in Ireland. This historical introduction was, however, only jam for the fact-loving American public; the pill came at the end, coated with the interesting information, thrown in absent-mindedly, as a kind of postscript or afterthought, that the sheets, towels, damask tablecloths, napkins, etc., manufactured in our hand and power looms (trade-mark an Irish harp surrounded by a garland of flowering flax) would be found exhibited – not, of course, with a view to sordid commerce, but merely as objects of aesthetic and educational interest – in the household-linen-and-white-goods department of Messrs Klein & Seager Inc., three floors down, elevator no. 6.

And having, as Florence Steinetz on more than one occasion remarked, 'shot off my face' to some such effect not once but several times in the course of an afternoon session, I would take my hat and coat, descend in the elevator, and walk home past the blazing shop windows of Chestnut Street and Walnut Street, to dine under the glittering chandeliers of M. Heyner's French restaurant and wonder what the devil in the course of my varied career I would be up to next.

Statues Round the City Hall, 1939

C.S. LEWIS
1898–1963

BELFAST, EARLY TWENTIETH CENTURY

I was born in the winter of 1898 at Belfast, the son of a solicitor and of a clergyman's daughter. My parents had only two children, both sons, and I was the younger by about three years. Two very different strains had gone to our making. My father belonged to the first generation of his family that reached professional station. His grandfather had been a Welsh farmer; his father, a self-made man, had begun life as a workman, emigrated to Ireland, and ended as a partner in the firm of MacIlwaine and Lewis, 'Boiler-makers, Engineers, and Iron Ship Builders'. My mother was a Hamilton with many generations of clergymen, lawyers, sailors, and the like behind her; on her mother's side, through the Warrens, the blood went back to a Norman knight whose bones lie at Battle Abbey. The two families from which I spring were as different in temperament as in origin. My father's people were true Welshmen, sentimental, passionate, and rhetorical, easily moved both to anger and to tenderness; men who laughed and cried a great deal and who had not much of the talent for happiness. The Hamiltons were a cooler race. Their minds were critical and ironic and they had the talent for happiness in a high degree – went straight for it as experienced travellers go for the best seat in a train. From my earliest years I was aware of the vivid contrast between my mother's cheerful and tranquil affection and the ups and downs of my father's emotional life, and this bred in me long before I was old enough to give it a name a certain distrust or dislike of emotion as something uncomfortable and embarrassing and even dangerous.

Both my parents, by the standards of that time and place were bookish or 'clever' people. My mother had been a promising mathematician in her youth and a BA of Queen's College, Belfast, and before her death was able to start me both in French and Latin. She was a voracious reader of good novels, and I think the Merediths and Tolstoys which I have inherited were bought for her. My father's tastes were quite different. He was fond of oratory and had himself spoken on political platforms in England as a young man; if he had had independent means he would certainly have aimed at a political career. In this, unless his sense of honour, which was fine to the point of being quixotic, had made him unmanageable, he might well have succeeded, for he had many of the gifts once needed by a parliamentarian – a fine presence, a resonant voice, great quickness of mind, eloquence, and memory. Trollope's political novels were very dear to him; in following the career of Phineas Finn he was, as I now suppose, vicariously gratifying his own desires. He was fond of poetry provided it had elements of rhetoric or pathos, or both; I think *Othello* was his favourite Shakespearian play. He greatly enjoyed nearly all humorous authors, from Dickens to W.W. Jacobs, and was himself, almost without rival, the best raconteur I have ever heard; the best, that is, of his own type, the type that acts all the characters in turn with a free use of grimace, gesture, and pantomime. He was never happier than when closeted for an hour or so with one or two of my uncles exchanging 'wheezes' (as anecdotes were oddly called in our family). What neither he nor my mother had the least taste for was that kind of literature to which my allegiance was given the moment I could choose books for myself. Neither had ever listened for the horns of elfland. There was no copy either of Keats or Shelley in the house, and the copy of Coleridge was never (to my knowledge) opened. If I am a romantic my parents bear no responsibility for it. Tennyson, indeed, my father liked, but it was the Tennyson of *In Memoriam* and *Locksley Hall*. I never heard from him of the *Lotus Eaters* or the *Morte d'Arthur*. My mother, I have been told, cared for no poetry at all.

In addition to good parents, good food, and a garden (which then seemed large) to play in, I began life with two other blessings. One was our nurse, Lizzie Endicott, in whom even the exacting memory of childhood can discover no flaw – nothing but kindness, gaiety, and good sense. There was no nonsense about 'lady nurses' in those days. Through Lizzie we struck our roots into the peasantry of County Down. We were thus free of two very different social worlds. To this I owe my lifelong immunity from the false identification which some people make of refinement with virtue. From before I can remember I had understood that certain jokes could be shared with Lizzie which were impossible in the drawing-room; and also that Lizzie was, as nearly as a human can be, simply good.

The other blessing was my brother. Though three years my senior, he never seemed to be an elder brother; we were allies, not to say confederates, from the first. Yet we were very different. Our earliest pictures (and I can remember no time when we were not incessantly drawing) reveal it. His were of ships and trains and battles; mine, when not imitated from his, were of what we both called 'dressed animals' – the anthropomorphised beasts of nursery literature. His earliest story – as my elder he preceded me in the transition from drawing to writing – was called *The Young Rajah*. He had already made India 'his country'; Animal-Land was mine. I do not think any of the surviving drawings date from the first six years of my life which I am now describing, but I have plenty of them that cannot be much later. From them it appears to me that I had the better talent. From a very early age I could draw movement – figures that looked as if they were really running or fighting – and the perspective is good. But nowhere, either in my brother's work or my own, is there a single line drawn in obedience to an idea, however crude, of beauty. There is action, comedy, invention; but there is not even the germ of a feeling for design, and there is a shocking ignorance of natural form. Trees appear as balls of cotton wool struck on posts, and there is nothing to show that either of us knew the shape of any leaf in the garden where we played almost daily. This absence of beauty, now that I come to think of it, is characteristic of our childhood. No picture on the walls of my father's house ever attracted – and indeed none deserved – our attention. We never saw a beautiful building nor imagined that a building could be beautiful. My earliest aesthetic experiences, if indeed they were aesthetic, were not of that kind; they were already incurably romantic, not formal. Once in those very early days my brother brought into the nursery the lid of a biscuit tin which he had covered with moss and garnished with twigs and flowers so as to make it a toy garden or a toy forest. That was the first beauty I ever knew. What the real garden had failed to do, the toy garden did. It made me aware of nature – not, indeed, as a storehouse of forms and colours but as something cool, dewy, fresh, exuberant. I do not think the impression was very important at the moment, but it soon became important in memory. As long as I live my imagination of Paradise will retain something of my brother's toy garden. And every day there were what we called 'the Green Hills'; that is, the low line of the Castlereagh Hills which we saw from the nursery windows. They were not very far off but they were, to children, quite unattainable. They taught me longing – *Sehnsucht*; made me for good or ill, and before I was six years old, a votary of the Blue Flower.

If aesthetic experiences were rare, religious experiences did not occur at all. Some people have got the impression from my books that I was brought up in strict and vivid puritanism, but this is quite untrue. I was taught the usual things and made to say my prayers and in due time taken to church. I naturally accepted what I was told but I cannot remember feeling much interest in it. My father, far from being specially puritanical, was, by nineteenth-century and Church of Ireland standards, rather 'high', and his approach to religion, as to literature, was at the opposite pole from what later became my own. The charm of tradition and the verbal beauty of Bible and Prayer Book (all of them for me late and acquired tastes) were his natural delight, and it would have been hard to find an equally intelligent man who cared so little for metaphysics. Of my mother's religion I can say almost nothing from my own memory. My childhood, at all events, was not in the least other-worldly. Except for the toy garden and the Green Hills it was not even imaginative; it lives in my memory mainly as a period of humdrum, prosaic happiness and awakes none of the poignant nostalgia with which I look back on my much less happy boyhood. It is not settled happiness but momentary joy that glorifies the past.

To this general happiness there was one exception. I remember nothing earlier than the terror of certain dreams. It is a very common trouble at that age, yet it still seems to me odd that petted and guarded childhood should so often have in it a window opening on what is hardly less than Hell. My bad dreams were of two kinds, those about spectres and those about insects. The second were, beyond comparison, the worse; to this day I would rather meet a ghost than a tarantula. And to this day I could almost find it in my heart to rationalise and justify my phobia. As Owen Barfield once said to me, 'The trouble about insects is that they are like French locomotives – they have all the works on the outside.' *The works* – that is the trouble. Their angular limbs, their jerky movements, their dry, metallic noises, all suggest either machines that have come to life or life degenerating into mechanism. You may add that in the hive and the ant-hill we see fully realised the two things that some of us most dread for our own species – the dominance of the female and the dominance of the collective. One fact about the history of this phobia is perhaps worth recording. Much later, in my teens, from reading Lubbock's *Ants, Bees and Wasps,* I developed for a short time a genuinely scientific interest in insects. Other studies soon crowded it out; but while my entomological period lasted my fear almost vanished, and I am inclined to think a real objective curiosity will usually have this cleansing effect.

I am afraid the psychologists will not be content to explain my insect fears by what a simpler generation would diagnose as their cause – a certain detestable picture in one of my nursery books. In it a midget child, a sort of Tom Thumb, stood on a toadstool and was threatened from below by a stag-beetle very much larger than himself. This was bad enough; but there is worse to come. The horns of the beetle were strips of cardboard separate from the plate and working on a pivot. By moving a devilish contraption on the verso you could make them open and shut like pincers; snip-snap – snip-snap – I can see it while I write. How a woman ordinarily so wise as my mother could have allowed this abomination into the nursery is difficult to understand. Unless, indeed (for now a doubt assails me), unless that picture itself is a product of nightmare. But I think not.

In 1905, my seventh year, the first great change in my life took place. We moved house. My father, growing, I suppose, in prosperity, decided to leave the semidetached villa in which I had been born and build himself a much larger house, further out into what was then the country. The 'New House', as we continued for years to call it, was a large one even by my present standards; to a child it seemed less like a house than a city. My father, who had more capacity for being cheated than any man I have ever known, was badly cheated by his builders: the drains were wrong, the chimneys were wrong, and there was a draught in every room. None of this, however, mattered to a child. To me, the important thing about the move was that the background of my life became larger. The New House is almost a major character in my story. I am a product of long corridors, empty sunlit rooms, upstair indoor silences, attics explored in solitude, distant noises of gurgling cisterns and pipes, and the noise of wind under the tiles. Also, of endless books. My father bought all the books he read and never got rid of any of them. There were books in the study, books in the drawing-room, books in the cloakroom, books (two deep) in the great bookcase on the landing, books in a bedroom, books piled as high as my shoulder in the cistern attic, books of all kinds reflecting every transient stage of my parents' interests, books readable and unreadable, books suitable for a child and books most emphatically not. Nothing was forbidden me. In the seemingly endless rainy afternoons I took volume after volume from the shelves. I had always the same certainty of finding a book that was new to me as a man who walks into a field has of finding a new blade of grass. Where all these books had been before we came to the New House is a problem that never occurred to me until I began writing this paragraph. I have no idea of the answer.

Out of doors was 'the view' for which, no doubt, the site had principally been chosen. From our front door we looked down over wide fields to Belfast Lough and across it to the long mountain line of the Antrim shore – Divis, Colin, Cave Hill.

This was in the far-off days when Britain was the world's carrier and the lough was full of shipping; a delight to both us boys, but most to my brother. The sound of a steamer's horn at night still conjures up my whole boyhood. Behind the house, greener, lower, and nearer than the Antrim mountains, were the Holywood Hills, but it was not till much later that they won my attention. The north-western prospect was what mattered at first; the interminable summer sunsets behind the blue ridges, and the rooks flying home. In these surroundings the blows of change began to fall.

First of all, my brother was packed off to an English boarding school and thus removed from my life for the greater part of every year. I remember well the rapture of his homecomings for the holidays but have no recollection of any corresponding anguish at his departures. His new life made no difference to the relations between us. I, meanwhile, was going on with my education at home; French and Latin from my mother and everything else from an excellent governess, Annie Harper. I made rather a bugbear of this mild and modest little lady at the time, but all that I can remember assures me that I was unjust. She was a Presbyterian; and a longish lecture which she once interpolated between sums and copies is the first thing I can remember that brought the other world to my mind with any sense of reality. But there were many things that I thought about more. My real life – or what memory reports as my real life – was increasingly one of solitude. I had indeed plenty of people to talk to: my parents; my grandfather Lewis, prematurely old and deaf, who lived with us; the maids; and a somewhat bibulous old gardener. I was, I believe, an intolerable chatterbox. But solitude was nearly always at my command, somewhere in the garden or somewhere in the house. I had now learned both to read and write; I had a dozen things to do.

What drove me to write was the extreme manual clumsiness from which I always suffered. I attribute it to a physical defect which my brother and I both inherit from our father; we have only one joint in the thumb. The upper joint (that farthest from the nail) is visible, but it is a mere sham; we cannot bend it. But whatever the cause, nature laid on me from birth an utter

71

incapacity to make anything. With pencil and pen I was handy enough, and I can still tie as good a bow as ever lay on a man's collar, but with a tool or a bat or a gun, a sleeve link or a corkscrew, I have always been unteachable. It was this that forced me to write. I longed to make things, ships, houses, engines. Many sheets of cardboard and pairs of scissors I spoiled, only to turn from my hopeless failures in tears. As a last resource, as a *pis aller,* I was driven to write stories instead; little dreaming to what a world of happiness I was being admitted. You can do more with a castle in a story than with the best cardboard castle that ever stood on a nursery table.

I soon staked out a claim to one of the attics and made it 'my study'. Pictures, of my own making or cut from brightly coloured Christmas numbers of magazines, were nailed on the walls. There I kept my pen and inkpot and writing books and paint-box; and there. . .

> What more felicity can fall to creature
> Than to enjoy delight with liberty?

Here my first stories were written and illustrated, with enormous satisfaction. They were an attempt to combine my two chief literary pleasures – 'dressed animals' and 'knights-in-armour'. As a result, I wrote about chivalrous mice and rabbits who rode out in complete mail to kill not giants but cats. But already the mood of the systematiser was strong in me; the mood which led Trollope so endlessly to elaborate his Barsetshire. The Animal-Land which came into action in the holidays when my brother was at home was a modern Animal-Land; it had to have trains and steamships if it was to be a country shared with him. It followed, of course, that the medieval Animal-Land about which I wrote my stories must be the same country at an earlier period; and of course the two periods must be properly connected. This led me from romancing to historiography; I set about writing a full history of Animal-Land. Though more than one version of this instructive work is extant, I never succeeded in bringing it down to modern times; centuries take a deal of filling when all the events have to come out of the historian's head. But there is one touch in the

History that I still recall with some pride. The chivalric adventures which filled my stories were in it alluded to very lightly and the reader was warned that they might be 'only legends'. Somehow – but heaven knows how – I realised even then that a historian should adopt a critical attitude towards epic material. From history it was only a step to geography. There was soon a map of Animal-Land – several maps, all tolerably consistent. Then Animal-Land had to be geographically related to my brother's India, and India consequently lifted out of its place in the real world. We made it an island, with its north coast running along the back of the Himalayas; between it and Animal-Land my brother rapidly invented the principal steamship routes. Soon there was a whole world and a map of that world which used every colour in my paint-box. And those parts of that world which we regarded as our own – Animal-Land and India – were increasingly peopled with consistent characters. . .

It will be clear that at this time – at the age of six, seven, and eight – I was living almost entirely in my imagination; or at least that the imaginative experience of those years now seems to me more important than anything else. Thus I pass over a holiday in Normandy (of which, nevertheless, I retain very clear memories) as a thing of no account; if it could be cut out of my past I should still be almost exactly the man I am. But imagination is a vague word and I must make some distinctions. It may mean the world of reverie, daydream, wish-fulfilling fantasy. Of that I knew more than enough. I often pictured myself cutting a fine figure. But I must insist that this was a totally different activity from the invention of Animal-Land. Animal-Land was not (in that sense) a fantasy at all. I was not one of the characters it contained. I was its creator, not a candidate for admission to it. Invention is essentially different from reverie; if some fail to recognise the difference that is because they have not themselves experienced both. Anyone who has will understand me. In my daydreams I was training myself to be a fool; in mapping and chronicling Animal-Land I was training myself to be a novelist. Note well, a novelist; not a poet. My invented world was full (for me) of interest, bustle, humour, and character; but there was no poetry, even no romance, in it. It was almost astonishingly prosaic. Thus if we use the word imagination in a third sense, and the highest sense of all, this invented world was not imaginative. But certain other experiences were, and I will now try to record them. The thing has been much better done by Traherne and Wordsworth, but every man must tell his own tale.

The first is itself the memory of a memory. As I stood beside a flowering currant bush on a summer day there suddenly arose in me without warning, and as if from a depth not of years but of centuries, the memory of that earlier morning at the Old House when my brother had brought his toy garden into the nursery. It is difficult to find words strong enough for the sensation which came over me; Milton's 'enormous bliss' of Eden (giving the full, ancient meaning to 'enormous') comes somewhere near it. It was a sensation, of course, of desire; but desire for what? Not, certainly, for a biscuit-tin filled with moss, nor even (though that came into it) for my own past. 'Ιουλίαν ποθῶ [O, I desire too much] – and before I knew what I desired, the desire itself was gone, the whole glimpse withdrawn, the world turned commonplace again, or only stirred by a longing for the longing that had just ceased. It had taken only a moment of time; and in a certain sense everything else that had ever happened to me was insignificant in comparison.

The second glimpse came through *Squirrel Nutkin*; through it only, though I loved all the Beatrix Potter books. But the rest of them were merely entertaining; it administered the shock, it was a trouble. It troubled me with what I can only describe as the Idea of Autumn. It sounds fantastic to say that one can be enamoured of a season, but that is something like what happened; and, as before, the experience was one of intense desire. And one went back to the book, not to gratify the desire (that was impossible – how can one *possess* autumn?) but to re-awake it. And in this experience also there was the same surprise and the same sense of incalculable importance. It was something quite different from ordinary life and even from ordinary pleasure; something, as they would now say, 'in another dimension'.

The third glimpse came through poetry. I had become fond of

Longfellow's *Saga of King Olaf*: fond of it in a casual, shallow way for its story and its vigorous rhythms. But then, and quite different from such pleasures, and like a voice from far more distant regions, there came a moment when I idly turned the pages of the book and found the unrhymed translation of *Tegner's Drapa* and read:

> I heard a voice that cried,
> Balder the beautiful
> Is dead, is dead —

I knew nothing about Balder; but instantly I was uplifted into huge regions of northern sky, I desired with almost sickening intensity something never to be described (except that it is cold, spacious, severe, pale, and remote) and then, as in the other examples, found myself at the very same moment already falling out of that desire and wishing I were back in it.

The reader who finds these three episodes of no interest need read this book no further, for in a sense the central story of my life is about nothing else. For those who are still disposed to proceed I will only underline the quality common to the three experiences; it is that of an unsatisfied desire which is itself more desirable than any other satisfaction. I call it Joy, which is here a technical term and must be sharply distinguished both from Happiness and from Pleasure. Joy (in my sense) has indeed one characteristic, and one only, in common with them; the fact that anyone who has experienced it will want it again. Apart from that, and considered only in its quality, it might almost equally well be called a particular kind of unhappiness or grief. But then it is a kind we want. I doubt whether anyone who has tasted it would ever, if both were in his power, exchange it for all the pleasures in the world. But then Joy is never in our power and Pleasure often is.

I cannot be absolutely sure whether the things I have just been speaking of happened before or after the great loss which befell our family and to which I must now turn. There came a night when I was ill and crying both with headache and toothache and distressed because my mother did not come to me. That was because she was ill too; and what was odd was that there were

75

several doctors in her room, and voices and comings and goings all over the house and doors shutting and opening. It seemed to last for hours. And then my father, in tears, came into my room and began to try to convey to my terrified mind things it had never conceived before. It was in fact cancer and followed the usual course; an operation (they operated in the patient's house in those days), an apparent convalescence, a return of the disease, increasing pain, and death. My father never fully recovered from this loss.

Children suffer not (I think) less than their elders, but differently. For us boys the real bereavement had happened before our mother died. We lost her gradually as she was gradually withdrawn from our life into the hands of nurses and delirium and morphia, and as our whole existence changed into something alien and menacing, as the house became full of strange smells and midnight noises and sinister whispered conversations. This had two further results, one very evil and one very good. It divided us from our father as well as our mother. They say that a shared sorrow draws people closer together; I can hardly believe that it often has that effect when those who share it are of widely different ages. If I may trust to my own experience, the sight of adult misery and adult terror has an effect on children which is merely paralysing and alienating. Perhaps it was our fault. Perhaps if we had been better children we might have lightened our father's sufferings at this time. We certainly did not. His nerves had never been of the steadiest and his emotions had always been uncontrolled. Under the pressure of anxiety his temper became incalculable; he spoke wildly and acted unjustly. Thus by a peculiar cruelty of fate, during those months the unfortunate man, had he but known it, was really losing his sons as well as his wife. We were coming, my brother and I, to rely more and more exclusively on each other for all that made life bearable; to have confidence only in each other. I expect that we (or at any rate I) were already learning to lie to him. Everything that had made the house a home had failed us; everything except one another. We drew daily closer together (that was the good result) — two frightened urchins huddled for warmth in a bleak world.

Grief in childhood is complicated with many other miseries. I was taken into the bedroom where my mother lay dead; as they said, 'to see her,' in reality, as I at once knew, 'to see it'. There was nothing that a grown-up would call disfigurement – except for that total disfigurement which is death itself. Grief was overwhelmed in terror. To this day I do not know what they mean when they call dead bodies beautiful. The ugliest man alive is an angel of beauty compared with the loveliest of the dead. Against all the subsequent paraphernalia of coffin, flowers, hearse and funeral I reacted with horror. I even lectured one of my aunts on the absurdity of mourning clothes in a style which would have seemed to most adults both heartless and precocious; but this was our dear Aunt Annie, my maternal uncle's Canadian wife, a woman almost as sensible and sunny as my mother herself. To my hatred for what I already felt to be all the fuss and flummery of the funeral I may perhaps trace something in me which I now recognise as a defect but which I have never fully overcome – a distaste for all that is public, all that belongs to the collective; a boorish inaptitude for formality.

My mother's death was the occasion of what some (but not I) might regard as my first religious experience. When her case was pronounced hopeless I remembered what I had been taught; that prayers offered in faith would be granted. I accordingly set myself to produce by will-power a firm belief that my prayers for her recovery would be successful; and, as I thought, I achieved it. When nevertheless she died I shifted my ground and worked myself into a belief that there was to be a miracle. The interesting thing is that my disappointment produced no results beyond itself. The thing hadn't worked, but I was used to things not working, and I thought no more about it. I think the truth is that the belief into which I had hypnotised myself was itself too irreligious for its failure to cause any religious revolution. I had approached God, or my idea of God, without love, without awe, even without fear. He was, in my mental picture of this miracle, to appear neither as Saviour nor as Judge, but merely as a magician; and when He had done what was required of Him I supposed He would simply – well, go away. It never crossed my mind that the tremendous contact which I solicited should have any consequences beyond restoring the status quo. I imagine that a 'faith' of this kind is often generated in children and that its disappointment is of no religious importance; just as the things believed in, if they could happen and be only as the child pictures them, would be of no religious importance either.

With my mother's death all settled happiness, all that was tranquil and reliable, disappeared from my life. There was to be much fun, many pleasures, many stabs of Joy; but no more of the old security. It was sea and islands now; the great continent had sunk like Atlantis.

Surprised by Joy, 1966

GEORGE BUCHANAN
b.1904

COUNTY ANTRIM, EARLY TWENTIETH CENTURY

My father's a clergyman – small, with dark brown moustache; a voice unexpectedly rich. He lives at Kilwaughter, near the Antrim coast. His parish is wide. There are two churches nearly ten miles apart. At breakfast on Sunday he's worried, every delay annoys him. He's afraid, with his slow pony-trap, of arriving late for the services. To any child who comes late for breakfast he complains, 'How do you expect to get to church in time?' He breathes heavily, and offers breakfast to the offender.

Now he cuts a slice from the loaf. 'This bread,' he says, 'is too stale for Communion.' Another loaf is fetched, from which he cuts a new slice; he divides this into tiny cubes, which he puts into a tin box, for the altar.

It is time to go, my mother runs upstairs and downstairs. 'Have you got your keys? Your glasses? Your sermon?' After each question has been repeated, my father says, 'Yes.'

Outside on the gravel, white-bearded Finlay holds the pony ready in the trap. My father, plucking at the reins, says, 'Go on, Simon.' The trap emerges from the avenue and goes five miles over small hills on a road between thorn hedges and rusty wire.

Already for ten years my father has worked in this soft damp place, with sunny, but never hot, summers, under bosomy clouds – where bramble, wild parsley, dandelions, celandine, primrose, congregate and flower in their seasons – here, at a corner of the sea. A couple of miles away over the fields, there is the blue North Channel. From this road you can't in fact see the shore; the sea appears, then, to have no sand or rocks skirting it but to be edged by the green country.

'It's going to rain,' my father predicts. 'You can see the coast of

Scotland too clearly.' It's bad to see Scotland too clearly. Far off, in the distance, its promontories lie on the water like half-collapsed balloons.

In my father's sermons run passages like this:

> Day after day, week after week, month after month, year after year, one plods a section of the way as a treadmill. One sees the same old faces, the same old places. One longs for change and progress. But nothing happens.

Does he wish that anything *should* happen? He has accepted routine in a secluded world. If at times he becomes impatient it doesn't mean he wants to depart from monotony. Impatience is the spirit's faint rebellion, its demand for novelty, which, whenever experienced, it is his duty to quell.

One Sunday resembles another; only the weather is different. Today the sun is warm, the hedgerows afford little shade; the sun accentuates the smell of horse.

On a small hill is a huge Spanish chestnut, reputed to have been sown by a Spanish sailor, wrecked after the Armada disaster. Beside it stands the little church, surrounded by dark elm, yew-tree, sycamore, tombstones and grass. Carrying gilt-edged prayer books, people go up the hill in twos and threes. A sextoness gossips at the door.

Inside the porch, beside the font once used by Dean Swift, a man pulls on the bell-rope. 'Sun. . .day. . .Sun. . .day. . .' sings the bell. Those who are late hurry.

In the wooden pews sit farmers, farm-hands, a few gentry, wives, children. Choir girls stare down at their friends. They rise and sing 'O day of rest and gladness'. Everyone stands, within the pink walls under the arched wooden roof.

In the east window a red-cloaked Christ is blessing various figures – women, children, a prisoner in chains. Yellow words on the glass spell: COME UNTO ME ALL YE THAT LABOUR AND ARE HEAVY LADEN AND I WILL GIVE YOU REST.

The people stand, kneel, sit, as they have always done. My father repeats words that have been endlessly repeated: 'O God who art the author of peace and lover of concord. . .' The choir, dragging the tune, sing: 'Peace, perfect peace, in this dark world of sin. . .' We are emptied of anxiety for the future; we become affectionate towards everyone.

In the sermon my father urges us to be more obedient to God's commands. It's extraordinary the amount of submission he calls on us to give. Do our faces in the pews show signs of a drowsy enthusiasm? Beside me, my mother looks at the rings on her hand. Is she, too, responding to the spell of renunciation? Years ago at the university she belonged to a group of clever spirits. Now she often says to us: 'God is our Father. We are his children. Everything hangs on that.' She's anxious that God the Father should say that she has been a good girl.

The sermon continues. We, resigned, in the country, are not to worry if our lives are obscure.

Are there many among us disappointed men and women eating our hearts out, unrecognised and unknown?

If I pray to God to make me rich or grant me a title, and if I use lying and selfish means to enhance my comforts, then I cannot expect God to be with me.

The sermon is over. My father takes off his spectacles and walks to the altar. The choir sing the last hymn. . .

From over the crest of a small hill a sound of shots comes to our ears. We advance and see something which has changed the complexion of a hitherto tranquil field. A rifle range, with elaborate wheeled targets, is there; four prone men are firing; others, wearing military belts, stand behind them. We understand that these are Ulster Volunteers in training for a possible civil war. They wear badges inscribed NO SURRENDER.

Ping-ping! The shots strike the targets. The volunteers are learning how to kill.

For a time we stand in the hedge, watching. Then we step in among them to pick up some of the bullet-cases that litter the grass.

'Let's have a shot,' I say.

'Not today, sonny. By the hokey, you'd shoot yourself!'

It's the period of the British Constitutional Crisis. Ireland is about to be granted Home Rule by a Liberal Parliament; but, at the instigation of English Conservatives, armed opposition to this has been organised in Ulster, through the Orange Order, composed of Protestant workers. With these rebels, my father tends to side. The Orange workers are docile towards the English industries that use them; and industry brings advantages. 'It is better to build a new factory than an alms-house,' my father says, with a picture in mind of impoverished, pre-industrial parts in the south of the island.

Moreover, he's a Protestant. Protestants are people who have taken a few steps away from old dogma towards liberty of thought. (They don't necessarily wish to advance further.) They hate and fear their former 'bad' selves, the serfs of strictness. A self-governing Ireland would so carry them back, they think – a fear carefully played upon by interested politicians.

In the rectory my mother says: 'We have found leaders to take up our cause.' She's referring to Sir Edward Carson whose eloquence sways the crowd. She shows us a pen. 'With this,' she says, 'I signed the Covenant [a pledge to oppose Home Rule]. You will show it to your grandfather with pride.' Evidently life has become noble and heroic. 'We live in stirring times, when a small province has the courage to face a large Empire.'

We look at the pen. We repeat the slogans such as *No Surrender,* which are being repeated around us.

My father holds a service specially for the rebels. Wearing military equipment, they file into the pews. In the east window the glass Christ still offers rest; but today the church is dedicated to *unrest.*

Is my father, who studies so much to be submissive, attracted by the insubmission of the Orangemen? He who deprives himself of initiative and audacity, who says 'not my will but Thine' – would he be inclined to regard a little rebellion as a relief? Some shadow of truth may lie in these speculations. More accurately, perhaps, rebellion isn't in him; his support of the Ulster Volunteers may be rather a further act of submission – this time, not to God but to his milieu.

In his sermon he says:

> As yew trees used in ancient times to be planted in the shadow of churches, so that our ancestors might at any moment cut the national weapon from ground hallowed by God's worship and their father's graves, so our churches come forward to cheer this movement and lend sanction by a solemn service and bless the uplifted hand.

After the service the men march jauntily down the hill. . .

Coming out from an amateur theatrical performance in Larne, my mother finds the main street lined with members of the volunteer force. She recognises and questions a pedlar who has often called at the rectory. Heavy with pride in his duties, he says slowly: 'Go you home to bed, and ask no questions.' She continues to ask him, and he concedes: 'All you need to know is that the Ulster Volunteers are doing their duty. We're out all over the country tonight.'

On her way home she passes a stream of cars and lorries, with full headlights, that are racing in the direction of the harbour.

And all through the night, on the road beside the rectory, we can hear the cars and we can see the trees constantly illumined by their headlamps.

In the morning it is understood that an extraordinary event has occurred. A ship from Germany landed a cargo of arms at Larne Harbour. The police barracks were surrounded and the telephone wires cut. Already the arms have been distributed to points through the province, some being concealed under chancel floors in Protestant churches.

From this night the rebellion passes beyond the stage of play-acting.

In an old castle beside the coast, still in the parish, we have rooms during August. Through windows in the immensely thick walls we overlook the beach. How I love the sea! At night I hear it roaring softly outside. I dream of swimming in green tides among black rocks. In the morning I jump out of bed and gaze through the window, set in the immense thick wall, at the half-moon of sand with breakers falling over upon it.

At breakfast my father reads from the newspaper that Germany has invaded Belgium, and that Britain has declared war on her. Germany has entered upon a European campaign, encouraged by the civil dissension in Britain that roared the other night past our gates.

I know nothing about war. Our history books give an impression that the world contains one invincible power, the British Empire. How can the Germans be so foolish as to make war against it? They must *know* they'll be beaten! I think of hussars in pretty helmets riding out to victory, as usual; and this is not only certain but also exciting and brave. . .

Along a grey Belfast street battalion after battalion, dressed in khaki, swinging their right arms high, make a roaring noise of feet, as they beat the stone surface. Fife and brass bands play. One band strikes up a rattling Orange tune:

> Slitter-slaughter
> Holy water
> Sprinkle the Papishes
> Ev-er-y-one. . .

Another drones out the homesick songs of war:

> Pack up your troubles in your old kitbag
> And smile, boys, smile.

Such war songs neither exalt battle nor jeer at an enemy; they're meant to console unhappy soldiers.

Watching the procession, we stand in a patch of garden before a redbrick house. Dick and I climb a plane tree, whose bark is black with grime, whence we obtain a wide view. 'You won't miss much,' my father observes.

The spectators cheer; but my father, with his parish in mind, is filled with the excitement of dismay. These are men of our own province marching as a public spectacle through the city before sailing to a war. They're the former rebels, transformed into the Ulster Division. Their own suits, belts, rifles have been put aside; now they wear the uniform of the British Army; now they'll fight in France side by side with those whom, a few months ago, they were prepared to shoot. Their illegal German rifles have gone to the Belgians, to be turned against the German senders. Events have taken a twist.

Bursts of shouting from the sheeplike crowds rise along the street. Have they no other attitude to these obviously doomed men but imbecile cheers and the waving of penny flags on bamboo-sticks? Have the raw soldiers themselves no other attitude to their applauded predicament but one of jokes and sloppy refrains?

Although my father is sorry for them, he cannot help remarking on their better health and comportment, the result of military discipline. 'Left. . . right. . . left. . . right,' an officer, proud of his new rank, calls stridently.

Dick studies his pocket compass. 'They're marching due north-north-east.'

Why have we been brought? Is it our duty to see men march out for a cause? It is understood that for men to march to war like this through an excited city is noble in the extreme. We have heard often enough *dulce et decorum est pro patria mori*; and saying it in accordance with the law of elision, *dulc' et decor' est pro partria mori,* we believe it implicitly. This scrupulously pronounced echo from the past makes us gaze with respect at these troops, who bear no resemblance to Roman legions but are red-faced Irishmen in tunics.

We say to one another: 'Suppose we ran away and told a lie about our ages, we might be taken as recruits.'

'They have *boys* as buglers. Look at that boy!' A child-faced bugler passes.

'Unfortunately,' we have to admit, 'we can't bugle!'

We discuss how it might be possible to make ourselves look older, as old as seventeen or eighteen.

The procession ends.

The last man appears slightly ridiculous. There follow a few dogs and urchins. Then the crowd closes in. Tramcars, with drivers striking the gongs with their heels, begin to grind again along the street.

My father says 'Come down!' to us in the tree.

'Are you going now?'

'Yes, we're going.'

Our clothes are marked by grime from the branches; and I'm feeling sick.

The railway train, carrying us, puffs along the coast from Belfast to Larne. In the pony-trap we jog over the miles to the rectory, which, with so many men drained away from the province, seems lonelier among the fields. . .

While we, outside our school studies, still play and contemplate nature and feel in contradiction to an unnamed philistinism, romantic signs more violent than ours begin to show in other parts of the island. Irish nationalism, rooted in the soil, has taken to arms – not, as with the Ulster rebels, to maintain and keep the industrial connections, but to sever them. Led by a poet, Padraig Pearse, it is an astonishing outbreak in an apathetic time. Yeats's refrain catches the nature of the moment:

> All changed, changed utterly,
> A terrible beauty is born.

Of course we don't realise that this revolt can express a mood similar to our own: we're children; it's an event as far off as Dublin and condemned by our elders; it has nothing to do with what goes on in our hearts. Yet however anxious we are for the insurrection to be reduced, we can't fail to perceive excitement in that handful being shelled in Dublin Post Office, of whom Pearse speaks in a manifesto:

> If they do not win this fight, they will at least have deserved to win it. But win it they will, although they win it in death. Already they have won a great thing. They have redeemed Dublin from many shames, and made her name splendid among the names of cities.

This is Easter 1916.

The rebels are defeated; and several leaders, including Sir Roger Casement, put to death.

This is a year of death, indeed, for the Irish. In July those men whom we saw marching through Belfast are obliterated in France. At the command of English generals, the Ulster Division hurls itself to be mown down, across impossible terrain at Thiepval.

So end, for the most part, those kindly, obstinate, easily deceived neighbours of ours. The houses are full of mourning; and thousands of women walk in black dresses. . .

Green Seacoast, 1959

I am seventeen-and-a-half. I have begun work in the office of a morning newspaper in Belfast. The *Northern Whig* was founded in 1824 as 'a political journal devoted to the advocacy of Liberal principles'. F.D. Finlay, the first editor, suffered two terms of imprisonment in 1826 and 1832 in the course of his struggle for various reforms, including that of Catholic emancipation. After 100 years the newspaper has changed its character, is hardly Whig any more. It submits to the prevailing political line, which is Conservative and Unionist (the word Unionist meaning unity with England, not with the rest of Ireland). I can't say that I'm in favour of its now changed politics. What I'm there for is to gain newspaper experience. Every evening from 7 p.m. to 2 a.m. I work in the office near the docks, not far from the Albert Clock. What late hours! On leaving the office I am obliged to walk nervously to my distant digs through a city under curfew.

Shots. . . buildings on fire. . . this is night-time in Belfast during the Troubles.

For centuries Ireland was a subjugated colony of England. The resistance movement against the occupying power, stimulated by the attempted coup d'état of 1916 in Dublin, grew in force, and by 1920 had won a partial independence for the country, under the terms of which the island was divided into two parts. At the time of which I am writing – in the southern part dissatisfied nationalists are still continuing their fight against England. But in the northern part a loyalist (loyal to England) government has been established, and has been greeted with outbreaks of violence from nationalist opponents. This violence leads in turn to widespread reprisals from the loyalists. To deal with the disorders British troops have come in; and Belfast is almost continuously under curfew.

At night the streets are empty and are patrolled by armoured cars, as I go home. Sometimes a sentry lets me walk past him for 50 yards and then recalls me, for the pleasure of making me come back to show my permit. He is a B Special. He has his own way of enjoying night duty.

When I arrive and am about to open the door of the house where I lodge, I imagine gunmen waiting, perhaps behind the gable or inside in the hall. I say to myself: 'You must control these fears.' And next day quite likely I read that an hour before or an hour after my passing some 'outrage' has been committed in one of the streets: perhaps a family has been lined up and shot by raiders. I am only a few minutes or a few steps, it seems, from the raging murder.

In this respect the *Northern Whig* isn't innocent. Leading articles refer to reprisals and may appear to suggest them, articles written by a grey-bearded Englishman who wouldn't hurt a fly. He is disgusted, for example, at James Joyce calling the sea 'snot-green' in the first chapter of *Ulysses*. As a comment on our climate he walks about the office wearing gumboots.

I'm in the subeditors' room. The copy slides down a chute from the creed room and falls in front of the chief subeditor, who puts some of it on a pin and passes some of it to the four or five subeditors to prepare for the printer. John Shaw, the chief subeditor, with a white moustache, pads about in carpet boots. 'Now, young fella-me-lad, here's something for you to do. See what you can make of this story. It ought to be cut to ribbons.' He's my patient instructor. (In subediting you don't write, though you often rewrite; you sort, select, cut, adapt other people's information; put headlines on it. You have to be accurate, keep everything brief, and you don't have much time to change your mind as the newspaper is made up page by page.)

While we are working, we hear shots in the street, and the windows are filled with a glow from buildings which are on fire. 'Another bad night!' someone says.

One of the subeditors, Alex Riddell, keeps *The Oxford Book of English Verse* in a drawer and takes quotations from it for his articles in the weekly edition. He gives me this advice: 'Never allow anything into the paper that isn't right by your standards. Even a Pro. Par. [Provincial Paragraph] must be perfect in its own way.'

'Ha! Can it be?'

'You try.' He says that a writer's duty is to take a positive attitude towards even these humble tasks of expression. So with news of some farm fire in Tyrone I rewrite the sentences as carefully as if I were translating from *The Greek Anthology*.

Another subeditor, Larry Morrow, is more my age: we arrange to meet in a café. Alex Glendinning, my schoolfriend, comes there too. He is now in the linen trade. He says: 'I feel as if a voluminous web of cloth were gathering about me.' He talks as in printed sentences on a page. When he tells a joke, you can almost hear the punctuation.

Larry and I go on from the café to the newspaper office. Journalism is like the labour of Sisyphus: there's a rebeginning every night. 'Our most careful sentences by midday already lie in somebody's lavatory.'

In the front office a woman known as Gold Tooth is screaming: she is drunk and has been picked up by the police who are waiting for their van. This well-known prostitute is lying on the floor, trying to catch my foot as I step past her to my work.

We sit, crossing out, rewriting the long-winded copy. 'Orr of Ballymena sends screeds about nothing. . . Ritchie of Bangor is nearly as bad. . .'

'Slash it! Slash it!'

'I *am* slashing it.'

Larry reflects: 'This place needs bursting with something other than bombs. We have enough of those.'

89

Outside, the fires, the distant explosions. Why does the fighting still go on?

The new Treaty between the South and England (which was ratified in Dublin early in 1922) has been followed by a further subdivision of the South, into those for and those against the Treaty – so grave that it has led to a civil war. I have already been a boyish supporter of the rebels. Now our taste for nationalism is troubled by this tragic civil war. Our own part of Ireland, the North, has been excluded from the rest: our island has been partitioned. We don't feel that one part, and not the other, is Ireland; to us, both parts are Ireland. Our northern contribution surely will be, not to deny that we exist, but to exist well, and hope for unity. The 1920 Act envisages that the two parts may one day find a link and converge. 'Work with what you have', the law for poets, is not a law for extreme nationalist revolutionaries, who are fixed on what they have not. If there were less belief it might be better. It's the unbelievers who are gentle, not the believers.

We are talking too much. The chief subeditor shouts: 'Stop your jaw! Get on with those Provincial Paragraphs.'

I boil a kettle in a room beyond the case-room: I'm the junior and must make tea for the others.

A sports reporter, Parker, filling his pipe from Shaw's tobacco pouch, holds up a handful of the brown tobacco which looks almost like seaweed. 'Did you wade far out for it?' he says. Pointing to the leader-writer's door, he asks: 'How's Nebu? [short for Nebuchadnezzar: a reference to the leader-writer's beard] Has he written his piece yet?. . . I could write his stuff with my eyes shut.'

'Your copy looks like that.' Larry points to the reporter's account of a football match, reads out a phrase: '. . . piloted the ball between the uprights. . .'

Parker smiles. 'That's the stuff! Take my word for it, you half-cooked Alfred Lord Tennyson! You couldn't do better yourself.'

There are plenty of jokes of this and other kinds: I am guilty of one of them. On the telephone I talk in an assumed voice to the reporters' room: 'This is Ritchie of Bangor,' and I dictate some information about a gruesome event, and my words are carefully taken down in shorthand by Bob Orr, BA (he is always referred to with the BA). Later I go to the reporters' room and tell him what I have done. He rushes at me. He is six feet tall. Fortunately I manage to put him down on the floor; at the same time breaking a chair. Bob Orr, surprised, calls me Sandow and says: 'You ought to take up wrestling as a profession.'

Morning Papers, 1965

PATRICK KAVANAGH
1904–1967

COUNTY MONAGHAN, EARLY TWENTIETH CENTURY

The name of my birthplace was Mucker; some of the natives
wanted to change it to Summerhill which would have been worse.
All who could do so without risking the loss of their scant mail cut
'Mucker' out of their postal address altogether. The natives of the
place were known far and near as Muckers, which in after years
was rhymed obscenely by corner-boys. The name was a corrupted
Gaelic word signifying a place where pigs were bred in abundance. Long before my arrival there was much aesthetic heart-
aching among the folk who had to put up with, and up in, such a
pig-named townland. In spite of all this the townland stuck to its
title and it was in Mucker I was born.

Astrologers anxious to read my stars have now and then
queried the hour and date of my birth. I always gave them somebody else's stars to read so that the horoscope mightn't put me out
of humour with my dreams. But to those who may desire to cast
for me my horoscope now I will say: my stars are events in time,
things that happened and could not have happened to one born in
the sixteenth century. The date of my birth is cut on the tablets of
common existence.

The railway line to Carrick was visible from our back window.
One hundred yards from our house was the railway gate-house
and level-crossing where the Mucker Road joined the county
highway. The railway was important: we set our clock by the
three-thirty train. My father said the three-thirty was the only
train you could depend on. It was the only train that had a
connection to make. The other trains started just when the driver
felt in the humour, and made no important connections except the
pubs where the driver, fireman, and guard quenched their smoky

thirsts. We possessed the only clock in the townland. It was an old clock, Father bought it second-hand for half-a-crown thirty years earlier, and the old woman from whom he bought it had herself bought it second-hand forty years earlier still. That clock was as touchy as a spoiled child; it would only go for Father. Not even Jock Brickle, the wandering clock-repairer, could make it keep time. Once indeed Father did let Jock try his hand at the old timepiece. Jock took it asunder. When he reassembled it there was one wheel for which the clock-repairer could find no place. He tried to fix the wheel in sideways, angle-wise, and turban-wise, and while so engaged the old clock started tick-tock, tick-tock.

'There was a wheel too many in yer clock,' Jock said.

The clock continued to go but when the hour came to be struck there was no response. Father dissembled the clock again and reinserted the extra wheel.

'That finishes me with Jock Brickle,' he said. Of course Father had a watch, but that was a private affair, and had no communal importance. All the neighbours passing our house called in to inquire the time.

At the other end of the Mucker Road, out of sight of the railway, was another clock. It wasn't very reliable as it was set by the bread-cart. The 'Bumper' Rooney, the bread-server, was sometimes late and sometimes early. Our clock was dependable, never more than a half-hour fast or slow. In any case time hardly mattered much. The sun rose and set in a land of dreams whether the clocks were right or wrong.

My part of Ireland had a poet at one time, a poor ragged fellow whom no respectable person would be seen talking to, but he left doors open as he passed. The peasant folk knew the lore and strange knowledges of God and Greece that they didn't know they knew. From the lips of simple old women I heard phrases of whimsical prophecy and exciting twists of language that would delight the heart of a wheelbarrow or a modernist poet.

When I was born the people weren't expecting a poet. They already had one, self-styled the Bard of Callenberg and his satiric rhymes were about as much as they could stomach.

Tailor Magrane putting in the long buck stitches
And Carpenter Hamill cutting his timber out of the ditches.

That was how the Bard of Callenberg summed up the local tailor
and carpenter.

The people didn't want a poet, but a fool, yes they could be
doing with one of these. And as I grew up not exactly 'like
another' I was installed the fool.

I was the butt of many an assembly. I hadn't then read the
wisdom of King Cormac Mac Art – 'Never be the butt of an
assembly.' At wake, fair or dance for many years I was the fellow
whom the jokers took a hand at when conversational funds fell
low. I very nearly began to think myself an authentic fool. I often
occupied a position like that of the Idiot in Dostoevsky's novel. I
do not blame the people who made me their fool; they wanted a
fool and in any case they lost their stakes.

Being made a fool of is good for the soul. It produces a sensitivity of one kind or other; it makes a man into something
unusual, a saint or a poet or an imbecile. I often used to regret not
having been born among the mountains or by the sea. Then I
might have been brave enough to drink to excess the wild wine of
fantasy. And I thought, too, that it would be a fine thing to be
reared in a workhouse – fatherless, motherless, and so free from
the net of love.

Many of my neighbours treated me with cruelty and derision,
but against that I have had – not friends – lovers. Anybody who
cared for me cared a great deal for me.

When I arrived in Mucker the natives were beginning to lose
faith in the old, beautiful things. The ghost of a culture haunted
the snub-nosed hills.

The parish priest was the centre of gravity, he was the only man
who was sure to go to heaven. Our staple diet was potatoes and
oatmeal porridge. Porridge had only recently taken the place of
potatoes and buttermilk as the national supper.

Though little fields and scraping poverty do not lead to grand
flaring passions, there was plenty of fire and an amount of vicious
neighbourly hatred to keep us awake. Most of the neighbours had

at one time or another gone to law chiefly for trespass.

'Show me good fences and I'll show you good neighbours', is a saying we had. The fences in Mucker were bad stone-ditches that a lame duck could cross. Neighbours often went to law over the right-of-way to a well. Never was there a case for abusive and threatening language. There was language abusive enough though. Each person was keeping up spite to at least two of his neighbours.

We had two families that we didn't care a great deal for, though in the end everybody got too lazy for hating.

My father was a shoemaker in the good days when a pair of shop boots were an insult to any decent man's feet. He was a small, lively, intelligent man and had among the people a reputation for learning almost as great as the schoolmaster. He played the melodeon till he was forty. He then got married. His passion for music was strong and even after his marriage he found crevices in among his cares in which to play. He was fond of reading but – peace to his soul – he never really got beyond the stage of *Titbits* and *Answers*. I am sorry when I think of all the creations of the mind that he could have enjoyed.

My father loved me and I loved him, but he didn't like my daydreaming way of living. He said I'd end my days in the workhouse if I didn't change my gait of going. Like Solomon he was a firm believer in the virtue-giving qualities of the rod, except that he used a strap, and many's the flogging I got from him, most of which I deserved; for I had none, or very few, of the qualities that go into the making of a perfect child. I was a bit of a lazy-bones, a bit of a liar and a bit of a rogue.

'Let me at him,' Father would say. 'Let me at him till I knock the daylight out of him.' He wouldn't be very well pleased if he was let at me. As our kitchen was his cobbler's shop there was always someone to stand between me and my father's anger. I was only afraid of my father when he had his spectacles on. He is dead a good many years now, yet as I write these words I know he is beside me, encouraging me to go on and win to be a great writer. I can see him smile and he isn't wearing his spectacles.

My mother was a simple peasant woman, twenty years younger

than Father. She was without any schooling but was very shrewd, a good judge of men and animals, and the best measurer of unknown quantities I have ever known. From my father I have inherited the spirit, from my mother the material garment of wisdom. In our house the two most important subjects were the saying of the Rosary each evening and the making of money. Ours was a united house, there was only one purse let it be full or empty. In other houses the man held to what he could make from cattle or corn, the wife would have to supply the kitchen from the proceeds of butter and eggs. Everybody was poor and proud. My parents didn't know anything to be proud of, so they just carried on. All the small farmers had as income was the price of a pig or a calf every twelve months. We had no land but into our house came what is known as the 'dropping shilling'. My parents were great experts in making the hens lay in winter – the hens of the neighbours only laid when the birds in the bushes were laying and prices at their lowest.

There were nine children in our family. All our names are to be found in the calendar of the saints: it was to that calendar Father went in search of a name when a child was born, and not back to some dubious ancestor with a name like a gnarled stick.

My father wrote the history of his family for me on a sheet of foolscap. I have often wondered since if he hadn't some instinct that I should some day give it the permanency of print. It was a romantic story of his father who had come out of the West to sow the wild, vigorous seed of Connaught among the little hills of south Ulster.

Because I knew I had the manuscript to read any time I only scanned it once. I put it in what I thought a safe place in the bottom of a large delf jug – a preposterous heirloom that was never in use. When my father was dead a month I looked in the jug and it was empty: and whether it was the handmaid of Prudery or Cleanliness swept it away I do not know. I was filled with grief as I never now could have a copy.

All my early memories are evening memories close to bedtime.

The haze of years is kind to sharp jutting stones.

I was in my mother's arms clinging with my small hands to the security of her shoulder. I saw into a far mysterious place that I long associated with Wordsworth's ode on immortality. I believed for many years that I had looked back into the world from whence I came. And perhaps I had.

But examined in the light of honest reality what I had really seen was the secret side of a cupboard. It was a sort of press which only opened one door, and the end of the not very accessible top-shelf was filled with rent receipts and curtain rings and such like.

Not very long ago I have looked into that same cupboard where it lies in an outhouse discarded, and the rent receipts are still there, a good deal yellower than they were and their corners mouse-eaten, and the curtain rings are there, too, though the rusty base metal has eaten away most of the brass veneer.

Of such is the Land of the Immortals. . .

A county council quarry was opened in our vicinity. Among the quarry-men was one man named Bob. He was a stout fellow of thirty, brown-eyed and very quiet. For three months he passed our house on his way to work before we spoke to each other. He was usually reading a book – an Irish grammar. He was studying Gaelic.

Then one evening he came in to have his boot repaired. Bob was a flame. He touched the damp wood of my mind till sparks began to dance.

He talked on unusual themes. He mentioned Canon Law, syphilis, and irregular verbs. He recited verse, bad verse by critical standards, perhaps; Longfellow's *Evangeline* and a translation of Dante by – I think – Cary.

He had tried his skill at verse-making himself. One poem of eleven lines he gave me; there were meant to be twelve lines, but he couldn't get the last line. 'For the past six months I've been trying to find that line,' he told me.

'Beside an Irish rath,' was the nearest he could get.

'It's a great poem as it is,' I told him, 'a real masterpeice.' And I thought so at the time. We were then standing in the shadow of Rocksavage wall, close to the crossroads from which the wild laughter of young men came. It was a moonlit evening in October and the air was filled with the fragrance of over-ripe blackberries and elderberries.

'Aren't they the gets?' I said, referring to the boys at the crossroads.

'They're true Irishmen,' he said.

Bob gave me a long lecture on the beauty of *Alice in Wonderland* and *Gil Blas*.

Down among the slabs of basalt rock, when Bob was in the quarry, thought took wing. The listeners in this academy of stone hunger were fed.

'What is God?'

'God's a man.'

Bob's conception of God, whatever it was, must have been a million-forked tongue of truth.

'What would the priest say if he heard us?' some fool was sure to say. And Bob would tell them that their conversation was truly religious. Bob was asked a long time afterwards who was the cleverest man he had ever met; he said I was. Lucky for me I didn't hear of this opinion till my mind had developed a resistance to vanity.

A neighbour of mine – a young fellow who lived alone in a fine house – had a large stock of inherited books. I used to visit him in the winter evenings. He loaned me books. We would sit by his fire long hours discussing literature. I did most of the talking, and I shudder when I think of the flood of poetic silliness I let loose on my friend. We agreed that 'The Siege of Corinth', by Byron, was sublime. I it was who suggested the word 'sublime'.

'Sublime, that's exactly the word,' my host said. I envied this fellow his stock of books. The fine old volumes lay blue-moulded around the floor and tables. Burns's poems and a huge history of Rome stood on the hob. On top of a bag of flour lay – in the company of some copies of the *Wide World Magazine* – Shelley's *The Cenci*. It was the fashion in fancy houses to have a big book on the parlour table. This man had several big books on his parlour table, but it wasn't for vanity.

'Two is company, three is a crowd,' the saying goes. There is deep intimacy when two men sit by a winter fire. When a third enters – though he be of close spiritual kindred – the whole fabric of familiar sweetness and innocence comes to pieces.

This often happened to us. Some fellow was sure to come rumbling in his hob-nailed boots up the cobbled yard to our door. A bull to the china-shop of the angels.

'Anybody inside?'

'Come in.'

If the fellow who entered had leprosy or was a lunatic with a gun I wouldn't be half as vexed. And he would more than likely be breezy with good humour. He would be entirely unconscious that he was treading on holy ground. He would be sure to lift a book and turn over the pages before he sat down.

'Aw, holy fiddlesticks! What the divil does that mane?'

It might be Milton's *Paradise Lost,* for that chunk of poetic theology was in my friend's library.

We wouldn't tell him what the book was.

'Take a sate,' the man of the house would say.

Then the talk would turn on the loud wheel of present day. I could talk that kind of talk, too, but it went against the grain of my soul. So that when I talked everyday-talk I was the most vulgar man in the company.

This man's house was quite close to my own. I was lucky, for had it been miles distant I should have gone there to read the books, and more than that to unload myself of my poetic whimsies. There were so few to whom I could talk.

He gave me the works of Pope. In this edition the poet was given as Mr Pope. I liked Pope. His essays on Man and on Criticism were good strong truths in rhyme. At the crossroads on Sunday afternoon I recited with enthusiasm to a crowd of farm-folk.

> Of all the causes which conspire to blind
> Man's erring judgment and misguide the mind,
> What the weak head with strongest bias rules
> Is pride, the never-failing vice of fools.

My hearers understood and appreciated this. Some of them were very eager for knowledge. We might have had some very metaphysical debates if there were not always in the crowd one of those ridicule-making fellows whom poor Ireland still continues to produce.

My sister was attending the convent school. She had many books dealing with the craft of verse.

Intermediate Poetry and Prose, by Father Corcoran, D.Litt., was one I remember. I thumb-marked that book. I studied iambics, trochees, rhyme and stanza. I counted the feet in the verses I read. I tried to write verse myself, but the number of feet per line varied to break my heart. Once I wrote a complete poem and sent it to a weekly paper which had a Poet's Corner. I was in wonderful humour the next week when I saw my initials among the list of those whose poems had been rejected. It was recognition. I never imagined that the editor would as much as recognise that my writing was verse, even for the waste-paper basket. I was getting on.

I made a lot of ballads. I sang them at dances, and part of one at a wake. I remember at the wake how I had just the first verse sung when the Rosary broke out in the room of the corpse.

> Thou, O Lord, wilt open my lips
> And my tongue shall announce Thy praise.

We all dropped on our knees.

Some of the girls at the dances got romantic about me. I really believe that one of them fell in love with me. The boys laughed at my songs, though not all. Some of them said I 'was the makings of a very good comic'.

My first song celebrated the drinking of a half-barrel of stout. I remember four lines.

> Farrelly fell over the barrow
> At the gable-end of the house
> And the singing and ructions were awful
> Around the half-barrel of stout.

To relations in America I wrote letters in rhyme. 'I see you have a new Tom Moore,' one of the Yankees wrote to my father.

As I wandered about the roads and fields I composed my verses. I was spreading dung in drills for turnips in a field belonging to

100

Red Pat. Red Pat was not at home. I was alone. I got my tea in the field. Sitting beside a heap of steaming dung I drank the tea and afterwards felt in great poetic form. I had lately been reading of a poet who made a poem about a telegraph pole. I started making a poem on an old wooden gate which guarded a field I knew. For every drill of dung I spread I made a line of verse. I kept adding to the poem till it was of grand size. I sent it to the editor of the local paper. The next week my poem appeared.

ADDRESS TO AN OLD WOODEN GATE

Battered by time and weather, scarcely fit
For firewood. There's not a single bit
Of paint to hide those wrinkles, and such scringes
Tear hoarsely down the silence – rusty hinges.
A barbed-wire clasp around one withered arm
Replaces the old latch with wanton charm.
This gap ere long must find another sentry
If the cows are not to roam the open country.

There was a whole column of similar quality. I cannot remember the rest. It wasn't too bad. The readers of the paper didn't like it. They wanted sentimental verse about the gallant sons of Erin or something like that.

Everyone who had an old wooden gate – and that was half the parish – claimed that it was *their* gate I had slandered.

I sent some verse to the Poet's Corner of a Dublin paper. It was published. Part of the rules of the Corner was that the author's address as well as name must be at the bottom of each poem. This rule left the poets open to a lot of fan-mail. I got books of tickets to sell for charitable purposes. From priests and nuns these tickets came.

An Irish woman in Wigan, England, wrote asking if I would do some research into her family history for her. Her mother's people were natives of Monaghan, she said, and she would love to know if there were any of the name in the place now.

A fellow wrote to me from Chicago:

101

DEAR FRIEND,

I read your poem entitled 'A Memory' in the Irish paper. I
have never found this sense in writing before.

The weather here is very bad for the past two weeks, but I
think we will have a dry spell soon.

Wishing you great success in your writing.

> I remain,
>
> Yours sincerely,
>
> HARRY J. MILLIN

I replied to this letter. Then my distant admirer began to flood
me with letters and piles of comic papers. Some days I got half a
dozen letters from him. He sent me a Sunday-school paper in
which he had inserted an advertisement in praise of me. It was a
double-column advertisement about six inches square:

GREETINGS:

FROM HARRY J. MILLIN TO PATRICK KAVANAGH,

POET, IRELAND.

It was headed thus in heavy black type. There was a lot of small
print which said big things about my poetic genius. I was suffering
from chronic poverty at this time and I wrote to H.J.M. for
money. I had hopes that he might be a mad millionaire. He
replied:

DEAR FRIEND,

This is the first letter of this description I have ever received. I can only afford to send you one dollar. I am only a
poor lift-man in a hotel at fifteen dollars a week.

> Yours sincerely,
>
> H. J.M.

I lost contact with him shortly afterwards.

Verse-writing was getting a grip on me. It grew unawares like an insidious disease. But I wasn't satisfied. There was something dead and rotten about the verse-world in which I moved.

Of Yeats I had not heard. Not one of the contributors to our Corner had heard of him either. Yeats, AE, Colum, Stephens, and all that crowd, if their names ever came through the dense wall of prejudice, to us would have been just a gang of evil men who were out for a destruction of the Catholic Faith. No nun or priest would send books of lottery tickets to such men.

We were very pious poets. Many of the poems in the Corner were religious. The Blessed Virgin, St Patrick, St Bridget, the Sacred Heart, and others of lesser nimbus power provided themes for our verse. From Brian Boru to Dan O'Connell we sang the praises of the saints of Irish nationalism as well.

We were the biddable children of Kathleen Mavourneen – but for me at least the grey dawn was breaking.

It was the last days of August 1927. We had grass-seed for sale. I had cut the hay with a scythe and scutched it on the bottom of a tub. It yielded me four bags, which I had sieved and winnowed in the breeze and sun. I was proud of my grass-seed – it was white and clean. My father, who was in his second childhood then, seemed as proud of me as I was of the grass-seed. Second childhood is like that.

'Ye'll be takin' it to Dundalk,' he said.

'Tomorrow,' I answered.

Selling the grass-seed was my special prerogative. I could do as I liked with myself and the money.

A man passing looked at the seed. 'Very dirty,' he said, 'a lot of hair-grass in it.'

This after all my sieving.

I went to get the loan of Carr's ass on the evening of Sunday – the market was next day. The ass was already promised.

'The Charger has him,' I was informed. 'Charger' was the nickname of a neighbour.

'Get Maggy Quigley's ass,' they advised me; 'he's a very good stepper.'

Maggy lived up a long lane. Her ass was an old creature and the cart was still older. 'It's a danger to be safe in Maggy's cart,' people used to say.

'We don't lend the ass to anybody,' she stated when I declared my business. She waited till the importance of the ass and cart should have time to sink into my mind. 'But on account of who ye are we'll let ye have Darby.'

The ass was lying before Maggy's door with his two forepaws stretched out in front and his eyes closed. He wasn't a promising beast to drive to Dundalk.

'Do ye see that pole there?' Maggy said, pointing out to me a long pole laid across the gap in the stone ditch. 'If Darby gets an aisy day he jumps that pole during the night, but if he's abused he lies out there on the rock.'

I promised to treat Darby well.

It was considered a good-stepping horse could make Dundalk from our district in two-and-a-half hours. I left at five o'clock in the morning as I calculated getting in around nine. I over-rated Darby's powers; he was nearly as bad as the ass of the song:

> With blood-stained powers
> It took him two hours
> To travel each mile of the road.

Darby wasn't just as bad as that, though he was bad enough.

Sitting on top of my four bags of grass-seed, I jogged down the Mucker Road between the tall poplars at a pretty speed. I had given the ass two full porringers of oats, a temporary rejuvenation to his old blood. He cocked his ears and swayed pleasantly between the shafts. It must have been an early harvest that year for much of the corn was gathered, and in one or two haggards the threshing mills were set up.

The morning was chill, still, and the crevices of the land were grey. There were two stars in the western sky. When I turned eastwards for Dundalk, leaving the poplar-lined road, the dawn was before me, a grey dawn breaking above the Irish Sea, and in my mind a grey passionate dawn was breaking too. I was becoming aware of new beauty.

For the first two miles Darby travelled on the steam of the oats. Then the weariness of age returned to his bones. It took him half

104

an hour to climb Mahera Hill. I got down and pushed at the tail board.

'Foolish fella,' a man who was yoking a horse to a cart said when he saw me. 'Don't ye know,' he explained, 'that the more you push the less the ass will pull?' I might have known, for I had wide experience of the ass-temperament. The man who spoke was getting ready for the market himself.

'How's the time going?' I inquired.

'It's hittin' round half-six,' he said, 'but ye'll have lavings of time.'

Darby trotted down the hills passing out horse-carts drawn by hairy-legged Clydesdales. 'Short and sweet like an ass's gallop', is a good saying: the hairy-legged Clydesdales recovered the lost ground and passed out of our sight on the top of the next hill.

The sun was up before I got to the town. A double row of carts laden with grass-seed was queued up in Park Street. I tried to get in before a woman who was holding an ass by the head. She looked quiet enough but was far from it as I soon found out.

'Ye brat,' she sort of squealed, 'is it tryin' to knock dacent people outa their turn ye are? People that's after losin' a night's sleep.'

'I have only the bare four bags,' I pleaded.

'Four or twenty-four, it's all the same to me,' and she pulled on the rein to narrow the gap between her and the cart in front. There was nothing for it but go to the end of the row and learn patience.

The rows of carts moved very slowly towards the market crane because of late arrivals, whom well-wishers were letting cut in further up. Around me people were complaining. 'It's a damn shame, that's what it is.'

I strongly supported the speaker. 'It's all that,' I said, 'and a good deal more.'

There was a lot of talk about politics, and right behind me two young men were confabing about last night's dance.

'I think I could go with her if I went all-out.'

'I think you might.'

'I seen Tom on the job again.'

'Aye, the oul' clown, some people wouldn't know when they

105

were insulted. Paddy Kirk tried his hardest for Josie Duffy and he might as well be idle.'

'No go for Paddy.'

I came opposite a newsagent's shop, and was glad. 'Keep an eye on that ass,' I told the fellow before me.

Searching among the papers on the counter I came across a periodical dated a few weeks back. 'What kind of a paper is this?' I asked the newsagent.

'Something like *John Bull*,' he said.

It was the *Irish Statesman*. Returning to my ass, I opened the paper and read.

The first thing my eye fell upon was a review of a book by Gertrude Stein. I read a quotation and found it like a foreign language, partly illuminated by the Holy Spirit. There was mention of a man called Joyce. I was a little surprised to find that his Christian name was James and not P.W. or Robert Dwyer. P.W. Joyce had written a history of Ireland which I had read at school and his brother Robert Dwyer Joyce, whom I knew from a song of his – three lines of which I remember:

> Where the stream leaps down
> From the moorland brown
> And all on a May-day morning.

'Any stir on the paper?' a fellow asked me.

'Plenty,' I replied. 'Gertrude Stein is after writing a new book.'

'Quit the coddin'. How's the markets goin'? My sowl, this looks like a bad pit today.'

> They shall sink under water
> They shall rise up again,
> They shall be peopled
> By myriads of men.
> Paris and Babel
> London and Tyre
> Re-born from the darkness
> Shall sparkle like fire.

I didn't understand AE's poem except in a vague way, the last line: 'Shall sparkle like fire'. Later I heard from AE himself that that poem had a commonsensical meaning, but for me on that August morning in Dundalk Grass-seed Market it had a meaning and a message that had come from hills of the imagination far beyond the flat fields of commonsense.

On that day the saints of Ireland, political and theological, lost a strong supporter. I never wrote for the holy poets again. How I fared with my four bags of grass-seed hardly matters. Sufficient to say I sold it, afterwards visiting an eating-house, viewed the sights of the town from the gaol to the distillery chimney and down to the quays, bought a packet of cigarettes, yoked Darby to the cart and gave him his head. How long it took us to get home I do not know, for I was wandering among the hills of a timeless world. It was an Eden time and Eve not violated. Men were not subject to death. I was happy.

> Paris and Babel
> London and Tyre
> Re-born from darkness
> Shall sparkle like fire. . .
> Faery shall dance in
> The streets of the town
> And from the sky headlands
> The gods looking down.

The Green Fool, 1971

LOUIS MACNEICE
1907–1963

COUNTY ANTRIM, EARLY TWENTIETH CENTURY

Hark the lying angels sing. Every man's birth might be a Messiah's but is it? All this nine months' trouble and forward-looking in order to produce, so the psycho-analysts tell us, a backward-looking child who longs again for the womb. Never to come out of the quarry to be made into a pillar of the temple or into more likely a paving-stone for pavement artists to draw on and blind beggars to spit. To be unpolluted, unused. But it can't be helped anyway, here we are and hail Pollution!

Memory cannot go back that far, fades into myth, I find myself walking down a long straight passage hung with bead curtains. Through one curtain after another, like sheets of coloured rain, but I notice very little in the passage, only at the end there is a staircase. I go up it several flights, at the last floor but one there is a small window of cheap, stained glass which throws a stain on the floor mingling with the pattern of the worn-out linoleum. The last flight of the stairs is uncarpeted and the top is all but dark. The top is a blind alley, a small lobby without any doors and the roof sloping down as in an attic. It smells very fusty. Close in under the roof, but I can hardly see it, is a trunk, an old-fashioned trunk with metal studs on it. On the lid of the trunk there are initials but I cannot see if they are mine. Anyway the trunk is locked.

There were five of us in the family – my father and my mother and my sister and my brother and I – but there were many more people in the house. The red soldiers, for instance, who by day were tiny, you could knock them over with a finger, but by night they were ten-foot high, came marching straight for you, drumming, and not the least change on their faces. There were people too in the cracks of the ceiling, in the mottling of the marble mantelpieces, in the shadows of the oil-lamps and the folds of the serge curtains.

The first house looked out on the harbour which was noisy and dirty, the salt pier on one side and the coal pier on the other, and beyond it there were sails on the lough and I never knew where they were going but I took it it was somewhere good. The nursery was at the back of the house and looked down on a coal yard; there was a frayed red bell-rope swinging on the wall which went 'See-saw, Margery Daw' as it swung and my aunt was called Margery who hit my sister with a hair-brush.

The second house was in a garden, enormously large (an acre), with a long prairie of lawn and virgin shrubberies and fierce red hens among cauliflowers run to seed, and the other side of the hedge was the cemetery, you could hear the voice of the minister tucking people into the ground. The dining-room was sombre red and the drawing-room was faded yellow; in the dining-room there was a harmonium and in the drawing-room there was a piano and, if my mother drew up her chair to either, something would come out like a cloud – a 'Green Hill Far Away' which was the same as the 'Fairy Mount', a round grass knoll near the yarn-mill, the mill where I could see through the windows the savage, champing machines which would hunger and wait for me at night.

My mother was comfort and my father was somewhat alarm and my sister wore yellow shoes and a bow on her hair and my brother, who was a Mongolian imbecile, could not say many words but could mimic the gardener; the gardener, people would say, was touched in the head. I was the youngest. My mother made cakes in a big yellow bowl in the kitchen, the mixture was yellow and sticky and sweet, she would stir it around with a spoon and it came higher and higher up the inside of the bowl till a dollop would catch on the rim and then I was allowed to taste it.

There was always a sense of loss because things could never be replaced. There was a golliwog lost in the shrubbery and a teddy bear who fell into the soot-heap and in the first house there was a spotted horse called Dan who failed to come with us when we left. Later I took my sister's doll, with a pink frilled dress and big blue eyes, and built her a house out of coloured bricks on the table but she was too heavy for the house, the walls fell down and over the edge of the table and she went with them and broke and was hollow inside. And my mother kept being ill and at last was ill all the time.

Before she got ill I used to get in her bed in the morning and there was only one thing I disliked in her room. That was a little cone-shaped straw basket, trimmed with pink ribbon, which hung on the wall and in which she put the hairs that came out from her head in the comb. Whereas the little net pocket in the wall above the berth in the cabin on the boat that went to Wales was pleasant to look at, for in that she put her small gold watch.

I liked all ladies and they made me show off. Until I learnt the name for it. One day, when I was about four or five, I was telling two ladies to watch me spring-clean my pockets when my sister came in, very cross, and said '*You're showing off.*' After that Showing Off became something terrible and I kept myself to myself.

Pleasure was bright and terror had jagged edges. My father would seat me on his knee and imitate the train from our town to Belfast, chugging and whistling and stopping at all the stations – Trooperslane, Greenisland, Jordanstown, Whiteabbey, Whitehouse, Greencastle, Belfast. And then the train back again – Greencastle, Whitehouse, Whiteabbey, Jordanstown, Greenisland, Trooperslane, Carrickfergus. That was pleasant but what my father did by himself was frightening. When I was in bed I could hear his voice below in the study – and I knew he was alone – intoning away, communing with God. And because of his conspiracy with God I was afraid of him.

Things project other things, that was the trouble. The oil-lamp in the nursery made a brown stain on the ceiling which no one could get off; and when my mother put her hands together, made rabbits on the wall, how was I to know they would not stay when she took away her hands? I wished my mother would not encourage them but was too frightened to tell her I was frightened. And Annie the cook had a riddle which began 'What is it that goes round and round the house?' And the answer was the wind but, though I knew that was the answer in the riddle, I had a clammy suspicion that in fact it might be something else. Going round and round the house, evil, waiting to get me.

Going to Wales was too far back – it was walking along white planks, they may have been deck or they may have been esplanade, there was hot buttered toast too and hooters and buckets – but Portstewart is the holiday I remember, we went there twice but the times have fused together. It is a little seaside resort on the north coast of County Londonderry a few miles west of Portrush. On the train I was anguished because I had forgotten my toy boat but when we got out at the station a thrill came up in my stomach because I was really There. Outside the station there was a flowering bush of buddleia and my father produced a little bag of preserved ginger. The ginger was sweet too though it bit, brought tears to the eyes, but the buddleia was sweet only, sweet. Only where was the sea? I might have cried because the sea was not at the station but they said it would only be a little while now and I pattered along the road, my mouth full of ginger, and suddenly around a corner or over a crest came a strong salt breeze and a rich smell of herring and there down below us was blueness, lumbering up against the wall of the fishermen's quay, ever so or never so blue, exploding in white and in gulls.

We stayed in a house looking over the sea, there were tramcars running by the window and jellyfish melting on the beach and further along an enormous castle on a crag with a dangerous path going round it; one day we were climbing fearfully along this path with the sea boiling below us far among rocks when I saw to my horror two people in the boiling sea and curious pink bladders growing out from under their arms; I asked my mother what they were and she said they were wings. Wings! It was all too much to take in. Like the golf course along the river Bann. The turf there was crisp and buoyant to walk on but it had its queerness too. There were iron red things sticking up out of the Bann and my mother said they were waterworks but I caught my breath when we came near them, and there were also little red flags growing up out of the ground, flapping away to themselves and punctuating the distance.

111

On the roads we would come to signposts and my mother would read the name and say, 'That goes to Coleraine.' I liked the name, translating it into cold rain, and, when I asked my mother what it was, she said, 'Coleraine is a watering place', so I knew my translation was right. Everything nearly was joyful except when we went to watch the fishermen pull up their nets and caught in the nets there were several dead gulls. But I made myself forget them, collected shells with my sister. Then one day before we left I had a revelation of space. We were walking along a road between high walls and I could see nothing but the road and the air on the road was quiet and self-contained. On the top of the walls, on the contrary, there were long grasses growing in the stonework and these were blown out, combed, by a wind which I could not see. I wondered what was over those walls and I thought that it must be space. Not fields or roads or houses but an endless stretch of a windblown something, something not I nor even my father and mother could ever, however we tried, walk to the end of. . .

The cook Annie, who was a buxom rosy girl from a farm in County Tyrone, was the only Catholic I knew and therefore my only proof that Catholics were human. She worked very well and fast and filled in her spare time doing Irish crochet work. We would watch the shamrocks and roses growing from her crochet hooks while in a gay warm voice she would tell us about Five-miletown where she came from and the banshees and fairies and cows of the Clogher Valley. They had nice rhymes out there – Lisnaskea for drinking tea, Maguiresbridge for whiskey – and County Tyrone sounded like a land of content. Annie in fact was always contentful except when she had palpitations. And we were content with Annie.

One day, however, my mother engaged what was called a Mother's Help. My brother and I were busy laying pebbles along a little ledge outside the conservatory porch when the Mother's Help came up the drive. She was small and lean and scrawny, quite unlike Annie, her face was sour and die-hard Puritanical, she had a rasping Northern accent. The daughter of a farmer in

112

County Armagh, she knew all there was to be known about bringing up children; keep them conscious of sin, learn them their sums, keep all the windows shut tight and don't let them run for it is bad for their hearts.

It was the end of *laissez-faire*. Miss Craig nearly pulled your ears off when she cleaned them and she always got the soap in your eyes. When she carried you off in disgrace your face would be scratched by the buckle on her thick leather belt. Though small she was strong as leather and we soon developed new reflexes when we saw the slaps coming. Believing in economy she made dresses for my sister out of the funeral scarves with which my father was presented at funerals. Obsessed by a righteous hatred of the Common Cold she loaded us down with perspiring layers of clothing. In spite of this my sister kept catching cold and Miss Craig would jeer at her bitterly, say she would never live to grow up and they would write on her tombstone 'Here lies Old Snivelly'.

It was Miss Craig who brought Hell home to me. Being one of a rector's family I had heard it mentioned before but it had never been cardinal; Miss Craig made it almost the Alpha and Omega, hell-flames embroidered her words like Victorian texts. I realised now that I was always doing wrong. Wrong was showing-off, being disobedient, being rude, telling stories, doing weekday things – or thinking weekday thoughts – on Sundays. I had done so much wrong I knew I must end in Hell and, what was worse, I could imagine it. Sometimes when Miss Craig had jerked me and thumped me into bed she would look at me grimly and say: 'Aye, you're here now but you don't know where you'll be when you wake up.'

Miss Craig, however, had her glamour. County Armagh was not so romantic as County Tyrone but it was also somewhere unseen and Miss Craig told us of the will-o'-the-wisps that went skipping around in the bogs. Also she had a trunk which she would unpack for us sometimes for a treat; the contents were always the same but we always looked forward to seeing them. There was a photograph album – yellow snaps of gaitered and whiskered farmers – and a heavy Bible with a brown binding (always a novelty, for the Bibles we knew were all black) and at the bottom of all was a little parasol which took to pieces. We never even wondered what Miss Craig was doing with a parasol, Miss Craig who had hair on her face and whose style of dress was not only plain but repulsive.

My mother became steadily more ill and at last she went away; the last I can remember of her at home was her walking up and down the bottom path of the garden, the path under the hedge that was always in shadow, talking to my sister and weeping. I had no part in this, I did not know what it was all about. Later I visited my mother in hospital and she offered me a box of chocolates. Something evil came up in me – I knew it to be evil, although it was quite different from the wrong-doings for which I was going to Hell – and I refused to take the box. I wanted the chocolates very much and also I wanted to be gracious to my mother, but something or other made me spite myself and her and stand there surly and refuse. When I got home the box was there (someone had brought it back furtively) and I was filled with remorse and remembered the other time with the poplar twigs. That had been a fresh spring morning and everyone well and gay and my father was perched on a ladder clipping the arbour which was made of little trees we called poplars. The long sprays fell on the ground with light green lively leaves and I gathered some of them up to arrange in a jam-jar. But one of my twigs was too long, whenever I put it in the jar the jar fell over. My mother came up smiling, folded the twig double, put it in the jar and the jar stayed upright. And I was outraged, went off in a sulk.

At the age of five, while my mother was away, I made my first rebellion. Thursday was Mrs McQuitty's Day and we always had stewed steak. Mrs McQuitty, the charwoman, was very stout and friendly, she had a son who was a fisherman and she had given us our cat but she had to have stewed steak. I could not bear stewed steak, I found it too tough to swallow, had to keep the pieces in my cheek till after dinner, then spit them out in the shrubbery. So one spring Thursday, as we were spending the morning with Annie raking up new-cut grass, I planned that, when the gong went, I would hang behind and hide and have no steak. So the gong went

114

and I hung behind, crawled in under some laurel bushes at the side of the lawn. In a few minutes they came out and called for me but I did not answer. This was achievement, I felt, something entirely new, I had planned to do something outrageous and the outrage was working. The steak too must be getting cold.

There was a great hue and cry, Miss Craig and Annie and Mrs McQuitty screaming all over the garden but they never looked under the laurels; I was proud to be so clever. 'There he is now,' Miss Craig cried suddenly, 'I see the red cap on him in the cemetery.' So they all stampeded to the cemetery hedge but, whatever it was red, it was not my cap. I could feel ripples of delight going over my face as I lay snug under the laurels drawing patterns with my finger in the dried crumbly soil. Dinner-time – steak-time – was past but I was not in the least hungry, would lie there all afternoon; the experience was too precious not to exploit to the full. Mrs McQuitty and Annie brought out a carpet on to the lawn right in front of me and began to beat it, with great wicker bats; the thud of their strokes reiterated around me and the dust rose up in the sunshine. A terrible thing, Mrs McQuitty kept saying, me to be lost and my mother ill and away. Sure he may be killed on the roads; the master has the polis out looking for him.

I was a little scared to think that the polis were after me; maybe, I thought, I am in for a lot of trouble. I lay very quiet and left it to fate. I might not have come out for a long time had there not been a scratching and a blustering behind me in the nettles and there, broken out from the henyard, were the hens led by the rooster. The rooster looked like the Devil with his great scarlet wattles and crest and he was leading his hens straight into my hideout. It was too much for me, I scrambled out to the lawn and was caught. Miss Craig told me I was bound for Hell and my father told me it was very wrong to make everyone so frightened and I ought to think of my mother.

Adventure did not pay and life settled into routine. In the morning I would have my lessons from Miss Craig in a small nursery with the window shut tight. On the walls there hung a multiplication table and a calendar with a picture of John Peel and a coloured picture from the *Sphere* of Queen Mary dressed for her coronation; I liked Queen Mary very much because of her jewellery and I liked John Peel for the names of his dogs. Sometimes Miss Craig would put a new nail in the walls and the plaster would drop out. One day I picked up what looked like a piece of sugar and ate it and Miss Craig said at once it was plaster, I was a bad wicked child and would die. She was always talking of dying, and in winter when the trees in between were not in leaf, would marshal us at the window to watch the funeral processions on their way to the cemetery next door.

In the afternoon when it was not raining too hard (which it often was) we would walk with Miss Craig up the road up the hill behind our house to a point called Mile Bush and back again. Always – or nearly always – the same walk because Miss Craig disliked going through the town; you never know what you might catch. We walked very slowly because of my brother and Miss Craig kept saying, 'Don't drag.' My sister and I were agog to see something new, if only a horse drinking at the water-trough, but everything was usually just the same except that the hawthorn hedges which were flaming green in spring were jaded by autumn and in winter were barren black with raindrops ricocheting from twig to twig. Miss Craig, however, would tell us stories, always on the pattern of *Jungle Jinks,* the children's comic section in *Home Chat*; my brother was Jacko and I was Tiger Tim and my sister (Miss Craig's one original contribution) was Careless.

When we got home we would have tea in the nursery, strong tea thick with sugar, and sometimes before we went to bed Miss Craig, for a treat, would give us thick beef sandwiches with mustard or a cold drink made from cream of tartar. Possibly our diet, though it was not the cause, was one of the conditions of my dreams. These got worse and worse. Where earlier I had had dreams of being chased by mowing-machines or falling into machinery or arguing with tigers who wanted to eat me I now was tormented by something much less definite, much more serious. There was a kind of a noise that I felt rather than heard, 'ah. . . ah. . . ah', a grey monotonous rhythm which drew me in towards a centre as if there were a spider at the centre drawing in his thread and everything else were unreal.

'Oh God, I do not want to have any dreams. If I am going to go to sleep, do not let me have any dreams. And if I am going to have dreams, do not let me go to sleep, God, please I will do anything if only You keep me awake.' But I always went to sleep all the same. One night I woke up and yelled, my father came up from downstairs, there was light and his voice, he told me nothing would hurt me. I felt quite safe when he had gone but next morning Miss Craig was very angry; my father had forgotten to go down again to the study and had left the lamp burning there all night. I was a very wicked boy and might have burnt the house down.

There were also the terrors of Church. The church, was cruciform, and the rectory pew, being the front pew of the nave, looked out on to the space where the chancel and the nave and the two transepts met. The transept on our left was on a higher level and was reached by a short flight of steps; the end wall of it was occupied by a huge Elizabethan monument to the Chichester family who had then been the power in the land. The father and mother, who were each very large, knelt each under an arch, opposite each other, praying; below them, much smaller, was a Chichester brother who had been beheaded by the rebels, and between them, like a roll of suet pudding, on a little marble cushion was a little marble baby. None of these marble people worried me at all; what I disliked were the things that hung high up on the wall on either side of the monument's narrower top. A decayed coat of mail, a couple of old weapons, a helmet. I could not see the coat of mail when I was sitting, thanks to the solid front of the first pew in the transept, but, whenever I had to get up, there it would be, older and older and deader and deader, yet somehow not quite dead enough.

On the other hand if I looked down the chancel there was a rich old widow who always wore black and whom therefore I took to be blind. And blindness was not a misfortune, blindness was evil magic. When I was sitting down I could not see her either as she was hidden by the reading-desk, so the morning service became an alternation of agony and relief, but the relief itself shadowed with the knowledge that soon we should have to stand up again and there I should be, exposed to the blind old lady on the one hand

117

and the coat-of-mail man on the other.

Our best antidote to these terrors and depressions was the gardener Archie, in whose presence everything was merry. My father did not think of him in that way, as Archie, whose professional pride was easily wounded, would sometimes absent himself for weeks out of pique. But for us nothing that Archie could do was wrong and he cast a warm glow upon everything he touched. We would anxiously wait in the morning for him to appear – he rarely turned up before noon because of his rheumatism – and, whenever we could escape from Miss Craig, we would encircle him in the garden and listen to him, as my father called it, romancing.

Archie romanced largely about himself, always in the third person – 'Archie's the great fella now, aye, Archie's the queer fella for work, ye wouldn't find his like, I'm telling ye, not in the whole of Ireland. Sure he's the great fella.' His forte was cutting hedges; no-one in the world could cut hedges the way he could. He would take a long heavy plank and rest it on one of the steps of a stepladder at one end and a wooden box or two at the other and he and I would stand up there as if we were on a captain's bridge and the hawthorn sprigs would leap from his shears as he rambled along in a voice that was half singing, going over and over again about the gentlemen's places he had worked on and his wife Maggie and his canary and King William and the Twelfth of July.

For Archie, though he could neither read nor write, was a great Orangeman and played a flute in the Twelfth of July procession. Until, that is, his rheumatism made him unable to march. The Orange Lily was his fitting emblem, for he took a childlike delight in the gaudy and was naturally histrionic, would sometimes turn up in the morning with a small Union Jack in his cap, level his blackthorn stick at a crow, sight along it and pull an imaginary trigger, then say, 'I'm a Frenchman', and stand to attention and salute. He had snow-white hair and beautiful pure blue eyes and on his gnarled and abraised ring-finger he wrote an imitation gold ring.

Even when we would not see him it assured us that life was good to hear him sharpening his scythe on the hone or mowing the

118

lawn with the machine, mowing from a standing position because of his rheumatism, a shrill silver noise as he pulled it back and a deeper purring or snoring noise and a clack as he thrust it forward. Then we could imagine the emerald dance of the grass in the air which would afterwards be piled in heaps and become quite other than itself, no longer luminous and fresh but coagulated into lumps so that if you thrust your arm into the heap, you found inside it a perspiring animal warmth.

Archie preferred children (whom he called bairns) and cats and birds to grown-ups, but he would engage in badinage with Annie and Miss Craig, both of whom he called Maggie after his wife. With us his conversation was lyrical and interpersed with snatches of verse remembered from the kindergarten – 'A bee met a wasp once runnin' by' or 'The cat sat by the barn-door spinnin''. Each spring when he cut the hedge between the garden and the cemetery a polished granite obelisk would reappear looking over at us. Then Archie would shake his fist, say, 'Thon's a bad ould fella'; sometimes he would identify this obelisk with a blackleg gardener whom my father had employed once while Archie was privately on strike. He had also his moments of moralising, was a good Temperance man as well as an Orangeman, would speak with contempt of the whiskey-drinking corner boys with their big stomachs and their great white faces. And sometimes he would point at the sky and say, 'I believe in the Good Fella Up There,' or point at the thin moon that appeared in the sky before twilight and say, 'Thon's the Good Fella's lamp.'

If he did not have us for an audience he would do his romancing to the cats or else to the robins that waited around him for worms and his singsong voice would echo around the garden – 'Archie's the great worker; ye wouldn't find his like in County Antrim.'

The Strings are False, 1982

PATRICK SHEA
1908–1986

Newry in 1922 was a town with a hangover. The atmosphere was sour and full of hostility, the people divided denominationally and politically, each side resentful of things past and suspicious of the other side's every move, apprehensive about the future. The A Specials in ill-fitting uniforms, formidably armed, were there in large numbers; on duty in the streets, racing through the country-side in a variety of vehicles, standing guard over important instal-lations, watching and searching and sharply observing the towns-people.

Although this was one of the few areas which John Redmond's Nationalist Party had held against Sinn Féin in the 1918 elections, the republican movement had since taken a strong hold in the district. With the coming of the Special Constabulary and the 1920 Act which placed the town in Northern Ireland, Sinn Féin and the IRA had grown in strength. Police had been ambushed and killed on one occasion in the main street of the town; there had been savage reprisals by the Specials; some of the town's menfolk had sought refuge across the border; some were, under orders made possible by special legislation, prohibited from re-turning to their homes in the North. There had been curfew which kept the resentful townspeople indoors after dark; we were told about the young man from the South, suspected of being con-nected with the IRA, who had been taken from his lodgings late at night and whose cries had been heard by the curfewed people as he was dragged through the deserted streets to a shed on the Armagh Road where, on the following morning, his monstrously mutilated body was found. We saw the line of Protestant houses at the foot of the Camlough Mountains which the IRA had burned out in a fierce night raid in which several of the occupants had been killed. Nearby two brothers, one of them mentally defective, had been taken from their cottage home and shot dead at the roadside because they were believed to be IRA men. A short time before we moved house Father spent some days in Newry making preparations for our move and on Sunday morning as he left the cathedral, in the main street, Wolff Flanagan, the Resident Magistrate, who had been to the same Mass, was shot dead virtually on the threshold of the church.

We arrived in the aftermath of these happenings. Except for the shooting of Wolff Flanagan, which was an act of delayed vengeance, the campaign of violence had, in fact, come to an end; peace had been restored by force of arms but the air was full of recrimination and mistrust.

Newry was very different from Clones or Rathfriland or Athlone. It was bigger than any of them, it had a ship canal along which small steam-driven vessels brought grain to the local mills, timber from Scandinavia and coal, for which Newry was a major distributing point, from the mines of Britain. Along the quay there were redbrick grain stores, coal yards, timber stacks, depots from which potatoes were exported to England and hardware and ironmongery warehouses owned by builders' suppliers and the importers of agricultural machinery and implements. The quay was a busy, noisy place, a place of fluttering pigeons and dark dust and many smells. The shops in the main street seemed always to be full and the Thursday market brought Belfast 'cheap-jacks' with their stalls and farmers with a variety of horse-drawn vehicles into the town.

Newry had a football team, and an operatic society which staged a light opera every winter in the Town Hall. It was there that I had my first experience of the professional theatre. Dobell's touring company played a 'season' of Victorian melodrama for two weeks each year; the plays in their repertoire were *A Royal Divorce, Under Two Flags* and *East Lynne*. In the intervals between acts Dobell's actors and actresses revealed themselves as singers and musicians and the soubrette, all dimples and waving eyelashes, came amongst the audience selling autographed photo-

121

graphs of herself and other members of the company. We also had visits from Charles Doran's Shakespearean Company and in the Newry Town Hall I saw Anew McMaster, then a young actor who had just started his own touring company, in a performance of Hamlet which made a lasting impression on me.

The Newry people were born performers. On the smallest excuse it was possible to organise an evening's entertainment from amongst the ample supply of people with talents to display. Newry was a town in which there was always something to be seen or something to do.

The Abbey Christian Brothers' School was very different from the high school in Clones. It was an all male school. Our classmates in Clones had been male and female Little Englanders, the pupils in the Abbey were republicans; almost every one of them and their teachers were believers in a political doctrine with which I had no sympathy. But my brothers and I were not unduly apprehensive about the conflicts which might develop. Jack and Tim and I were enrolled in the secondary school and Tom, who had not yet reached the age for secondary education, went to the primary school.

Looking back over the years I still feel a little pride at the logic with which we dealt with problems created by our minority attitude. One concerned Gaelic football which was officially the school game. The Gaelic Athletic Association was, we believed, politically motivated, many of its leading players and administrators were prominent in the republican movement, it had silly rules about who could or could not be allowed to participate in its activities and the republican tricolour was flown at some of its matches. Jack, Tim and I – without any guidance from our parents who did not dictate a family attitude in such matters – decided that we could not refuse to take part in a school activity but that we would not have anything to do with Gaelic football out of school hours. We played in school games but when the Abbey decided to enter a team in a local competition for boys' teams and all three of us were picked for the first match, we struck our names from the team list. Since we had made no secret of our feelings our action was accepted with little comment.

The fiercest outcome of our political differences was a bare-knuckle fight with a farmer's son. For half an hour he and I were allowed to belabour one another until a Christian Brother inter-vened and sent us home. We had reason to believe that he had observed the whole contest and appeared on the scene only when he felt that we had both had the hiding we deserved. When my opponent grew to manhood he joined the Royal Ulster Con-stabulary.

I was at the stage when the question of an occupation was beginning to impinge on my thinking. I knew that I was being well taught albeit under fairly Spartan conditions. Corporal punish-ment was freely used but my apprenticeship in the Deerpark School in Athlone had taught me to bear such trials philoso-phically.

In those years secondary education in Ireland was based on a programme of examinations (originally conducted by the Inter-mediate Education Board for the whole of the country) which were taken in successive years; Junior Certificate at fourteen, Middle at fifteen and Senior at sixteen. I had taken the Junior Certificate before we left Clones but Irish had not figured in my education there. It was a compulsory subject for all pupils at the Abbey. As I was neither a diligent student nor an Irish language enthusiast, the extra burden of making up the leeway in Irish became a matter for agitation. I pleaded with the headmaster to relieve me of a load which I assured him was prejudicing my whole future. I seemed to be on the point of creating a school record by being excused Irish when he found out that I was the son of a very fluent native speaker. My case was thereupon lost.

Much has been written and said about the Irish Christian Brothers. Some have sought to belittle their work but over the years since my first day at the Abbey my respect for them has grown. I know how high their reputation stands amongst present-day educationists; in earlier years when opportunities were few their contribution to the education of Irish Catholics must have been immeasurable. My schooldays were before the arrival of free secondary education. In the Abbey School we knew that when the envelopes were handed out at the beginning of the term more than a few contained no bills. One could never know who was getting free tuition but it was known that in a Christian Brothers' school a promising boy was not refused education because his father could not pay the fees.

During our early years in Newry the Boundary Commission was an unending topic of conversation, for Newry was one of the places which the nationalists confidently expected would be transferred to the Free State. That the area was predominantly 'nationally-minded' had been demonstrated in election after election; if the declared intention of adjusting the border 'in accordance with the wishes of the inhabitants' meant anything, Newry's future in the Free State was assured, or so argued the nationalists. And they were not alone in this opinion. One of the town's leading Unionists exchanged his Newry house for the Warrenpoint house of a republican businessman and it was generally understood that they had swopped houses so that when the expected change came each would be a secure citizen of his preferred state.

When members of the Boundary Commission, in a fleet of large cars, paid a visit to the town, people stood and watched them pass slowly through. Stories were told about the cool reception they had given to Unionists who had appeared before them to argue their case for the retention of Newry in the United Kingdom.

When, out of the blue, the *Morning Post* published what it asserted were the findings of the Commission, the news was greeted by the Nationalists with derision, for the article said that the Border would remain virtually unchanged. When there was no official denial of the *Morning Post*'s forecast, there were expressions of indignation. When it became clear that the Commission's recommendations had indeed been 'leaked' and that the high hopes which had been inspired by all the lengthy deliberations would be unfulfilled, there was dismay. After all the fine talk about majority opinion settling the destiny of Fermanagh and Tyrone and large areas of Armagh and Down and possibly leading to a united Ireland, the outcome was shattering. The southern Government, which had made no secret of its expectation of a profitable settlement, cried out in protest but the protests sounded hollow for one of the members of the Commission was a representative of the Free State Government. They had been crushingly wrong-footed.

The outcry died quickly, the Boundary Commission was quietly forgotten, and in time the Government of the Free State accepted the border as it had been drawn in 1920. Ireland, it was said, had been tricked again by perfidious Albion and for every Irishman with nationalistic aspirations, Lloyd George's place in republican Ireland's rogues' gallery was assured.

Newry had two cinemas, the Frontier and the Imperial, with admission prices of 4d., 6d. and 9d. In each of them there was a Saturday matinee to which we were admitted for 2d. Those were the days of the great silent epics, of Tom Mix and Buck Jones, Eddie Polo, Charlie Chaplin, Clive Brook, Harold Lloyd, Buster Keaton and many other pioneers of universal popular entertainment. In the newsreels we watched the closing stages of the Civil War in the Free State; the new Irish Army trundling its small cannons behind lorries, moving from town to town in armoured vehicles not unlike those in which the Black and Tans had travelled, spreading its hold on the country and ultimately forcing the Irregulars to give up the struggle.

During one lunch period I walked along North Street, a tumble-down part of old Newry, to the Butter Market and found myself in the midst of a hiring fair; a fair in which the merchandise was human beings. Those doing business were standing about in small groups, talking quietly; a sturdy man holding out for what he thought he was worth as a ploughman, a rosy-cheeked servant girl listening and nodding as the conditions of the offered engagement were explained to her by a farmer and his wife, a mother handing over her fourteen-year-old son on the understanding that in return for his apprentice labour on a farm he would be kept and given three meals a day and after six months she would be paid perhaps five or six pounds.

Hiring fairs were peculiar to the northern part of Ireland.

Happily they are held no more.

The most exciting event during my years in Newry was the public meeting at which Eamonn de Valéra was billed as the principal speaker. He was then in the political wilderness, having come out on the losing side in the argument about the settlement with Britain and not yet having propounded his formula for entering Dáil Éireann in the face of his stated objection to the compulsory oath of allegiance to the British Crown. The republican group which had organised the Newry meeting had put posters all over the district announcing that de Valéra would address the great gathering to be held in the Town Hall. But under an order made by the Northern Ireland Minister of Home Affairs, de Valéra was a prohibited person; the law said that he would not be allowed into Newry. The sponsors of the meeting said that come hell or high water, their star guest would be in the Town Hall on the night and at the time appointed; the unionists and the police said 'not bloody likely' and the townspeople awaited the outcome with light-hearted anticipation. Bets were laid about whether or not the great man would put in an appearance.

About ten days before the date fixed for the meeting the town was encircled with a ring of armed Special Constables who scrutinised every person and searched every vehicle coming into the town. Day after day we watched them peering into cars, climbing on to lorries, driving their bayonets deep into loads of hay and manure. One felt a certain sympathy for the distinguished fugitive as each day the ring got tighter, the search more diligent. It was impossible, it seemed, for any man, let alone one whose appearance was so well known, to penetrate these defences.

The Town Hall in Newry is built on top of the river which runs through the town; the roadway along the front of the hall is, in fact, a bridge. On the evening of the great meeting I was there in good time, sitting on the stone parapet directly opposite the front door of the Town Hall, well above the heads of those standing on the footpath. As the time for the meeting approached my friends and I watched the faithful arriving; earnest men and women come to greet one who to them personified incorruptible republicanism.

There was still twenty minutes to go when it was announced that the hall was full. The crowd outside got bigger and bigger, spreading out across Trevor Hill; from every direction they had come, people of every shade of political colour, many from country districts, some from neighbouring towns; they had come to cheer or to scoff or just to look on. By the time the town clock above our heads showed eight o'clock I was at the centre of a great multitude of people of all ages and conditions; a good-humoured, expectant gathering. Policemen and Special Constables were everywhere, watchfully moving amongst the crowd, standing in small groups, clearing a passage for the occasional car passing through.

We heard that the meeting inside the hall had started; it had been decided to begin without the guest of the evening. This announcement brought a derisive cheer from the 'antis' who interpreted it as acceptance of defeat by the organisers. Those who had been so sure that de Valéra would fulfil his engagement grew silent. Jokes about the missing leader were made. The hands of the clock moved to eight fifteen, to half-past eight, and the crowd began to show signs of restlessness; there was talk of going home. At a quarter to nine one of the cars moving through the crowd stopped in the middle of the roadway, only a few yards from where I was sitting, and de Valéra stepped out. There he was; unmistakably it was de Valéra himself, the tall dark-clothed figure, familiar to anyone who had read a newspaper; the long-jawed white face, the solemn, inquiring eyes looking unblinkingly over the heads of those around him.

The clamour of voices around the front door and the flashes of cameramen's magnesium flares brought to the far limits of the crowd the news that the impossible had happened, that the event which had held the town in suspense for a fortnight was taking place before their very eyes. A great clamour spread out from the centre to the furthest limits of the crowd; cheers and angry shrieks and much laughter and, at the centre of it all, almost within reach of where I sat, stood the great man himself, a look of guileless solemnity on his pale face.

The cameras flashed again as District Inspector Fletcher put his hand on de Valéra's shoulder and led him to the waiting police car which moved off with a banging of doors.

Eamonn de Valéra was not one of my heroes but walking home in the dark I was not the only one who might have said, in the words of Percy French – 'I cheered, God forgive me, I cheered with the rest.'

Next morning de Valéra was taken to Adavoyle railway station, then the last stopping place before the border, given a single ticket, and put on the Dublin train.

(I have sometimes wondered would the history of the difficult years between 1916 and 1923 be as it is if in 1913 the Intermediate Education Board had appointed the shortlisted candidate Edward de Valéra BA, to the post of Inspector of Schools. He lost on a split vote.)

My parents, like many Irish parents of their generation, were very ambitious for their children. Father had almost an obsession about security; for him the first test of a career was that it should be permanent and pensionable. He had known insecurity as a child, when his household was at the mercy of the climatic and economic hazards affecting life on a small farm at a time when there were no government subsidies, no state pensions for the old and no financial aid for the unemployed. The penalty for failure was the workhouse. Small wonder that the Royal Irish Constabulary was an attractive career for Irish farmers' sons.

The 1920s were lean years. We had seen the beginning of unemployment benefit and as we passed the labour exchange going to and from school the reality of unemployment was before us every day. The queues of idle men grew longer, business was bad, wages low and the opportunities for school-leavers were few indeed. Public scholarships were almost non-existent; in my last year at school two university scholarships, each of a maximum of £40 a year for three years, were provided by the education committee for County Down. Most of the boys at the Abbey School came from homes in which there could be no thought of finding the money to send a son or daughter away for a university education. The highest hopes were teaching, the bank, the civil service, the police force, the priesthood or one of the religious orders; the possibility of going into business was not discussed because such industry as there was in the district was not, even in prosperous times, on a scale which could provide worthwhile openings except perhaps for the sons and nephews of the owners. Not more than about one-third of those leaving school could hope to go straight into stable employment. This situation weighed heavily on parents like mine. As we grew up the question of what we would do for a living was increasingly discussed.

Throughout his schooldays Jack had let it be known that only a life at sea would satisfy him, but as he came nearer to working age and he realised that his wish would not be fulfilled, he declared that he would not work in an office of any sort. After much discussion and argument and advice tendered by friends, he submitted himself as a candidate for the Royal Ulster Constabulary, attended a series of interviews and tests first in Newry, then at the County Headquarters in Downpatrick, and finally at the Police Depot in Newtownards, and was accepted.

We had lived all our lives in small towns in which good employment opportunities were few and we knew that if we were to fulfil our parents' wish that we should 'get on in the world' we would leave home as soon as our schooldays ended. To everyone in our home that was accepted as a fact of life. Nevertheless Jack's departure left a blank, for we four brothers had been close together and he had been our leader, a leader with no respect for authority and a versatile talent for breaking rules. He found ways of getting into football matches without paying; if the owner of a fruit garden felt that his fencing was secure against marauders Jack found a way in and we followed; he questioned the rulings of teachers and policemen and, all too often, our parents. He was fearless and there had been moments in our young lives when courage was needed. When he went away we all thought of him, a boy amongst men, feeling the restraints of discipline to which he would not take kindly. Until then we had not been conscious of the orchestration of ideas which had existed between us. After he had gone our activities were less adventurous.

At this time I was wrestling with the problem of my own future. I was not a good student, my work at school had never been more than the minimum needed to keep me free of trouble with the teachers. But there had been moments of praise of which I took full advantage by granting myself periods of rest; the company of kindred spirits could always lure me away from academic pursuits. In any case it was not manly to be thought to be a 'swot' and I moved in circles in which it was more praiseworthy to be manly than to be 'clever'.

Everyone seemed to want to become a teacher. In those bleak, competitive days teaching looked an attractive occupation. Teachers, I was told, had good pay, excellent prospects, long holidays, short hours and respect. But I found the prospect of spending my days in the company of schoolboys unattractive. 'The Bank' was a possibility. The banks held examinations for which large numbers entered but it was generally believed that the jobs went to those whose sponsors had good accounts; that ruled me out. A local solicitor with a large practice suggested to my father that I should become apprenticed to him and qualify as a member of his profession. This pleased me because I had a secret ambition one day to study law but just then the prospect of five or six years during which I would be paid only a nominal wage and work for a series of examinations, was not in line with my thinking. Father, to whom the law was almost a religion, would have liked me to accept but I knew, as he must have known, that my continued dependence on him would have created problems for the two brothers and the sister who were following me. I suggested that I should sit for the Clerical Officers' examination in the Northern Ireland Civil Service. If I drew a blank the legal apprenticeship offer would still be open.

My candidature for the Northern Ireland Civil Service posed a special problem. Two boys from the Abbey had just sat the examination and, as they were amongst the brightest in the school, no-one was surprised when they were called for interview. Both were rejected. They had also entered for the Free State Civil Service and come high in the list of successes. There was a furious outcry about the treatment our candidates had got in Belfast. In the Abbey it was entirely understandable that we should see religious discrimination as the reason for the rejection of boys who throughout their school careers had shown exceptional ability. The headmaster made no secret of his opinion. He announced that he would not enter any more boys for posts at the disposal of the Government of Northern Ireland. Nevertheless, I decided to enter in the following year although the headmaster's decision meant that in preparing for the examination I would be on my own.

The candidates for the Civil Service Clerical Examination in 1926 filled the Great Hall in Queen's University and we all knew that of the hundreds there about two dozen would be called for interview and perhaps half of that number offered appointments.

I thought I did a good essay and I enjoyed my week in the city where the new Classic Cinema had an organ and there were orchestras in the Imperial and the Royal Avenue Cinemas. Our two picture houses in Newry had upright pianos.

After about a month I got a letter from the Civil Service Commissioners in Belfast inviting me to come for interview. This was good news; I had got into the final. But the interview carried twice as many marks as any subject in the written exam and this was the test which the school's candidates had failed in the previous year. I felt like someone about to take part in a duel.

The Civil Service Commissioners held their interview board in the Ministry of Finance offices in Donegall Square West. I was brought into a large waiting room where I found about ten candidates already assembled and waiting to be called before the board. I was in a grey hand-me-down suit, but they were in sober navy blues and browns and, in one or two cases, formal black jackets and striped trousers. They looked and sounded cheerful and confident, they seemed to know one another and they talked amicably about rugby football and dropped names which meant nothing to me. I felt a stranger in a strange place. I sat alone and read the morning paper because interviewers, I had heard, were very clever at testing one's knowledge of current affairs.

Every fifteen minutes or so a uniformed messenger would come to the door, call out a name and take one of the candidates away. I must have waited for more than an hour as candidates went and others arrived. I found myself getting angry. I felt gauche and inadequate and envious of the urbanity of the others and I thought about the Newry boys who had come here a year before and been sent home empty-handed.

At last my name was called and I was brought into a conference room with five very important-looking men sitting along one side of a polished mahogany table. (I didn't know that in those leisurely days the interview board for mere clerks was made up of four very senior civil servants and a Parliamentary Secretary.) The man in the middle seat invited me to sit in the chair opposite him. Their attitude was, somewhat to my surprise, genial and informal. Quite early I realised that I was not nervous; I was talking freely and actually enjoying myself. After about ten minutes of questions about my hobbies and world affairs and local news it was all over. Going back to Newry in the bus I felt light-hearted, not because I thought I had made a lasting impression on my questioners, but I was fairly sure that I hadn't lost ground. In any case the last trial was over, it had not been too severe and my future was now firmly in other hands.

There must have been a late delivery of mail in those days for I was coming from the tennis court in the afternoon sunshine when I met my father who had come to meet me and give me an official letter with my name on it. It told me very formally that I had qualified for appointment as a Clerical Officer in the Northern Ireland Civil Service.

Posts in the lower ranks of the Civil Service may be very small beer nowadays but in the barren 1920s success at the first attempt in an open competition was more than a minor triumph. In our small school I would be amongst the year's successes. I was elated, not because I was going to be a civil servant, for I had not the remotest idea what that meant in terms of work or responsibility or prospects, but because my future was settled. I was independent. I was now free to direct my own life.

Father suggested that I should go at once and tell the headmaster rather than that he should hear the news elsewhere. I called at the Brothers' house and the headmaster brought me into the 'parlour', a rare treat for a pupil. I confessed that, contrary to his wishes, I had sat for the Northern Ireland examination and I handed him my letter. He was delighted and generous in his praise of my achievement. He made me stay and have tea and cakes with him and I felt very privileged as he talked about the dizzy heights to which I might rise if I worked hard and led a virtuous life. And that was the end of my schooldays.

Voices and the Sound of Drums, 1981

SAM HANNA BELL

b.1909

COUNTY DOWN, 1920s

In my childhood I was fortunate enough to live for several years in the household of a small farmer, Alexander Gaw. Alexander was about seventy at the time, heavily bearded and his shoulders bowed by hard work. He divided his time between his five acres of land (or four, really, for one of his fields was marred by a whin knowe), and his harness-making business which he carried on in a lean-to at the gable of the house. His daughter 'took in flowering', that is to say, she acted as an agent for several of the linen firms in the city of Belfast, and distributed embroidery work to the needle-women of the district. These activities of the Gaws made their hearth a meeting place for their neighbours. In the evenings, when their day's work was done, the young men came with broken harness and wrenched buckles for Alexander's attention. The farm women, with their skirts kilted against the wet grass of the fields, would bring their finished embroidery. There was talk about the hearth of crops and markets, births and deaths, and if someone had brought a paper Alexander read it aloud, down to the *Government cheers* and *Opposition uproar*.

No-one outstayed his welcome. When all the transactions had been settled the company rose to go. Several of the young men and women found that their homeward road lay over the same paths, and where they had arrived singly, or in twos, now a little cluster of lamps moved over the dark fields.

When the last neighbour had gone, supper was set on the table. Alexander usually had hot buttermilk, the rest of the family, tea. When the meal was finished Alexander took down the family Bible and read a few verses. It was now evident why the evening meal was delayed until the neighbours had gone. This hour was reserved for the dignity and privacy of the family. When the reading was finished the family knelt at their chairs and Alexander prayed. Experience had taught the younger members of the household to rise from their knees reluctantly, as it were, and to stifle any sigh of relief. Alexander could withdraw hand and eye from heavenly contemplation with devastating speed.

Apart from the Bible, which he read regularly but temperately, I can remember only three other books in which Alexander Gaw showed any interest. They were Emerson's essays, *A Serious Call to a Devout and Holy Life* by William Law, and Robert Burns's poems; and the only pages of the poet unthumbed were the glossary. He had a picture of the poet hanging on the wall beside the fireplace.

Alexander allowed himself few relaxations. But there was one event to which he looked forward with as much pleasure as the youngest member of his household, and that was the annual cockle-raking excursion. I can still recall the excitement as we hunted for the short-handled cockle-rakes among the couplings and rafters of the byres and sheds. Then when the rakes were found they had to be cleaned and the teeth of six-inch nails replaced where they were missing.

Usually four or five neighbouring families joined in the trip and shortly after breakfast, when the house had been redd up and the animals and fowl provendered for the day, all the family would pack into the trap and drive out to the main road where at each loanenhead we would be joined by our neighbours until a small cavalcade of traps would be moving along the winding road among the drumlins that led to Castle Espie on the shores of Strangford Lough.

Children are fickle labourers, as any parent knows who has tried to cajole a small son or daughter into helping him in the garden. We were no better; after a tentative scratching at the sands we gave up our cockle-rakes and ran off to the rocks to hunt for flounders or tear away pennants of leathery seaweed in search for dulce. But all over the flat dull sands our elders were stooped, with petticoats and trousers rolled to the knees, raking away and dropping the fat round shellfish into the potato bags they dragged behind them.

Then we were set to gathering twigs and driftwood for the fire that would boil the tea kettle, and as we all sat around on the sheep-cropped grass one of the women was sure to stroke her bare feet and sigh and thank God for an occasional paddle in salt water, and one of the men, brushing the crumbs from his moustache, was sure to say, 'Aye, that's them washed for another year, Mrs McCoubrey!' and wink in such a way that we and Mrs McCoubrey and everybody else knew he was only joking, for such a joke, if misconstrued, might mean one trap-load less at next year's excursion.

By the time the crockery was scoured with sand and rinsed in a spring and the fire stamped out the lough was darkening, and the emerald glow fading from the Slave Rocks and the Island of Lost Sheep. A dripping sack of cockles was loaded on to the floor of each trap and in the rakers clambered, the women protesting, as usual, that their boots and stockings and skirts would be ruined on the cockle sacks.

When we got home we were sent across the fields to a neighbour's house with a calf's bucket of the shellfish. As everyone shared out there were cockles for supper in a dozen homes in the townland that evening. The big saucepan was put on the range or the pot hung on the crane and the cockles tipped in to stew in their own juice (some of the men would put two cockles hinge to hinge, unlock the shells and swallow the contents, but to boil the cockles first was the popular way to prepare them).

So far as our household was concerned the first sniff of brine had barely floated out of the pot when there would be a knock at the door and in would come the Man from the Lough and a crony (we children sitting patiently before our empty saucers and our buttered wheaten farl always hoped he wouldn't come *this* year, our elders knew better). The entrance and patter were always the same. He would take two steps into the kitchen, his eyes screwed up as though he were blinded by the light from the oil-lamp, take a look at Alexander's Sunday collar, tie and gold watchchain, pause, take a step back and say, 'Ach, I didn't know, Alec boy, have ye friends in?'

'Not at all,' Alexander would answer patiently, 'we're just back from Castle Espie. Come on in, the two of ye –'

'Ach now, Alec, we wouldn't like to do that! I was just out on my pad wi' James Orr here,' and he indicated a face glooming at us round the door like a harvest moon that had risen out of joint with the calendar.

'Well come in anyway, now that you're here and share a cockle.'

'W-e-e-l –' With murder in our eyes we watched him giving in with a good grace. 'Mebbe the wife was going to make an early night of it?' and he turned on her as false a smile as ever cracked a glutton's face. And Mrs Gaw, usually the most hospitable of women, would rattle the cockle pot angrily and cry, 'Will you come in for any sake and sit down! There's a draught blowing through that door would lift a bullock's feet off the floor.'

In they would come and sit down to rattling plates of cockles that by right of labour and inheritance were ours. And when they had finished and drawn their chairs up to the hearth we would fissle among their empty shells in the vain hope that one golden half moon had escaped engulfment under those ragged valances of moustaches.

Lying awake we listened to the bumbling drone of voices from the kitchen, the muted explosions of laughter, the chink of tea-cups. The talk would fall away into silence until someone would take up the story again, someone else would answer, and we would fall asleep to the antiphon of neighbours' voices round the hearth.

Erin's Orange Lily, 1956

JOHN BOYD
b.1912

'Education's easy carried' was a pronouncement I often heard in Portallo Street. Uncle Willie and Aunt Ida seemed to regard it as a self-evident truth, and none of the Boyds ever dared to contradict or challenge it, at least not in my presence. I might have questioned it myself if I'd known what it was supposed to mean, but like winning the scholarship, it remained a bit of a puzzle to me. I didn't even know what the word 'education' really meant; all I knew was that Dr Williamson had it because he was a clergyman; but somehow ordinary people never had a chance of getting it. For education cost a lot of money, more money than working-class families could afford. It meant going to school for another five or six years while other boys were out at work, some as message boys at five shillings a week – dead-end jobs they were called – and some as apprentices in the shipyards. But at least an apprentice had the chance of becoming a tradesman. My fear was that a scholarship might lead me nowhere, a fear shared by Father, who repeated for my benefit his belief that the most important thing in life was 'influence'. What 'influence' meant puzzled me; all I knew was that Father maintained that he had hardly any – not even in the County Down railway where he'd worked all his life.

The school chosen for me was the Royal Belfast Academical Institution, the only reason for the choice being its convenience: a tram ride brought me almost to its front gates, whereas the other secondary school meant an extra tram ride. I went to Inst in almost complete ignorance of what kind of school it was: all I knew was that no girls were admitted and this fact seemed to me to make it superior to the Methodist College, which was a mixed school. Only one scholarship boy from Mountpottinger chose

138

Methody and I assumed that that was because nobody had told him that girls went there.

Inst was very different from Mountpottinger. It had a well-kept lawn at the front and a muddy playing field and a bicycle-shed at the back. In the middle, between the main building and the common room, lay the quadrangle where hundreds of boys congregated in the morning before dispersing to the various classrooms and laboratories. Some of the senior boys were called prefects and were in the sixth form, studying for scholarships to universities. Everything was different: pupils travelled to school from all parts of Belfast and from towns like Bangor and Lisburn; and everybody had to wear the school cap which was quartered yellow and black. The new principal, an Englishman, was making Inst more like an English public school by having four houses – Dill, Larmour, Kelvin and Pirrie – with masters in charge of each house. Some of the staff were in favour of these changes and told us that the old school needed a good shaking up: others were of the opinion that the new principal had a lot of fancy ideas that the old school could very well do without. I, as a devotee of the *Magnet,* was of course in favour of the English public school system.

But one innovation did not meet with my approval: the compulsory wearing of the bright new cap to and from school. In the mornings I'd stuff it into my bag and put it on only when I reached the City Hall, after having made sure that no prefects were in sight. Coming back from school I wore it as far as the City Hall and then stuffed it into my bag again. The trouble with it was that it attracted attention far too easily: during my first term, when I didn't dare to break the rule, I had to suffer from attacks on it. A rough big lad would come up from behind, grab my cap, tramp on it and run off shouting, 'Who spilt the egg on yer cap?' It was safe enough to wear such a showy cap when you were in town, but not when you were walking along the Albert Bridge Road or Templemore Avenue. Although the discipline of Mountpottinger had moulded me into being the most timid of conformists, conformity had, in this instance, to give way to commonsense. And as I couldn't run the risk of losing my new cap, the school rule had to be disobeyed. It was the only rule I deliberately flouted.

At Christmas my first report arrived home and caused so much consternation that I would have left Inst if that had been possible. Father read it over and over again, comparing my marks with the average marks of the class and demanding why I'd performed so badly. Most damning of all was the judgement of the principal at the end: 'Very disappointing for a scholarship holder'. Mother, as usual, was much more understanding of my difficulties but, as usual, less than tactful towards Father and his puzzlement. To me she said, 'Don't expect your father to know anything about these things', a remark which was not calculated to improve matters between Father and me, or between Father and herself.

The truth was that we were all out of our depth, myself most of all. Released from the regimentation of Mountpottinger and suddenly given the freedom of Inst, I reacted by completely failing to adapt to my new environment. Inst was a different world. The classrooms were spacious, each of us with a separate desk; most of the masters were friendly and none had canes; in one classroom there was even a lower-form library containing all sorts of adventure and school stories. I was like a prisoner given unexpected liberty and immediately abused it; I did as little homework as possible and went unpunished; I daydreamed in class and found I was ignored; and after school I dawdled home with my cap stuffed in my bag. Once home, bag flung into our parlour, I forgot all about Inst until the next day. I was floundering unhappily between two worlds: the world of Ballymacarett and the world of a middle-class school where the masters came from Oxford and Cambridge, Trinity and Queen's, and the pupils from houses in the suburbs or farms in the country. I found no snobbery, no bullying and no unfriendliness, and I should have been able to settle down to my lessons, make friends and receive good reports at the end of each term. But I became apathetic, remained friendless, and sought refuge in Chatsworth Street and in my old haunts – the public library, the public baths, the Victoria Park, the Oval football ground on Saturday afternoons, the pictures on Saturday nights.

The only building I frequented at Inst was the gym, where I was singled out by the instructor, Sergeant Watkins, for being athletic on the 'horse'. I loved to race to the springboard, bounce high into the air, complete a somersault and land safely on the mat where the watchful sergeant waited.

'You've the makin's of a first-class gymnast, young fella,' the wrinkled sergeant told me, wiping the sweat off his forehead. 'The arms need to be strengthened, but the legs is good, an' the body's trim. Join my extra class.'

I loved going to that gym class, held when lessons were over and the school deserted, apart from a few boys kicking a ball in the back field, or one or two boys riding in front of the bicycle-shed. The sergeant would make us march and run, jump the horse and climb the ropes and bars until we were lathered with sweat and he was breathless. Then he'd dismiss us in his gruff army voice, 'Clear off, boys! Time's up! Away an' do your homework – else you'll get me the sack!'

It took me about two years to feel that I belonged to Inst, and during that time my reports gradually improved. I became interested in chemistry and physics, enjoying the experiments and recording the results in imposing black notebooks. In particular, I loved the sight, smell and atmosphere of the laboratories – the polished wooden benches scarred from previous experiments; the Bunsen burners with their adjustable flames; the beautifully shaped flasks and mysteriously potent bottles which we were taught to handle carefully; the surrounding apparatus in cupboards which whetted our appetite for scientific research.

We respected our master – 'Beaky' Manning – because he kept good discipline without intimidating us. But one master, an Englishman with a rasping, lisping accent, occasionally took the class, and dissipated the relaxed atmosphere with his ill-temper. I still remember his snarling reprimand, 'Boy, where were you bwought up?' He would pause, and a silence would fall over the class who were familiar with what was to follow: 'You weren't bwought up, you were dwagged up from the guttah!' No matter to whom the insult was directed, I wilted under the sting of it, conscious that Lord Street and 'The Gut', and their drunken fights on Friday and Saturday nights weren't far removed from the gutter.

But Inst made no distinction between scholarship holders and the majority of pupils whose parents paid their fees. Indeed those of us with scholarships tended to be favoured; we were expected to bring academic distinction to the school, and many of us did; but some of us – those uninterested in games – were called 'swots'. There was no danger of my being called a swot: I loved all kinds of games – soccer, rugby, cricket, handball – and would spend part of the summer term training for the annual sports held in Osborne Park on the Malone Road. To my surprise and disappointment I discovered I was a poor runner, without speed or stamina, and therefore useless at field events. But I also discovered that I was one of the best cricketers of my age in the school and soon got selected for the third eleven. It was my aptitude for games rather than my academic capability which enabled me to adapt to Inst.

If the repressive atmosphere of Mountpottinger was responsible for my timidity and diffidence, Inst was responsible for increasing my feelings of self-consciousness and social inferiority. Though there was no snobbery at Inst, I was becoming a snob – by which I mean I was more and more conscious of belonging, by birth and upbringing, to what I regarded as an inferior class. I lived in a house and street I was ashamed of, while most of the boys I knew at Inst lived in villas in quiet suburban avenues; my father wore dungarees and worked in the railway, while their fathers were business men, doctors, dentists, architects, teachers, civil servants; and their mothers – whom I'd seen at the Christmas concert and at sports' day – wore expensive-looking clothes and spoke with a semi-English accent.

More and more I withdrew from playing games in Chatsworth Street. No more football with a sixpenny rubber ball or cricket with a bat made from a rough plank and chalk markings on the wall for wickets. Now I played cricket on a prepared grass pitch with a real bat and in white flannels, shirt, and shoes; and instead of playing knock-up football in the muddy 'wee field' I played rugby in proper togs and with the luxury of a shower after the game. The long winter evenings I spent indoors, reading or doing my homework. . .

Sex played a subterranean part in the life of Inst during the years I was there. Emotional friendships between younger and older boys were common but these affairs were, I imagine, nearly all natural to adolescence. At thirteen or fourteen I experienced two emotional affairs. For some months I worshipped from afar a dark-haired pudgy boy called Savage who spent his early mornings playing handball but not, alas, with me. My role was that of a morose spectator, too shy to participate in the game. Morning after morning I rose early and cycled to school for the sole purpose of mutely admiring my favourite at play. To my fervid imagination he possessed all sorts of virtues, and my joy would have been immeasurable if he had recognised my presence and invited me to become his partner and his friend. But I'd no such good fortune: I was ignored. Not a single glance from him fell in my direction, until a year later when he sat beside me in an English class and began chatting to me. My delight turned out to be short-lived. To my dismay I became aware that Savage had a pimply complexion, a rasping voice and ugly fat knees. When he begged me to help him with his homework I discovered he was both lazy and stupid. In short, he bored me and I changed my desk to get away from him.

My second affair was equally disastrous and even more mawkish. I was attracted to a slightly younger boy appropriately enough called Kidd who, because we lived in the same direction of the city, cycled across the Albert Bridge with me. For some reason I've forgotten, I nicknamed him 'Tinkerbell' and those journeys homewards with the wind in our hair and our caps stuffed in our pockets were, for me, pure bliss. Then, after a couple of ecstatic months, these same journeys turned dull and I no longer looked forward to them. Instead girls began to attract me. The problem was of course getting to know them at close hand as it were; to explore the mystery.

There was no mystery about boys; for after rugby games we all stood naked, flipping wet towels at one another, comparing our genitals and laughing at obscene jokes which we all thought to be excruciatingly funny. I remember one pale-faced youth with an aquiline nose and a sly manner who boasted of the sexual conquests he made every Friday evening. He played centre three-quarters in the first fifteen, and when he performed poorly during the Saturday game we attributed his failure to his debilitating exertions of the evening before. But as he usually played well – else he wouldn't have retained his place – we always cast doubt on his tales. 'Oh well, you needn't believe me,' he would remark, with a wink and sly look. 'But if I didn't go out with women on a Friday night I'd play like an international. Instead I turn up like a wet rag – no spunk in me at all.' We half-believed him, we envied him, and we implored him to keep off his wild women before any of our important Schools' Cup matches. Probably he was a virgin, but certainly he had a good imagination.

Though we all talked of 'women' we meant girls; and by 'girls' most of us meant schoolgirls from Victoria College or Methodist College; girls studying for the same exams as ourselves and playing hockey instead of rugby. Nice, respectable girls who were willing to chat and giggle with us and who would stand on the touch-line at Osborne Park on Saturdays and cheer us whenever we scored a try or a goal, lingering around after the game, in twos or threes, so that they could gang up with us and go giggling along the Malone Road. I never had much luck with these girls, possibly because my attention had to be partly on my bicycle which always seemed to get in the way. Usually as soon as we reached the Old Stranmillis Road I gave up the pursuit, said 'Cheerio' to everybody, and proceeded up the hill alone. Unfortunately none of the girls lived in the same part of town as myself, so the only way to get near them was to meet them in the 'gods' of the Opera House. And if you were lucky and cunning you might find a place behind a girl and when the lights went down you could make her comfortable by letting her sit between your legs, and later imperceptibly manoeuvre yourself so that she lay cradled against you. Such experiences were disappointingly few and never led to much more excitement other than a stroll up and down Great Victoria Street and an ice-cream in the Continental Café; which altogether constituted a fairly daring night out. There was little chance of anything serious following on these casual encounters. Even though you were sometimes given a promise that you could see her again the next Saturday night, your girl would call over her

144

shoulder on departing, 'Perhaps'. And with the uncertainty of that 'perhaps' you lived in hope until Saturday at last came and the longed-for face was nowhere to be seen in the crowded gallery of the Opera House.

Out of My Class, 1985

ROBERT GREACEN
b.1920

'Ven' was the name which my mother and her two sisters used
when they met in a coven and talked about my father. They could
safely use it when the old boy was within hearing distance; he
never cottoned on, and thought perhaps they were gossiping
about someone they had known in the old days in Derry. 'Ven'
was an abbreviation for Venezuela, and they sometimes giggled as
they spoke the longer form. This nickname seemed to cause them
infinite amusement; it helped them to overcome their contempt
for somebody they considered a drunken failure. I never did find
out why they had chosen this particular nickname. Perhaps he had
once read out a news item or something of the kind from the
'Tally' – as everyone called the evening paper, the *Belfast Telegraph* – that had to do with the South American republic. Children sometimes ask a lot of questions; but about some matters
they wisely keep quiet, believing that acceptance is best. They
know that grown-ups will not answer certain questions truth-
fully. I never heard the old man refer to Venezuela or South
America, for his terms of reference were strictly local. He had
never been further away from base than London and I remember
him telling me about a big railway station there called 'Houston'
or so I imagined him to say. Perhaps he unconsciously picked up a
cockney porter's rendering of 'Euston'.

Father was one of five children – John, James, Robert, Henry,
Elizabeth Ann and Samuel – born in the second marriage of a
typical Presbyterian 'small farmer' in County Monaghan. They
moved two or three times, I believe, but for some years lived in the
neighbourhood of Cootehill. A more prosperous and educated
branch of the family had settled in the town of Monaghan – one of

146

them was to become the chairman of the County Council, but we never had any truck with grand folk of that kind. Father's name incidentally, was Henry; and it was given to me as a second Christian name, though plain Robert suits me fine. My paternal grandfather looked the patriarch, white goat beard and all. I do not know what persona he presented to his sons and daughter, but on the occasions I saw him I regarded him with awe – he was a sort of rural Jehovah, thunder-voiced, or, if not quite that, one of the immortals from Mount Olympus who had lived and ruled despotically for hundreds and hundreds of years.

In actual fact I am not sure whether Grandfather was as stern as all that, but that was the impression I had as a small boy. I avoided him as I would have avoided a collision with a big puff-puff. Father himself had somehow or other struggled out of the harshly frugal parental nest – though it did not strike me as being one of singing birds – and attempted to make his way in the narrow Ulster world with only a national school behind him and an early-developed, un-Presbyterian taste for liquor, a liking he never lost. (One of his brothers, my uncle George, was a lifetime teetotaller, and the others only drank occasionally, at weddings or around Christmas.) 'Many's the bit o' business was done over a wee drink,' Father used to say. Or again he would ask, 'Would you tell me a clever man that couldn't take a drink?' A rhetorical question indeed, to answer which would have invited a cuff on the ear. Mind you, when I got a bit older, I wanted to say: 'Yes, Bernard Shaw – and he doesn't eat meat either! He's famous, too!' But I knew that Father had no use for Bernard Shaw whom he regarded as immoral, partly because he had written an exposure of his parents. Father had once said, 'Imagine the oul' idiot makin' a laughin' stock of his own parents! He'll surely go till hell for it.' Apparently at the age of seventeen Father could down his whiskey with the best, or worst, of them. If success in business depended on a man's ability to drain his glass fast and often, then Henry Greacen's name would be inscribed far above that of Isaac Wolfson. Alas, alas!

Father had tried farming without success. As his sister, my Aunt Lizann – Elizabeth Ann – said, 'Harry's heart was never in the

147

moilin' and toilin'.' That was only too clear. He wanted quick results. Crops would not grow fast enough or tall enough; prices in the market were never high enough; farming was a hard, dirty grind at which nobody grew rich. As a young man he had tried his luck in one of those new-type 'creameries' started by people like Sir Horace Plunkett and AE as the basis of an Irish Rural Co-operative Movement. This work was more to Father's liking. He enjoyed it and the prestige which came from being the manager of a creamery. He used to talk about a 'Father Poland' (that's what it sounded like but the name was probably 'Boland') he had been friendly with in those days, although Father was normally somewhat suspicious of those who 'dug with the wrong foot'. Perhaps the priest was something of a Graham Greene character. I know that Father was held in esteem in at least one of these jobs, for he always carried round with him a presentation gold-cased watch which had a copperplate inscription on the inside cover that referred in a stiffly respectable phrase to his qualities as a creamery manager. This watch was often consulted to know whether the pubs were about to open or shut. One of my early delights was to have him hold it to my ear so that I could hear the tick-tick-tick.

But Father was not a man to remain content with managing a small country co-operative. His eyes scanned wider horizons; he looked at the world, like the sage Dr Johnson, from China to Peru – or perhaps it was from China to Venezuela. He never travelled far, but, for all that, was more of a traveller than those who have actually viewed the Golden Gate. There was, after all, the non-conformist obsession with money to be reckoned with. If you made money you were, *ipso facto,* a good man, one whom the Presbyterian God had favoured. If not, why, you were little better than an RC ('Father Poland' excepted) who would do appallingly wicked things like attending Sunday football matches or go dog-racing at Dunmore Park! Thus, there was life on the one hand, the dream on the other: the unending grind at disagreeable chores; and the counter-feeling that racetracks and whiskey (and perhaps a bit surreptitiously, slyly, lovely women) were around the corner. Had not other country boys, foresaking plough and spade and hoe, made their way in the big redbrick city and ended up as pot-bellied aldermen who golfed at the weekend with highly elevated gents such as bank managers and solicitors and doctors?

Frankly speaking, during Father's lifetime I never understood him, nor did he understand me. We lived for the most part in a thick fog of non-comprehension. To me he was a darkly-brooding, narrow-jowled, moody man, who to my disgust chewed twist tobacco and spat out the liquorice-coloured juice, drank a great deal of noxious-smelling whiskey and believed that a man who had not made a 'fortune' was 'no bloody good'. He lacked the gift for happiness or enjoyment. My mother and her sisters kept harping on the theme of his addiction to the bottle, and spoke with bated breath of the sinfulness thereof. I did not know so much about the sinful part of it – anything nice seemed always to be a 'sin' – but drinking was obviously something that made a man miserable. Why does he do it, I thought, if he does not find it *enjoyable,* if it makes him sick? I had yet to hear of Sigmund Freud.

But Father being a good 'Prod' in his heart (not that he was a kirk regular) was damned if he would do anything so fiendishly Papist or foreign as enjoy himself! My mother liked fun far more than he did, and delighted in what she called 'droll stories'. She liked innocent amusement so long as it did not cost too much, for there were bills to pay. Pennies had to be counted – and even halfpennies. In the years when we ran 'The Kenilworth', a newsagent's shop, we used to get a free cinema pass for displaying showcards of the current films. My mother and I, rigged out in our second-best clothes, would go off together to see films such as *The Silent Hour* which starred her great favourite, the very gentlemanly George Arliss, the very model of a model English gentleman. Earlier I had been taken to see *Ramona* by Aunt Tilly in – of all places! – the Clonard, right in the heart of Rome, you might say. The mission bells were indeed calling!

Father came to a film once or twice, but he insisted – much to my chagrin – on leaving in the middle of the 'big picture' saying he could not make head or tail of it. Like most of his relations he thought the silver screen a lot of high-falutin' nonsense, a veritable fraud perpetrated on decent people – Uncle George considered this wonderful never-never land nothing more than 'a wheen o' oul' shadows mugs pay to gape at'. Another time I wheedled Ven into getting as far as the Classic, that palace of romance to my eyes. He hesitated at the box-office, decided against and pressed a half-crown into my sticky palm with the words 'Better in your pocket than in some fat oul' showman's.' I could have wept. Excitement was what I hungered for, not a coin.

To an uncritical cinema-goer like myself, any and every film was vastly exciting. I could be as happy in the 'Pop' on a Saturday afternoon, watching a Western among the scruffy, smelly, jostling, orange-sucking young plebs, as in one of those swish new establishments that impressed me far more than any cathedral had ever done. The 'Pop' may have been rowdy and the noise a bit too much at times to allow one to hear the film dialogue properly, but it had the advantage of costing exactly one penny, merely a 'wing'. Matinees at posh places might cost as much as fourpence or even fivepence. All right for the nobs, but obviously the kind of place I could only visit as a very special treat. As I got a bit older mere shootin' and killin' and ridin' on the range, with a dramatic chase before the villains were brought to justice, began to seem like kids' stuff. The sophisticated world began to entrance me. What posh rooms – more like baronial halls than anything else – these high-class Yanks lived in and how they drank their cocktails with poise and charm! With what insouciance the elegant English actor could carry off a situation in which I would have curled up and died with embarrassment! How enviable were these lives that were played out against a Manhattan or Berkeley Square background! Nobody there worried about whether something cost sixpence, unlike the drab, damp, taxi-less, evening-gownless world where one queued for a fish supper (price fivepence) in Joe's steamy saloon near the 'Pop'. I liked grandeur, swank, pretentiousness, no doubt because such attitudes contrasted so violently with the horrible pinching and scraping that went on around me. The world symbolised by revolving doors that led into Grand Hotels of the Vicki Baum/Arnold Bennett type had a glamour far removed from the atmosphere of McMahon's Select Bar or Ross's pawnshop with its aroma of camphorated clothes. I was tired of existing. I cried out for LIFE or what I mistakenly took to be LIFE. Father believed, as I developed into adolescence, that my head had been turned with nonsense I read in the boys' magazines we sold in the shop, and picked up from the gossip columns of the London newspapers; and no doubt it was. Not only that, but I was at the stage where I read any tit-bit I could find about sex, and viewed with delight photos of naked ladies I came across in journals devoted to the cult of nudism. But the world of high-life was only a temporary aberration, and soon I was to become too serious by half, and be filled with zeal for reforming the world. Nudist magazines were to be replaced by intellectual nourishment represented by the *Irish Democrat* (to which paper I contributed my very first article, 'A Youth's Views on Education') and those limp-cover books issued by the Left Book Club. But that time was not yet.

Ven and I were at loggerheads as usual. He denounced me for always having my nose stuck in a book or newspaper or magazine. My eagerness to understand the world around me (not just in a dry, academic way, but in a real human sense) left him cold. Nor did he forgive me for taking naturally to those uppish garments known as pyjamas – 'pan-jams' he called them contemptuously – introduced into our household by my Aunt Tilly whom he loathed and I loved. I knew somehow that the lovely actresses would despise a boy who slept in his shirt, and the approval of ladies was for me far more important than that of Ven. Father still slept in the shirt he wore all day long. His ancestors had done the same thing, assuming they all had shirts to their backs, which I rather doubt. What was good enough for honest men was good enough for Ven. Why wear fancy clothes when you were asleep? The more he sneered the more adamant I became. He complained that my shoes – he wore boots – had 'pointy' toes and that I looked 'a regular show' in my 'white trousers' – these were simply grey worsted pants, though not as wide as I would really have enjoyed having. Nor did he like the 'classy' polite way I learned to talk at 'Methody', using big words, foreign phrases and schoolboy slang in a manner that obviously indicated a 'swelled head' and would never have passed muster anywhere near Cootehill. I began to be grammatical and say 'he's gone' instead of 'he's went' which showed that college affectation had insidiously crept in. Worse still, I began to pronounce English in a slightly anglicised way. That was also wrong. The more critical Ven became the more determined I was to make myself as different from him as I could, especially since these new directions had the warm approval of Aunt Tilly, who wanted me to be a gentleman like the McCreas whom she said were 'all doctors and clergy'.

There was daily evidence of his dislike for me and his feeling that fundamentally I sided with the feminine McCrea establishment, with its good humour, snobbery, conformity, hard work and relish in innocent amusement. Yet at times during a troubled boyhood – dark and haunted, yet not without an innate belief that one day I would live the life of Larry, far, far away from the Newtownards Road – a temporary bond would spring up between us, as it did in earlier days when I sat on his knee and combed his dark, grey-flecked hair. In the long, timeless evenings of July and August I would take the beloved football I had obtained by collecting a set of cards from a boy's paper and off the two of us would go for a tram-ride that brought us to a destination such as Bellevue or Glengormley. We would hurtle through the still evening air surveying the now inactive city from the top of – no, not a tram – a red chariot rocking its way ever onwards, that thrilled and pulsated with the energy of some elemental force. Those tram-rides were pure ecstasy. It was the route homeward that I feared, when he called at pub after pub for 'just a wee minute'. With tears in my eyes we would come back to the shop eyed by disapproving or amused neighbours.

Ven once went for about a week into a nursing home off the Lisburn Road, an institution that specialised in the treatment of nervous diseases. There he had electric shock treatment. I went to see him there and for the first time in my life played table tennis, that very genteel middle-class game. Within a few weeks of coming out he was, in my mother's words, 'at it again. Paralytic!' When she uttered words like these she would first raise her eyes to heaven and begin to snivel, drying her eyes with her apron. I would go hot and cold, feeling a little angry, very afraid and thoroughly ashamed. Then would come the scenes that occurred regularly and made me as tense as an old maid who wakes up to find a man under the bed. During these theatrical interludes Ven would rant obscenities at Mother or even strike her, or in a tantrum throw his food into the fire, or threaten to beat me 'within an inch of my life' or assert that Mother and her relations had dissipated the 'fortune' that he had made, and that he would have the law on the McCrea villains and leave them penniless. All these and more threats came out of an abysmally deep reservoir of alcoholic aggression, despair and self-pity. 'They ruined me, the McCreas have ruined me,' he would inform people who could not care less. Shaw remarked that home is the girl's prison and the woman's workhouse. It was certainly a workhouse for Mother. 'Home Sweet Home' seemed an ironic phrase or else one coined by people out of touch with reality. It was a place I was always glad to leave, and to which I returned with some misgiving. It was sour-smelling and affectionless. Fortunately from time to time I retreated to Aunt Tilly's where the atmosphere was always warm and cheerful, only shadowed by Ven's latest misdeed.

Home was where one slept and little more than that. Schoolmasters at least dispensed a rough justice. They could be respected, or most of them could. Their punishment was seldom unduly severe and seldom undeserved, whereas Ven was arbitrary and one never knew what might happen if he lost his temper. Like some of our politicians he exercised power without responsibility. Authority – Ven's excepted – was not too bad, and after the first rebellion of youth and early manhood, authority in its various forms is something with which I have had little difficulty in coming to terms. Not for me the lifelong urge to be 'agin the Government'. Coming from a household where civil war and alarms of one kind and another were to be expected, I came early to believe in Henry Miller's dictum: 'Peace, it's wonderful!'

Not that I was altogether a peace-at-any-price or *danegeld* boy in the incessant war against Ven, which was sometimes cold, sometimes hot. As in all wars, there came a crisis, a turning-point. It happened one summer day in 1935 when I was not quite fifteen. I had been out in the back yard breaking up into sticks a number

153

of wooden boxes in which goods had been delivered to the shop. This was something Ven used to order me to do when he was a bit high. I resented his manner of ordering it to be done, and the way his pale, dissatisfied face would press to the window to see the job was being carried out to his satisfaction. As a matter of fact I rather enjoyed the task in itself; and I liked to do it well, always having had an instinctive desire to excel. It was, as I recall, a warm August afternoon, and soon I had broken up all the boxes. A little out of breath from the hurried exertion, I brushed up the wood chips and put them in the bin. I threw down the hatchet with satisfaction after a job well done. I was pleased with myself and hoped now to sneak past the old man and into the shop to ask Mother's permission to go and visit Billy Davidson, a school pal who lived in the Malone Road end of town. This boy's father was a box manufacturer – I was a little flattered that a boy whose family actually had a 'skivvy' found me interesting, and Aunt Tilly encouraged me to get to know such people. I had my way to make in the world, she said, and influential friends would be all to the good. Then an ugly face appeared at the window, glaring at me with bloodshot eyes. Speak of the devil – if it wasn't the 'oul' lad', and in a bit of a paddy, too! What eyes! Had he escaped from Purdysburn or what? Out he rushed like a bull stung by a wasp.

'I didn't tell you to stop,' he screamed. 'You f—— idiot!'

'I won't do any more. I've finished the job in any case. And I've got a friend to see.'

'You're a bloody idiot – you an' yer fancy white trousers, an' yer grand college chums. A lot of oul' cissies.'

'And you're drunk,' I retorted. 'You're talking through your headgear.'

'Drunk, you impudent pup,' he screamed, 'I'll show you who's drunk, you f——, half blind get. You don't even know who yer Da is. He's down at the market sellin' oranges. Ask that oul' whore in the shop.'

'I'll kill him,' I thought, 'I'll kill him if he lays a finger on me, so help me God.'

He had struck me in the past. . . and I was afraid he might smash my nice new glasses into my eyes and blind me. As it was, it

154

was no fun being short sighted, and it handicapped me badly at games. Words would get me precisely nowhere. Action now or never! I picked up the hatchet and lingeringly touched its slightly jagged gleaming edge with my left forefinger. I was a-tremble with fear and anger. Then I spoke, slowly, deliberately.

'Get inside, you dirty lying drunkard or I'll cut you open,' adding for good measure, 'Whiskey Ven.'

He opened his mouth to say something nasty, but drunk as he was he read the word that shone behind my lenses. The word was murder. This was no play-acting and he knew it. Muttering incoherently, he turned, groped his way into the kitchen, and slithered into the swivel office chair. In a moment he fell off it on to the worn linoleum.

Feeling ashamed and angry I rushed into the house and out through the shop, not stopping to answer my mother's question as to where I was going. I ran wildly into the street, then turned left and ran. Past Kenilworth Street, past Fraser Street, past Cable Street, on and on, past Maidment's the greengrocers, on towards Connswater and the Holywood Arches. I glanced over at the Northern Bank where I carried the shop's weekly takings every Saturday morning. I carried my hundred pounds or more with dignity. Look at me now, a fugitive from Ven! The sun seemed to burn down as if to impede the progress of a malefactor. Old wives' tales came to mind. Had not Aunt Tilly once told me of the little boy who struck his parents, and how he died soon after of a brainstorm, and how even to this very day his fleshless hand stuck up out of his little grave. Oh yes, you had to 'Honour Thy Father and Thy Mother. . .' Yet how could one give honour where it was obviously unwarranted? Surely God was a just God? Nobody I knew could be asked to solve the dilemma, neither minister nor Sunday school teacher, for this was something which must at all costs be kept secret. I kept on and on, past grocers' shops and newsagents and pubs and butchers' shops and pawnbrokers and police barracks until at last I came to sedate houses along the route to Holywood. I stopped running, for the chances were now less that a 'peeler' would stop me and ask me to explain myself. How could a 'Methody' boy explain that he had wanted to kill his

155

father? It was inexcusable and would appal one of these black-suited pillars of law and order. Or supposing the headmaster in College Gardens heard of this hou-ha? Supposing Ven went to the head to complain about insubordination – heaven knows he had often threatened to go up to the school and disgrace me in front of my fine new friends. If I were expelled, what would become of me without having passed 'Junior' or 'Senior'? A life as a caulker in the Yard. Goodbye to my hopes of being a big man in London. London would callously close its gates to such a boy. These were my thoughts as I wandered, shirt sticking to my back, towards Holywood and the sea. . . Now in the open country, I climbed through a hedge and into a field. I wept bitterly for having wanted to kill Ven, for, despite everything he was my father. 'God forgive me,' I prayed fervently. And I repeated the Lord's Prayer with a sincerity very different from the way I gabbled it normally before jumping into bed.

It was chilly when I returned, sneaking past the 'New Princess' whose second house was just being let out. Tired and hungry and dishevelled I certainly was, but I felt strangely radiant and un-afraid. I had purged my crime. Not only that, but at last I had done something. I had stood up for myself and would now take what consequences came my way. The shop was shut of course when I arrived, so I rattled the letter-box with as much confidence as I could summon up. My mother came to the door. Her eyes were red, and she looked so much older than usual. I noticed the grey in her hair.

'Where were you, boy?' she asked. Her relief seemed to have an undertone of anger, a controlled anger, unlike Ven's.

'Out with a friend. Billy Davidson. We went to Holywood.'

'You look as if you'd been through a hedge backwards. Why didn't you say where you were going instead of rushing out like a mad thing? I was worried to death about you, Robbie. First your father, now you. . . The Greacens are all mad, I never saw the like of them, not like my people. . .'

'You should've known I'd be all right, Mother. Honestly I was. I wish you wouldn't treat me like a child. I wanted to get away from Ven, if you must know.'

She began to weep into her apron, a sight that always made me feel guilty, but I was powerless to do or say anything. Something in me wanted to comfort her, but I could not or would not. What did I care about this crazy world of grown-ups with their tears and anger and admonitons, don't-do-this and don't-do-that! When I grew up, I'd be off and I'd never come back. Never, never!

I went into the scullery, poured out a cup of buttermilk and made myself a big 'piece'. I ate hurriedly, standing. Without a goodnight to Mother I ran up the creaking stairs to the attic room where I slept. I didn't know if Ven had gone to bed or was still out, nor did I care. Then I lit my candle with a 'Swift' match – we had no electric light at the top of the house – and got into bed. I lay for a long time watching the shadows. Opening *Vanity Fair* I tried to read, but could not settle to it. Tomorrow was a new day, I thought. Perhaps I could re-learn to honour Ven as I should, perhaps not. It did not seem to matter much. Only a few more years and I would be out of the prison house, free to do as I pleased. I put out the candle and felt the darkness swathe me like a cloak – friendly and comforting.

About a week later I was coming home from having had tea at the house of a schoolfriend, for I was making every effort to cultivate the right people. Some book I had been reading stressed the need for contacts. I had every intention of making my way in the world and I had a contempt for those without ambition. For my part, I would have a shot at getting the best that was going. The idea of one man being as good as another – dear to many an average Ulster heart – was loathsome. I considered I was superior to most, and I wanted them to know it, too. Yet I sensed that that attitude caused resentment, even bitterness. Well, let it! I vowed that one day my achievements would outstrip those of the boys brought up on the Malone Road. In the past week things had taken a turn for the better in the place I called home. Ven had been off the booze for three whole days!

At the corner of Templemore Avenue I saw a group of people surrounding a navy-suited figure that seemed to have slipped into the roadway. A brown felt hat lay forlornly on the ground. As I approached I saw a man, red-faced and beefy like a cattle-dealer, holding in his clumsy hands a tradesman's bicycle with a big wicker basket above a low wheel. There was a sign under the bar that read: 'Cochrane: Flesher of Quality'. I heard the big man's shrill, angry voice splutter out:

'If drunken eejits get in my road it isn't my fault if I run them down.'

A weak voice from the ground: 'You. . . you. . . I'll. . . law on you.'

I came closer. Through my well-polished, steel-rimmed new glasses I realised with a shudder that the figure in the roadway was Ven. I thought of my mother's words and how nearly they had come true.

'May Ven never come home alive this day!'

I burned with anger and shame that I should be the son of such a man. How God had punished me and how I hated Him! But my anger found an earthly target – it flared up against the red-faced oaf who held the bicycle in his rough hands like a mother grasping her only babe – as if his wretched tradesman's bicycle were studded with diamonds! Summoning up my every bit of courage I pushed my way through the gawking bystanders.

'Look here, mister,' I said, 'clear off to hell you f—— baboon. He's my FATHER.'

Still burning with rage and shame, I pulled Ven from the gutter, shoved the brown felt hat on his head and dragged him home. When we got in, Mother started a tirade against drunkenness.

'Shut up, woman,' I said roughly.

Then I ran hell for leather up the stairs to my little room where I fell sobbing on the hard but familiar bed. It seemed to me as if I had been crying on and off for hours before I at last came to my senses, and decided to have a wash. I carefully brushed and combed my auburn locks, looking at myself appraisingly in the cracked mirror. I had pushed all thought of Ven out of my mind, and was dreaming instead of the golden world I should enter in the distant future and in some distant place. The world of famous men and beautiful women beckoned to me. . . and I knew they were all waiting. . . waiting for Robert.

Even Without Irene, 1969

SAM McAUGHTRY

b.1921

In all, my father signed on the *Dunaff Head* no less than ninety-two times, including the trip when she was torpedoed. A few of the trips were to the Far East, South America and Australia, but the vast majority of his voyages were to North America, where the Head Line's regular income lay.

This association was broken only because there was hardly any Head Line fleet left when the *Dunaff* went down. My father signed on with another company for the last ten years of his life.

For some reason, the Head Line forgot to thank him for his contribution, which, as a matter of interest, amounted to a hundred and forty recorded voyages in Head Line ships between 1904 and 1941, plus a conservative estimate of a further twenty in the seven unrecorded years before 1904.

That's one hundred and sixty trips. Mostly across the North Atlantic. There are seamen who did more for the Head Line, but I don't think the company wrote thank-you letters to them either.

. . . our Jim and I, who were considered to be far too young for such things, once had a fascinating time going through the record of Dad's voyages in order to pinpoint the dates on which each of our keels were laid, so to speak.

On 6 June 1910 the old man paid off from the *Glenarm Head* at North Shields, on which he had sailed for the previous four months on a voyage to South America and back.

Me and our Jim worked it out, when I was about nine and he was seven. Yes, we said. That's about right. Jack was born in March 1911. The kids in the street must be right about that stuff.

Two years later Dad paid off the *Ramore Head* after a two-

159

month trip to Canada. OK, let's see, said the two young researchers. Yes. Mmmmm. Mart was born in March 1913, was he not?

Marvellous. Here's yours Sam. Oh? Where, exactly? There. Look. On 17 June 1920, at the port of Belfast, Marriott McAughtry, fireman and trimmer, walked down the gangway of the SS *Melmore Head*, lately arrived from Montreal. He was glad to be home.

My date of birth is 24 March 1921, if anybody wants to know.

My father's father was a master mariner. That's how it was always referred to in our house: master mariner. Never sea captain. The old man's side of the family were all very proud of this. Especially his mother, Mary, my gramma.

'Your grandfather John McAughtry was a master mariner,' she used to say to me when I visited her in her little house in Shandon Street by the New Lodge Road.

For the life of me I could never understand why Gramma kept bringing this up. We hadn't two halfpennies to scratch ourselves with, so Captain John couldn't have been master of a very big ship.

Gramma was very old indeed, to my young mind. She commanded immense respect from our breed, seed and generation, not only because she had probably the highest IQ in the connection. Gramma, even in her eighties, was nimble of mind and deft in debate. She had a firmer grasp of politics and economics than any man of her acquaintance. Very likely she picked up the reading habit when she went to sea the odd time with my grandfather.

Incidentally, Captain John died at thirty-nine, drowned in Liverpool dock. We never bothered looking into the circumstances. Dad was sent to identify his body in 1897. He arranged for it to be sent home and then he took off at the age of fifteen, working down below, in some tramp or other. He didn't come home to Belfast for two years. And bingo went the chance of the Macs producing another master mariner. Gramma lost a lot of her fancy for Dad after that.

160

She was small and she wore long, black clothes. Her grey hair was pulled back in a bun. She wore rimless glasses with wool wrapped around the connecting piece so that it wouldn't cut into her nose.

The bottoms of her eyes were red crescents where the membrane had fallen downwards and the flesh underneath her chin had dropped so that it wobbled when she turned her head.

She was a tough old bird was Gramma. During the blitz on Belfast, when she was eighty-three, a 250-pounder dropped on to Shandon Street, bringing the house down around her. The neighbours dug her out of the parlour where she had been sleeping. Dusty and in a foul temper she was brought the few hundred yards to our house in Hillman Street.

'Here you are, Gramma,' my mother said, handing her a cup of tea.

'Have you anything else?' she asked, delicately. We knew what she meant.

'Try this,' said Mother, handing her a glass of brandy. She sniffed at it suspiciously, her face grimy and her hair and clothes covered in cement dust.

'Thanks, Lizzie,' she said. 'I hope you haven't watered it. It destroys it, you know,' and then she sank it in one, and that was the blitz dealt with.

It was a custom in our family that the job of washing and laying out the dead fell to Gramma. It was she who laid out Betty and Harry and Molly and the other Sam in our family. I happened to pass the bedroom door after Betty died and saw the naked little body lying on top of the bed whilst Gramma was holding her burial clothes up, examining them. I'll always remember that. Wee Betty looked so defenceless or something.

Gramma lived long enough to wash and lay out my own mother in 1946. She died herself not long after, and we worded her death notice with care: 'Mary McAughtry, widow of John McAughtry, Master Mariner. . .'

Whenever his ship tied up my father followed a strict ritual. As soon as he had finished wiping down the engines he came up on deck from the engine room and collected a bucket of hot water from the galley. He carried this up on to the fo'c'sle head, stepping over the two-foot high breakwater that ran slantwise across the deck. Then he descended into the port side of the fo'c'sle, where the engine-room crew had their quarters. There he undressed and scrubbed himself pink-clean.

Dressed in his shore-going navy blue suit, white shirt and black tie, he hoisted his long, seaman's bag on to his shoulder and went down the gangway, out into Whitla Street, and into Phil Maguire's pub nearby. With him usually were his pals the bo's'n and lamp-trimmer. In Phil Maguire's they bevied for a couple of hours.

Around about this time, his family were in a fine state of excitement, back in Cosgrave Street. This street was built on a steep hill that looked straight down on the docks, where the ocean-going ships tied up. Often it was possible to see from our street Dad's ship move slowly into view as she berthed. Her outline was unmistakable – all the Head Line ships carried the emblem of the Ulster Steamship Company, the Red Hand of Ulster on a white shield. The funnel and hull were painted black, and the upper works were white and yellow.

The shipping news in the *Belfast Telegraph* would have alerted us the day before the ship was due in any case, but all the way across the last leg of her journey I would have been following her course. Pinned up in the reading room of the Belfast Public Library was a copy of Lloyd's *Shipping Gazette,* and the noon position of Dad's ship was there. It was only a matter, for a school kid like me, of standing on tiptoe and looking for it.

'*Dunaff Head*, noon 25 January. Bar 40, vis. 15, NW Force 3, bound Belfast', it would say, giving the ship's position. I would sit on the hot pipes in the reading room, get my atlas out of my schoolbag, and check the noon position myself.

As the time drew near for the old man to arrive home, Mother was a sight to see. She, too, was scrubbed pink, with a touch of powder added. Her soft, dark hair was tied back in a bun. A brand new pinny was produced for each homecoming. She kept pulling and smoothing at this.

Mother was small, like Dad, and sonsy. At the least excitement a round spot would glow on each of her cheeks. They were there in her cheeks all right, in the run-up to Dad's homecoming. She would shush us kids when anticipation made us noisy, but we could see she was pretty thrilled at this time.

My goodness, they were in love, those two. In all my life I have never seen a married couple who were so much in love. There she was having given him ten kids, waiting at the door of our cramped little house, looking eagerly down the cobbled street for the taxi that would bring her man home to her from the sea.

When he arrived they would hug just inside the tiny kitchen, two small people, all dressed up for each other, in an ocean of love, with me and the other kids looking on and thinking the whole thing was absolutely smashing.

They didn't wait around too long downstairs at this stage. First Mother rushed to make him a cup of milky tea, while Dad produced silver for each of us out of his waistcoat pocket. Then they both went upstairs for the best part of a couple of hours.

And downstairs we young ones were steeped in contentment. Daddy was home from the sea. The house was full of a lovely smell of whiskey and Woodbines, and we had silver in our pockets.

Nobody in the world could have been happier than we were, when the *Dunaff Head* came home.

The Sinking of the Kenbane Head, 1977

ROBERT HARBINSON

b.1928

BELFAST, 1930s AND 1940s

There are no more weavers in Ballymacarrett.

Now, when the blasting lay-off siren wails above the screeching din of hammers and pneumatic riveters, the shipyard gates open. Into the dirty streets of the once quiet townland swarm the grimy workers. Pavements teem with youths and gaunt fathers, the air smells of a day's work, its grease and sweat. Hurrying with an unnatural speed, everyone is anxious only to get home to the kitchen sink and remove the stigma of toil. Afterwards, transformed, there could be a visit to the dogs, a session over pots of porter, or a game of marleys.

Big 'Ina heard the Albert strike four o'clock on a warm spring afternoon. Because of the great load that sagged heavily under her pinny, the air seemed oppressive. She felt hot and bothered, and thought of an ice from Leo's ice-cream parlour down the street. Before the men came spewing out from the yard there would be time to get a penny wafer. It did her good, so much good, that she decided to spend a second wing on another. And as she was licking it, a sharp pain gripped her and she realised the time had come to get Nurse Calvert. But barely had Big 'Ina got inside the door when I made my entry into the world.

The event was spectacular. Nearly eleven pounds I weighed. 'Ya've the muscles of a man,' said the district nurse when she congratulated Big 'Ina on having such a brute. My mother never forgot the nurse's remark. The years that followed were to prove that only those muscles would ensure our survival.

Not that the event shook the world – it had other things to think about. The gay twenties were coming to an end. On that very day Mr Churchill introduced his budget, a tax on imported buttons,

164

and a farthing off sugar. The Duke of Gloucester took his seat in the House of Lords, and another titled gentleman was arrested in Hyde Park when trying to share his seat with a lady of the town. Gay – but not for everyone. In Greece an earthquake rocked Corinth, a plague of locusts appeared on the shores of Galilee, and a hungry brat sought for Big 'Ina's breast. But for the small house in Ballymacarrett, the world was the baby.

When the young sire came down the street, ladder over shoulder with his bucket swinging from the end, Cissy, the first-born, ran to tell him the news. He bolted up the stairs and snatched up the purple-faced bundle. The squalling thing fulfilled his dearest wish of a son, and of course, it would be called Robbie after him. The excitement, localised in the dockside house, did not even reach as far as the clergy of the parish church. They, whose business was to disseminate hope and joy in our close streets, saw so many offspring coming into a hopeless and joyless world, and had become indifferent. Big 'Ina could wait, no rector was going to the house for *her* baby. When sufficient names crowded the list – a fortnight later – I was carried off to the big church round the corner that heaved its Victorian Gothic bulk above the mean dock houses.

That night many babies awaited baptism, and the curate was in a hurry to get started. Perhaps the church had chilled since the day's heat, perhaps his supper lay ready, perhaps despair at the despair of our world gnawed his soul. Anyway, I joined the first queue of my life, and so came into the heritage of the poor. Aunt Dottie, a cousin of my mother's, acted as my only godparent.

In Aunt Dottie's view Big 'Ina had 'come down' in the world by marrying my father, for their side of the family was comparatively well-to-do. My mother's parents both died and she was farmed out to an aunt who resented her intrusion. At the age of twelve Big 'Ina, properly called Georgina, went to work in the mill. Those muscles of which the nurse spoke, formed young. Though callous, the relatives maintained sufficient interest to oppose her marriage vigorously. In their opinion, the man she wanted was beneath her, and a reputation for wildness and an over-fondness of the bottle did not help. But in defiance, Big 'Ina and Robbie joined a church queue and got married, *en masse* with seventeen other couples. Afterwards they went off on a two-shilling excursion to Bangor and had a grand high tea at a Mrs McGowan's boarding-house, before returning to Ballymacarrett to start breeding.

When the aunts kept away, my father worked well enough and was popular with everyone whose windows he cleaned.

We left Ballymacarrett when I reached the age of five months, an age when I had already contracted a shipyard bark, the result, people thought, of the bronchitis that lingered about my young chest. My paternal grandfather died and left us his house on the other side of the city. It was rented, and though valued at no more than a hundred pounds, during the years that ensued we paid upwards of a thousand pounds for the scruffy little house, in coins so indignantly demanded every Monday morning by the rent clerk.

People considered the new house smart for it boasted two bedrooms and a return, though it is true only tiny ones. It stood so close to the railway that the whole structure shook from the foundations, day and night, from the passing trains. Out of the front bedroom where we all huddled together in the big brass bed, the window gave a view across a roof wilderness of near-slums whose only contact with heaven was by belching chimney-stacks that fingered the sky. It was to be the scene of my childhood until I was twelve. Bliss and tragedy were to fall on Big 'Ina's baby scarcely half-a-year old then. Later, he looked back on those years as the most wonderful of his life.

But the rows of houses did not go on for ever. Beyond them lay the Bog Meadows' marshy steppes where refuse heaps broke the flatness, and where the narrow, shallow Blackstaff river meandered, colourless and unmusical. Near its banks the tinkers camped. We at least held hopes in our heart – who knew, one day we might even have the chance of a council house. But the tinkers could not warm themselves with such a comfort, but only over reluctant fires that hissed in the drizzle outside their tents of rags.

God ordained that even the Bog Meadows should end and had set a great hill at their limit, which we called the Mickeys' Mountain. Among a knot of trees half-way up the flank a small cottage sheltered, and near by two fields were cultivated. Seen from the Bog Meadows they stood out amongst the bracken and heather like a giant hatchet. In terms of miles the mountain was not far, and I always longed to explore it. Somewhere, or in the hidden hills behind, lay the boot stuffed with goldpieces buried by Neeshy Haughan, who once upon a time robbed the rich to pay the poor, kindnesses ended by a hanging at Carrickfergus. What things might be bought with the highwayman's long boot of gold! But the mountain was inaccessible because to reach it we had to cross territory held by the Mickeys. Being children of the staunch Protestant quarter, to go near the Catholic idolators was more than we dared, for fear of having one of our members cut off.

I settled early on rebel dreams. My father was too much like Neeshy Haughan, wild and free. My life became embedded in his and I rushed to his defence whenever people attacked him on account of his wildness. Soon, when I grew to be five years old, tragedy struck at us. Playing with the tinker children in the Bog Meadows one day, I found some whitethorn blossom, and thinking to delight my mother, took it home. She recognised the evil omen and threw the blossom out. But it was too late. Before nightfall the hospital call came – Big 'Ina's fella had fallen from the top window of a house in the rich suburbs and broken his limbs. His head was spiked on the railings, his brain fatally damaged. He was twenty-seven years old, his wild music sung, his passion cased in plaster of Paris.

Then began the terrible days which have chased me down the long corridors of life ever since. For months he lay on the horse-hair sofa in the kitchen, delirious in body and mind. I can see him now, unable to join us in the brass bed, lying amid the bandages, and covered by his father's old lamplighter's greatcoat. He always wanted his melodeon near, though he could play it no more. And in my last memory of him, I see him on the sofa, where sometimes I would find odd coins that had rolled down the side. It was Christmas Eve, and my mother had gone to see my younger sister who had scarlet fever. Looking up I saw tears rolling down the unshaven face. I thought maybe he was sorry for having filled the house with vast terror earlier in the day, when my mother went near to wash him. Or perhaps his soul was fighting to be out in the Bog Meadows with his red-setter bitch, or playing his melodeon on the quayside as the emigrant boats sailed out from the harbour. Perhaps he wept because he realised that life was almost over, and he must leave the boys on the corner, the pigeons on the mangle in the back yard, the tin porringer of whelks from the Friday market and the little house in our row.

And so it was.

He never got free of the imprisoning plaster to go down to see friends off to America, his melodeon wheezing out 'God be with you till we meet again', or a good Orange bleat of 'Sons whose sires with William bled'. Before springtime came again he was taken, we thought, to hospital. Then one morning a sparrow flew down the parlour chimney and my mother knew the end had come. And sure enough the same day my father died.

We had an old saying, 'Happy is the bride the sun shines on; happy is the corpse the rain rains on.' Undoubtedly it meant happiness to him that his wrecked body, undermined by tuberculosis and the effects of hard drinking, to say nothing of smashed limbs and severed brain, could now rest. A thunderstorm swept across the city as he was taken very quietly away. I sat at the great-aunts', cloistered with Bible storybooks and an apple tart with six red candles because it was my birthday. But as the flails of rain lashed the windows I thought of the day's events. I had seen my mother borrow black stockings from next door, and knew why, dressed in the unusual clothes, she had taken us over to be at the great-aunts' until all was over. On my jersey sleeve, a diamond-shaped black patch had been sown, and my fingers wandered to pull and fidget the material. While the funeral was taking place somebody robbed our house. The window-cleaner's last possession, his ladder, disappeared. The neighbours rightly said that 'Poor Robbie went without a shammy to his name.'

Some days after, when we were all at home in our own house again, a relative brought what we called the 'grave-papers'. My mother put them in the marble-topped washstand upstairs along with the birth certificates and other family documents. I was told, as if I ought to know, that the family grave would now only hold one more adult, alternatively two of us children might be squeezed in.

Time, the unreckoned time of the young, swallowed our tragedy. Then I started school. The gloomy building and its dull chores did not interest me much, and after a taunting remark by my teacher, they became a special hate. The teacher, a great female Wolsey with triple chins and stomachs, was called the Tit Queen, a title awarded her on account of a most enormous bosom. One morning in the playground, my skylarking roused her wrath, and she resorted to sarcasm, and made the fatal remark, 'You're as mad as your father ever was.'

Some finely tensioned cord in me snapped. From then on I hated her, and all she represented, and became a rebel, very much with a cause. For years the taunt shadowed my life. The bitter words haunted me when, later, I got to know definitely that the 'hospital' had been a mental one, and succeeded in reading the death certificate's dread pronouncement, 'Cause of Death, General Paralysis of the Insane. Indefinite Certified.' How bare of humane feeling could officialdom be? The long, crisp certificate bore no mention of a young window-cleaner having an accident; did not even carry the merciful medical terminology to deaden the pain for the widow, still little more than a girl; not a thought did that bald piece of paper spare for the children who wanted him to come home, and rock them back and forth on his knee while singing:

> The Bangor boat's away,
> We've got no time to stay,
> So put on your coat,
> And run like a goat,
> The Bangor boat's away.

The memory of my father devoured me. Growing up did not separate me from him, for in doing so I grew to be like him. Everyone said, 'You're the spit of your ould da.' The loathed great-aunts employed this as a scornful term, and they did not only mean my facial structure which increasingly resembled his. But their contempt could be fought by spending long hours in the

169

cemetery, an activity they considered unhealthy.

But I knew that ordinary people regarded my father highly. 'Ordinary people' meant those whose hearts had not shrivelled, and whose emotions were not bottled in vinegar, and who had not got the money and killing respectability of the great-aunts. It pleased me immensely when an ordinary person recognised me as 'Robbie's wee craytur' or when I heard them talking and agreeing that my father had been a 'quare civil fella'. A grain of comfort for my mother came from the doctor who saw him die. Often she told us, I suppose because there was no-one else to tell, of the doctor's remark. She repeated with sad wonder that at the end, 'Robbie was like a lad of sixteen.' In death, the lines of anguish and suffering had been smoothed out. Nevertheless, the dashing youth with a cloth cap set at a cocky angle, his pockets full of rhubarb-rock, would come down the street no more to his small world – the world of the big brass bed and the children's lips like split roses that watered as he put hand to pocket.

Snow fell on the first occasion that my two sisters and I were taken to the cemetery by Big 'Ina. We were almost too small to keep pace as she hurried over the eddying, powdered snow to put a holly wreath on the still-new grave. Before we reached it, a melancholy bell tolled the closing time, so we began running. My younger sister was crying and I was afraid the gate would close too soon, and we would have to spend the night with the endless tombstones, the gargantuan angels and sarcophagi, and the cypresses looming out of the whirling flakes. But at last we reached the grave and my mother, leaning over the snow-covered knobbly earth, laid the ring of tough, shiny leaves, and we half-ran, half-walked back to the gates. We were the last out, and the man was cross for being kept late on Christmas Eve. Breathless from running, we passed under the weird street-lamps, our cheeks so hot that the snowflakes melted on touching them.

Working to provide for us through fourteen hours a day, seven days in the week, left my mother no time to go back to the cemetery, but the little plot had a willing guardian in me. Not that death was strange to me, for it often brooded in our streets, with wide bows of black taffeta tied to the knockers, blinds drawn for three days, and the collecting of pennies for wreaths of wax-paper flowers. The shining funeral horses, with froth dripping from their mouths, passed our house on their way home after a day's work, leaving a harvest of golden piles, which were quickly shovelled up for the orange lilies in the window-boxes. I was still a toddler when a small friend took me into the parlour where his grandmother was 'set out'. Because I had been a favourite of the old lady, he pulled the veil back from the coffin and told me I could have a last kiss.

In our own house we had a christening veil. As my face was very pale and unhealthy, hollowed by cavernous cheeks, and I knew nobody expected me to live long, I would dress up in a nightgown, put the veil over my face and play at funerals. Conversations I overheard often turned on my going first to the grave's remaining space. Solemn journeys to the cemetery continued through many years; I would not be drawn away from where my father lay. Not until I left Ireland, when sixteen, did I realise how desolate, how forlorn was the ugliness of those acres of the dead that once seemed so beautiful. Bitterly then, I wrote:

> It is there on the hillside,
> Despicable and disgusting,
> Like a white spreading sore
> In the flesh;
> A contradiction of life. . .

'No Pope here', 'Not an inch', 'God save the King', and 'Remember 1690' were signs we saw every day. They appeared in huge permanently painted letters on the gable ends of the streets round about. Although our street lay midway between Falls Road, the centre of everything Catholic in Belfast, and Sandy Row, the strongest Orange quarter, we were staunchly Protestant. Even ruder slogans against His Holiness decorated some gables; together with elaborate paintings, some twenty feet or more high, of coronation scenes complete with flowering robes, regalia, and recognisable portraits of King George V and Queen

Mary. The crossing of Boyne water by King Billy, with flying banners and flashing swords, was, however, the favourite topic for these vast outdoor murals.

We had a mural too in the back yard of our house, but only a painted crown on the whitewash under the window-sill. Higher up, only just visible, remained the fragments of King Billy's charger, the open Bible, a lurid eye through the clouds, Jacob's ladder, the rainbow, and Noah's ark, painted years before by my father while in a mood of patriotism. Whatever they represented religiously and politically, the pictures added a dash of colour and life to the drab mien of the streets.

We tried to reckon how much an ordinary Mickey would have to pay at confession for a week's sins. It was our firm belief that every sin had to be paid for in hard cash, and that was why so many Catholics were publicans – unlike so many others their tills were always full of cash.

For one particular crime we could never forgive the Mickeys: their hatred of the Bible. All Catholics were under orders, we were told, to burn any scripture they found, especially New Testaments. The old song supported us,

The intriguing Paypishes surround this loyal and ancient town
They tried you know not long ago to pull the Bible down
And to destroy it root and branch they often have combined
But from Sandy Row we made them fly like chaff before
    the wind.

What pride we enjoyed for living so near to Sandy Row – the Boys of Sandy Row, stalwarts of our Orange Order.

We imagined also that newly dead popes were embalmed like Takabuti in the museum, and then put on display as human money-boxes; and that when they were stuffed so full that not another penny would go in, they were canonised and became saints.

Takabuti, the Egyptian mummy, a house-mistress of a priest of Amunre, reclined in a case at the museum not altogether without a vestige of former dignity. She could never have imagined, three thousand years before, the tiny faces that would press so often against the glass of her exhibition table. Her hair and teeth, whole though shrivelled and discoloured, and her delicate foot complete with flesh and toenails, attracted as much attention as perhaps they had so long ago. Certainly the priest of Amunre could not have paid her more attention than we did. However, much as we loved Takabuti and her wimple of blue beads, other kinds of priests occupied our minds – those of Rome.

Crowding out any other aspects of history, our schools dinned into us over and over again the Protestant story. On leaving school, and that none too early for my liking, I had no notion of the world's past other than a few prehistoric tales and dreary details concerning our Protestant faith and the unrelieved darkness of Rome. The particular rack on which they tortured us appeared in the form of a small, buff covered booklet entitled *How we Differ from Rome*.

With what surprising, singeing pains my hands and fingers often smarted when a cane or strap was administered because on being asked 'How does Pope Honorius, writing in 1221, refer to the entry of the English into Ireland?' I could not furnish the correct answer. 'Pope Honorius states that "the English entered Ireland by the authority of the Apostolic See and made it obedient to the Church of Rome".' Really! No excuse could be offered, they told me so frequently, probably every day, certainly every week; I had no reason, on being asked to 'Quote from Pope Adrian's letter to Henry II', for failing to report that 'Pope Adrian states:– "While as a Catholic prince you intend to widen the bounds of the Church we are anxious to introduce a faithful plantation in that land" [of Ireland].' The complete horrid booklet had to be learnt by heart, before we could be upgraded to commit the Prayer Book catechism to memory, and finally present ourselves, suitably primed, for confirmation.

This picture appears black, but a lighter side did exist, a comic-relief provided by intimate details of the popes' private lives. Before we tumbled out of our cradles, we knew of the unspeakable behaviour by the pontiffs and their courts. The goings-on of the Borgias were as familiar as the affairs of the next-door neighbour.

Even proper history books, we were assured, disclosed the

antics at the papal court, with Roman strumpets running round and burning their bare bottoms on the great lighted candles of the Vatican. Nuns undergoing initiation were sometimes forced to play the part of these naked shepherdesses – until too old for orgies. Then they were given the flowing habits to cover up the singe marks on their buttocks and legs, and sent back to Ireland or wherever they came from. No wonder our preachers referred in horror to Rome as the Scarlet Woman! And little wonder amongst our first nursery rhymes was,

> If I had a penny
> Do you know what I would do?
> I would buy a rope
> And hang the pope
> And let King Billy through.

After all, our unswerving loyalty to the British crown was through King Billy – William of Orange, the man who defeated the Catholic Stuarts, the Irish and French, in the famous battle at the Boyne river.

From these allegiances the greatest spectacular event of the Ulster year took place on the Twelfth of July. How wise of William to win his battle at the height of summer, so that festivities in its honour through the centuries after could be held in sunshine and fine weather! How we children waited for that day, and for the day preceding, when the riot of decorations received finishing touches in the streets. A Union Jack hung from every house, and masses of bunting criss-crossed the street from upper windows; crowns and mystical triangles; crescent moons each with seven stars, and flaming suns with faces; the burning bush and David's sling and five stones; streamers; red, white and blue rosettes bloomed in a profuse garden of paper and linen.

Each street vied with the next in the splendour of the main piece, its triumphal arch. Spanning between two houses, bedizened with orange and purple streamers, the arch was studded with pictures of British royalty. The climax of these preliminaries to the Twelfth was the lighting of bonfires. In the manner of the English November Fifth, we had effigies of Catholic leaders, that had sat for weeks on street corners collecting pennies, and which were solemnly consigned to the flames like Guy Fawkes.

Before the ashes had lost their red hearts, the drums of Lambeg rolled like thunder through the summer night and ushered in our Glorious Twelfth. Day dawned; everyone was up early, ready to go out and see the sights and watch the traditional 'walk to the Field'. It was a public holiday, as important to us as the Fourth of July in the USA.

For miles along the Lisburn Road, thousands waited to see the Orangemen walk in procession behind elaborate banners painted with symbols of their secret society. To us Belfast boys, the Black men we looked for in the procession were not negroes, but the most respected holders of the highest rank within the hierarchy of the Order. Purple men followed them in precedence and lastly the ordinary Orangemen, all three wearing sashes coloured after their rank and bordered with a heavy gold fringe.

Everywhere orange colour flamed in sash and banner, and in the lily which people wore. They twined in bunches with sweet-williams on top of the standards, for the orange-lily was as sacred to us as the shamrock was to the Mickeys or Fenians.

> Do you think that I would let
> A dirty Fenian get
> Destroy the leaf of a lily-o,
> For there's not a flower in Ireland,
> Like King Billy's orange-lily-o.

Such sights! Such music, churning the Protestant blood in our veins! For my first eight Twelfths I had needs be content with trailing through the crowds, craning for a glimpse of glory, straining to see the cymbals flashing as zing-zing-zing they crashed in a flash of sun, pushing my way through a forest of arms and legs to catch the dozens of pipe-bands, the flutists, and the drummers. The drummers came between each Lodge, flaying the hides of the big bass drums from Lambeg, where, naturally, they made the finest drums in the world. The huge cylinders were painted and decorated in gold, red, and orange with figures and patterns, crests and royal coats-of-arms in a whirligig of colour and line. It

175

was considered a point of honour by some Lambeggers to beat the great drums so hard, and for so long, that wrists chaffed the drum's edge until the skin became sore or even until cuts and bleeding resulted.

As expression of loyalty to a Protestant throne it would have been hard to find anything finer. But as music the effect was open to question. Whether of pipes or flutes or brass, or simply four of the gigantic Lambeg drums, each band felt that responsibility for the day's music rested solely, and by no means lightly, on their shoulders. Consequently they blew, blasted, and banged as heartily as wind and muscle knew how. For a single band in isolation this would have been admirable, but since one band succeeded another long before the first one was out of earshot, closely followed by yet more, and all playing different music, the total effect was overwhelming.

Unsurpassable day! In the pomp's midst, we tried to see friends from our neighbourhood's Lodges, and waited especially for Nodding Will to come. He lived two doors away from us, was old and had a twitching, shell-shocked head. But he was also a Black man and because of this rode in state in an open landau, clad in his best dickie and Sunday bowler.

The very first time my mother allowed me to follow the Orange procession to Finaghy Field, where the brave followers of King Billy met, I lost myself. Holiday mood had seized everyone, money went like water, and so many lemonades and iced cakes were given to the lost boy that he was ill. But not so ill that he could not hear his name called over the loudspeakers, a thrill with an exquisite edge, the climax of climaxes, the gilding indeed of the orange-lily. The Field was Elysian for me on that first day, for I went round collecting hundreds of coloured bottle-tops, which I fastened to my jersey, so that by the time I arrived home, exhausted with excitement, I was as scaly as a crocodile.

But Orange celebrations did not occur only on the Twelfth, for later in the year children sat out on the back-yard walls, singing Orange ballads as the trains went by crammed with Black men going to the traditional closing of the gates of Derry. Although we enjoyed these celebrations as much as the grown-ups, we knew that serious feelings underlay the festivities. We had odd ideas on many things, but not about the reasons for these demonstrations.

In school nobody ever told us about Marie Antoinette or Marshal Foch, but we knew Louis XIV and Robert Lundy, the treacherous governor of Derry. We might not know the date of the French Revolution but we did know that in 1688, thirteen young men, apprentices in the city, closed the gates of Derry in the face of the Catholic soldiers. We would forget our avoirdupois tables, but we remembered well enough that during the famous siege a dog's head cost two-and-sixpence, a rat or a quart of horse blood one shilling, and a handful of chickweed one penny. Dogs were fattened on the dead, and sold for five-and-sixpence per quarter carcass. Our greatest bed-time story was of the fat gentleman who hid himself for three days because several of the garrison troops had looked on him with greedy eyes. It was our heritage, and we were proud of it.

Confident of the city's surrender, James II himself went outside the walls of Derry to receive it. Instead, the beleaguered Protestants lined the walls and shouted 'No Surrender', which we fancied still resounded in our own breast as we watched the Black men go off to the famous scene. On the gable walls, along with the murals of coronations and anti-papal slogans, 'No Surrender' was also painted. When we drank our lemonade we toasted,

> To the goose that grew the feather,
> To the hand that wrote No Surrender.

The passing of the years, which swept the heroic seventeenth century further and further away, also brought nearer the time when I could graduate from being a thrilled bystander to an actual member of the Orange Order. I joined a junior Lodge, a proud day indeed for it was the 'Loyal Sons of William', whose headquarters were in Sandy Row itself. To be reckoned amongst the Boys of Sandy Row who had made the Mickeys go 'like chaff before the wind', was high honour and laid grave claims on my own courage. And now I would most certainly get a good place in heaven and be able to see King Billy and the Protestant martyrs. Our Bible spoke of four-and-twenty elders before the great white throne, and we deduced that this meant King Billy and company, to whom also were given the key to the bottomless pit where the Mickeys would go.

At my Lodge enrolment ceremony I had to stand outside the sacred locked doors of the inner chamber, trembling and waiting in a gloomy passage. Then before the whole assembly wearing its glittering regalia my name was put forward and approved. The doors opened and my sponsors emerged to lead me in, keeping positions on both sides of me. I was marched through the columns of Loyal Sons. I was now shaking physically and almost incoherent as I swore to keep the Lodge password.

A concert took place afterwards, and I won first prize for declaiming the tale of the boy who stood on the burning deck. The Lodge wanted threepence for enlisting me, and I had only a penny. A bad beginning, to fall into arrears, but nevertheless I left the hall with an impressive penknife loaded with unusual blades and gadgets which must have cost at least two-and-sixpence. Such a possession had no appeal for me, and I gave it to Gandhi [another boy] in exchange for a tin of condensed milk.

Such a careless attitude could not be adopted towards the secret password. This frightened me very much, for I reputedly talked in my sleep. And my fear of divulging the special word was not because of loyalty to the Lodge, but rather fear that my sisters, or people in the hospital when I went in, would hear it, and tell it to their friends. And eventually Catholic ears would hear it and this would bring catastrophe on us, and we would be hounded from Belfast for breaking so solemn a vow. The Order's shadow fell everywhere in the city, and I kept the wretched word and felt separated from my family by the Lodge.

When I got home from my enrolment, little Helen wanted to know everything that happened, especially if I had had to ride the goat. Until then we had been as thick as inkle-weavers. But now the hocus-pocus of secret societies inserted a wedge between us. Big 'Ina overheard us and gave me a meaning look to keep silence, and I knew the Lodge doings must burn unrelieved in my breast, and Helen be content with a slap for presuming to inquire into such things.

Junior Lodges had their big parade on a different day from the elders, normally on Easter Tuesday; and we made an excursion by train, assembling again at the other end. Nothing could quieten us as we waited at the station, milling chaotically in orange sashes, dashing madly all over the place, mixing ourselves up with banner-bearers and bandsmen, and finally falling into the train as the whistle blew. There were always saucy girls on the train encouraging us to go with them to the carriages where the 'big kilties' from the pipe-bands sat, to find out how many of them were wearing trews under their kilts.

Over the years, the riotous outings merged into a general blur without detail except for a few occasions, such as when I could hardly walk in the procession. On the previous day I had been surprised taking flowers from a preparatory school garden, and a master had chased me for the best part of a mile. He never caught up, but the flowers cost me dear in the form of terrible blisters on my feet. For the outing I could not wear shoes, and set out in white plimsolls. In the train, someone took my overcoat by mistake and left me theirs which was too big for me. When we reached our destination I joined the march in a garment that came down to meet my plimsolls. The onlookers laughed as I trudged along in the pelting rain, holding on to a thick orange rope to steady our banner of King Billy on his white charger.

A sneaking feeling began inside, that perhaps the crowd's derision was well-deserved, for my odd appearance could hardly do credit to our cause. I tried to take my mind off it by concentrating on holding the banner steady, and listening to the band in front as it changed from 'The Sash my Father wore' to 'Dolly's Brae', while the band behind bombarded us with:

> On the green grassy slopes of the Boyne,
> Where King Billy and his men they did join,
> And they fought for our glorious deliverance
> On the green grassy slopes of the Boyne.

The parade always included some Orange champion dressed in seventeenth-century clothes and riding on a white horse to conjure before our very eyes a vision of King Billy himself. But on the

Easter Tuesday when I limped along in plimsolls the day's re-warding feature was to see the white horse rear up on his hind legs and throw the rider. He was a little, wide-moustached man, rather like the one in the famous nineteenth-century cartoon of Lord Randolph Churchill as 'King Randolph crossing the Boyne'. Off he went tumbling to the ground, his elaborate peruke flying. While two St John's Ambulance nurses rushed to gather him up, we speculated on the certainty that the Mickeys had attempted an assassination.

Only one real assassination took place before my eyes on an Orange Easter outing. Some of my fellow Lodgemen from Sandy Row set fire to a hayrick and out of the holocaust dashed a rabbit. Better sport than hay-burning ensued, and in a few minutes the poor creature was dead, wounded from the things thrown at it and from the pursuers' boots. When the warm, furry football was left to go cold, and the louts went off in search of other fun, I gathered the rabbit up, happy to be alone so that I could bury it in a wood. I took the red-white-and-blue rosette from my lapel and gave the rabbit a good Protestant funeral. And in my heart I could not forgive the Boys of Sandy Row for killing it.

Part of the day's thrill included leaning out of the train window to pick out which of the houses speeding by belonged to the Catholics. We could spot them easily enough for their gables, like ours, were painted. But the Mickeys' walls bore different signs – 'Up the IRA', 'Remember 1916', 'Silence is Golden'. The sign of the cross would appear on any blank space, and worse than any of them, 'God bless the Pope'.

The Pope! How we feared and hated him, we thought the Pope more terrible than Hitler when that German came to our notice, and certainly a greater evil than his disciple, Mr de Valéra. From the safety of the passing train we could boldly hurl abuse at the Mickeys' houses and their papish murals. Pushing to get a space at the compartment window we shouted 'To Hell with the Pope', a devout prayer on Ulster lips and a favourite one. As late as 1951 a member of parliament built a climax into an election speech with 'God save the King, and to Hell with the Pope.'

But God had not left us defenceless against the dreaded Roman

Pontiff. He had sent us Lord Carson to secure our Ulster freedom. Lord Carson was dead, and when the CLB parade brought me to St Anne's Cathedral, I sat with great awe near the new tomb. He was another of the four-and-twenty elders mentioned in the 'Book of Revelation', and would be found sitting on God's right hand at the Judgement Day. The least religiously or politically minded knew about Lord Carson as did the fervent, and all knew the song,

> Sir Edward Carson had a cat,
> He sat it by the fender,
> And every time it caught a mouse,
> It shouted, 'No Surrender'.

Our rhymes were like calypsos, endless, ingenious if monotonous, and dealing with everyday events whether political or not. Whenever anything new happened, then we found doggerel for the occasion. Mr Baldwin and an urging on to fight in Abyssinia appeared at one time. Mrs Simpson became the theme of endless variations. How our mothers had idolised the Prince of Wales! And although pictures of the Princesses, Elizabeth and Margaret Rose, with their corgies in Y Bwthyn Bach, the Welsh cottage, now filled the photograph frames in the parlour, we could sense the survival of the liking for Prince Eddie. Often the only contact maintained with the exile was through the medium of the Sunday papers. We scanned the pages for scandal or pictures.

Reaction to any incident concerning Protestant or Roman Catholic was always violent, nothing escaped notice and comment. When the new king ascended the throne his was our forsworn loyalty. And yet, in spite of such entrenched opinion, our ignorance of the Catholic world was profound. I, for instance, believed that Mickeys existed only in parts of Belfast and nowhere else except the Free State and Rome itself.

That many Catholics were living in London, or were allowed to live in London with our Protestant king, seemed impossible. The idea of a papist cathedral near the gates of Buckingham Palace would have been laughed at with scorn. So thought I, until coronation year. The celebrations burst over the city like a great coloured rocket, exploding in the drabness of our lives with a million sparks, a spectrum of excitement. Belfast went mad with patriotism. Even the Plymouth Brethren, so immured to anything but 'the word', published a coronation photograph on their Sunday tract.

Then we were presented with a magnificent coronation book, with close details of the ceremony, as well as pictures and diagrams of the important personages and Westminster Abbey, where it had all taken place. We prized the rare possession, and why not – for apart from religious storybooks won as Sunday school prizes, hymn-books, and a vast collection of Bibles, New Testaments and Books of Common Prayer, it was the only real book in the house.

But through the coronation book I learned of what seemed a terrible betrayal. Included in the pictures of the royalty involved was one of the Duke of Norfolk greeting the two princesses. In a blood-curdling Orange sermon we heard about the subtleties of Catholic scheming, and the preacher had included Norfolk by implication. And there he was, a Mickey, shaking the hand of the heir to the Protestant throne, King Billy's successor!

But there were other, worse things of sinister import. Not only did he hold the office of Earl Marshal (we did not know what this was, but no matter) but he was head of the nobility. If all the House of Windsor died, or were deliberately got out of the way, the Duke would be king, and the glorious freedom of Boyne water would indeed be lost!

How I imagined Norfolk to be scheming and counterscheming to win the crown, and send the country back to the days of Bloody Mary, whose history, besides that of Protestant martyrs, we had heard in school. Perhaps Norfolk would one day buy the confidence of a Buckingham Palace servant, who guarded the King night and day, and persuade him to steal the crown. I could see the vast, richly draped bedchamber, the Yeomen of the Guard, and tall plumed soldiers standing round the sleeping monarch, and his crown hanging on the end of his bed, next to his long underpants. The crown gone, life for us would be over. Was not that the reason why my mother, every year when the back yard was whitewashed, got a neighbour to freshen up the painted crown on the wall?

Such a pity for the lovely book to be spoilt like this. We would have liked to rip out Norfolk's picture and burn it, but this could not be done for the Princesses were on the same page and the King on the other side, and to remove them would be disrespectful. In fact, reflection showed it would have been disloyal, just as disloyal as the Mickeys putting their postage stamps on letters upside down as an insult to the Protestant throne. Instead, we gave the Duke a pair of horns and a nice tail with an arrow point sticking outside his rich coronation robes.

No Surrender, 1966

TOMÁS Ó CANAINN
b.1930

DERRY, 1940s

The other altar-boys were having a slipper fight in their long
narrow changing room before last Mass. Sean could hear them as
soon as he mounted the steps to the sacristy. He had his own
slippers rolled inside his white surplice under his arm. The noise
subsided as he opened the door quickly. He knew they'd think it
was Father Chapman, who was a deeply religious man. He liked
to compose himself in prayer before Mass, but the noise of flying
slippers hitting the walls next door would often bring him running
in angrily.

Barney Mackin, the chief altar-boy, came hurrying in from the
altar, where he had just left the wine and water cruets.

'Who's on candles today?'

Danny put his hand up to his mouth: 'God, I forgot it was me.'

'Well, get a taper and be out there quick: we're goin' on the
altar in a minute.'

Lighting candles for a weekday Mass was no trouble at all,
since they only lit two small ones down at altar level, but late Mass
on a Sunday was different: all six big candles in the brass holders
high up at the back had to be done.

'Give us a hand wi' the candles, Sean,' Danny asked.

They found two taper stumps on the window sill and stuck
them into the end of the long lighters, just behind the brass
snuffers. They knocked on Father Chapman's door and entered.
He had on the white robe, pulled tightly in at the waist with a
cord, and was reaching for the green vestments which had been
left ready on top of the pinewood cabinet.

'Well?' he said, not liking the disturbance.

'Could we have a light, Father?' Danny had on his 'innocent'

184

face as he spoke.

'The matches are on that shelf. I thought I said last week that candles were to be lit early on a Sunday.'

The match broke on the box as Sean tried to light it, and fell to the ground, still flaming. Father Chapman rushed across and stamped furiously on it.

'Give us those,' he said impatiently, snapping the box from Sean's hand. 'Bend the tapers away from the snuffer or there'll be no candles lit today.'

Barney Mackin opened the door for them and out they strode, side by side, carrying the lighters like rifles, but walking slowly, lest the draught extinguish them.

Sean hadn't expected the church to be so full, and they all seemed to be staring at him. His legs began to feel funny and he didn't know whether he should swing his free arm or not. He could see Danny's arm swinging, but couldn't get into time with it. It was ages before they reached the altar and genuflected together. He felt that one shoulder was higher than the other as he walked up the marble steps and round the back of the altar. This was his first time on Sunday candles and they seemed very high, even when he had mounted the back steps.

They had five candles lit at last, but Sean had failed with the sixth. He stretched as high as he could and rubbed the lighted taper back and forth on the distant top of the candle. He had no view of it himself, but Danny was standing back, watching closely for the first little glimmer of light. 'No good,' he whispered, shaking his head.

Sean saw his aunt down there, looking up at him, and Mrs Friel. Jim Meenan from Messines Park was pointing him out to his father. He had never liked that young fellow. Was nobody praying down there, he wondered, as he kept moving the light across the top of the candle. 'Please light. . . please,' he muttered, but the candle did not respond.

Barney Mackin came bustling out to the altar.

'Come down outa that,' he said in a whisper that could be heard half-way down the church.

Barney's height gave him an advantage with the big candles and this one lit up as soon as he touched it. Sean felt stupid.

'Father Chapman's leppin' in there,' Barney said, as he pushed Sean in front of him towards the sacristy door.

When he opened it he saw the altar-boys in pairs, facing him and ready to go out for Mass.

'You be on the door,' Barney Mackin said to him. He liked giving orders.

Sean stood there facing them all, his hand on the door-handle, ready to swing it wide open at a signal from the priest. Father Chapman was behind Barney Mackin, adjusting his biretta on his head. He didn't look happy.

But nobody could say the same about Danny. He had squeezed into the front row of altar-boys and was making funny faces at Sean. He knew that Father Chapman couldn't see him, so he got bolder and bolder.

Father Chapman was issuing his final instructions.

'Walk out slowly now and keep together: wait until I turn back to face the altar at the 'Orate Fratres' before you answer and. . .'

Danny had both hands up to his face, but with elbows pushed into his stomach so that Father Chapman wouldn't notice anything from behind. His fingers pulled the skin down from his eyes until the inner redness appeared beneath the big eyeballs and his thumbs pushed down his lower lip and the sides of his mouth. He stuck out his tongue and Sean's laugh exploded into Father Chapman's instructions.

The priest was on to him like a dog to a rabbit. His big hands came down on the curly hair and clenched firmly. He shook Sean backwards and forwards in fury until the biretta fell to the ground. Danny picked it up and almost pushed it into the priest's hands. Sean's spinning head was glad of the relief. Father Chapman replaced the shaking biretta on his head and gave the signal with a curt nod. He swung the door open and they all filed out. Sean followed them and shut the door. Why had he laughed in there?

The long prayers before Mass were over at last and the Latin had begun. '*Introibo ad altare Dei*,' intoned the priest and six young voices raced through the garbled reply: 'Damn quell toffee cat; you've a tutta may.'

186

He found himself thinking of the day Brother Sheehan heard about himself and Danny having started to serve Mass in Pennyburn. He brought them out in front of the class so that everybody could enjoy the Latin, close up, as it were. He himself would be the priest and Sean and Danny were to answer him.

They heard the familiar 'in tree bill tarry day' and they responded at speed with 'damn quell toffee cat: you've a tutta may'. This was well-trodden ground.

Brother Sheehan looked at them in surprise before he gave out the next priest's piece, beginning 'you'd a calmy days. . .' They both relaxed and waited for their next cue at the end of it: 'ate a low so, hairy may'.

Sean always liked the nice long response to that one as it gave the altar-boys time to get together and speed out the Latin. Danny and himself were beginning to enjoy the limelight as they answered.

'Queer two's days. Forty chewed a may. Quarry may plisty ate quarry: this is a shay dough. Dumb fidget main meek us.'

'That's enough,' Brother Sheehan said, closing his missal with a snap. 'Who taught you that gibberish?'

Their Latin teacher was Aidan Barry, who had learned it by rote from an older altar-boy, who in turn had learned it from Sean's cousin when St Patrick's Church, Pennyburn, first opened some ten years previously. His cousin had been an altar-boy in St Eugene's Cathedral before that, so they were all quite proud of their long Latin tradition.

Sean always thought they sounded great at Mass, with up to ten of them spitting it out at speed as a machine-gun might have done.

Father O'Loughlin, a very gentle and understanding person, didn't wait for them and they didn't wait for him – both parties had a job to do and each got on with it, as independently as possible. The priest was responsible for his own pronunciation and they were responsible for theirs. But Brother Sheehan did not share this tolerant approach and started giving them regular lessons in correct Latin.

'We can't say it like that, Sean,' Danny said later, shaking his head. 'They'll say we're stuck-up.'

Sean agreed with him, so they clung to the Pennyburn Latin tradition.

There were various jobs to be done after Mass. He helped Danny to put out the candles, but there was an ulterior motive for that. He had to see if old Mr O'Brien, the solicitor, was in the church.

Snuffing out the big candles was a lot easier than lighting them. As he quenched the last one he allowed himself to look across towards Our Lady's altar, with its rows of burning candles. His mother said that every one of them was a prayer. He could see the white head of Mr O'Brien bent in meditation. He was in his usual seat, about a dozen rows back. He would be praying there for another ten minutes at least. There was no hurry.

When they went into the sacristy Mrs Logan was there, trying to find out who had stuffed her son's immaculate white surplice up the chimney.

The Logans lived in Duncreggan Road and were a cut above average. Hugh had become an altar-boy at the same time as Sean and Danny, but things didn't work out well for him. The altar-boys from Governor Road and Phillip Street didn't like him. Maybe it was his carefully-polished shoes and clean hands. Sean himself could see no good reason for their active dislike of him, but Danny put his finger on it when he said, 'That Logan is a wild Protestant-lookin' fella.'

More than anything else, his shining-white starched surplice seemed to attract their wrath. It was the product of hours of loving care by a devoted mother. Twice it had been down the toilet in the little room beside them and now Mrs Logan had found it covered in black soot in the chimney of the altar-boys' room.

As Sean replaced the candle-lighter in the long cupboard, he was glad to hear Father Chapman telling her to come outside: only altar-boys and himself were allowed into that room. Anyway, she should have known better than to come disturbing a priest, but particularly Father Chapman, after last Mass on a Sunday. Hadn't he been fasting since last night? The priest might even eat the poor woman!

They were all in a hurry to get out now, in case she came back. Danny was pulling off his soutane.

'Are you comin' home, Sean?'

'No,' he said, 'I have to put fresh candles out in the candelabra. You go on yourself.'

'I'll give you a hand and we'll go out the main door afterwards, so that she won't see us.'

That was just what Sean did not want, but Danny already had lifted out a packet of new candles.

'Father Chapman told me not to put them out until he came back.' Sean hoped his black lie sounded convincing. 'You run on Danny and I'll see you this evening at Devotions.'

Danny put the candles down on the window-sill and ran out. As soon as Sean heard the bang of the outside door he peeped into the church, through the narrow slit at the side of the polished wooden door.

Mr O'Brien was still there, but seemed to be gathering up his rosary and prayer-books. Sean let the door shut quietly and went back to get the two packets of candles. He put his knee up against the wall to support the candles as he carefully opened the narrowest slit in the doorway.

Mr O'Brien came slowly out of the seat, genuflected right down, bent his head and carefully blessed himself. For an awful moment Sean thought he was turning to leave the church, instead of moving up the aisle as usual to light a candle to the Blessed Virgin.

He let the door close quietly again, hoisted the two packets securely under his arm, counted up to ten and opened the door, making as much noise as he could with the handle.

Mr O'Brien had reached Our Lady's altar by the time Sean was opening the low brass gates at the altar-rail. He left them open behind him when he saw that his quarry was already looking inside the candelabra for a candle and searching his pocket for the money to pay for it.

Sean recognised the right moment and smiled at Mr O'Brien, while he unwrapped his first packet of candles. He busied himself then, filling up the depleted box with new candles. As he turned for the second packet he heard the money clinking in the candelabra slot. He had the packet opened when Mr O'Brien squeezed a sixpence into his hand and smiled. Sean's heart jumped and he gasped with delight: not, mind you, with surprise, since it was the third time this had happened in three visits to the candelabra. He had not expected it the first time, of course, but he liked to remember what his mother was always saying about God helping those who helped themselves.

He could see Mr O'Brien praying earnestly to God for his intentions. Sean really did hope that the good man would get what he wanted, but maybe not for a while yet. . .

War was bringing prosperity to Derry. Hundreds of British soldiers and sailors had moved into Ebrington barracks, over in the Waterside, and had started to spend their money in the Derry shops: Fred said he'd heard that they were even giving cash to some of the Derry girls but, for some reason, his mother thought that wasn't right.

Sometimes they'd see a sailor and a girl going into the deserted billiard room at the bottom of the lane: they'd often find what looked like old white balloons in there the following morning. Jim Deeney, who was in Sean's class, said he knew what they were for, but when he told them they knew he was only fibbing. Nobody would believe his ridiculous version of what they did with them. Sean thought it all a very funny business.

Derry quay was lined with the Navy's grey-blue ships – destroyers and corvettes, with large painted numbers on their hulls. According to Jim's father they were assembling for a convoy, but it was supposed to be a secret. Everybody in Derry discussed the Navy's business in minute detail, for there was plenty of information available and no-one paid too much attention to the big posters that were going up on the Strand Road billboards with the warning 'Careless Talk Costs Lives'.

Derry was pushing its way out of a prewar obscurity and into the international scene. Sean and his mother listened to Lord Haw-Haw's broadcast one night and heard him telling the British

Navy to come out from behind the Golden Teapot, or Germany would blast them out of it. Sean knew what he meant: the Golden Teapot hung outside McCullough's shop in Waterloo Place and the ships were crowded in the docks behind it. It was exciting to think that Germany seemed to know so much about Derry. He just hoped the anti-aircraft gun on top of Bryce and Weston's factory would frighten away any Germans who succeeded in avoiding the barrage balloons that ringed the Derry sky.

His mother took in a lodger. He was Chief Petty Officer Pearson, a big fat 'regular' sailor who despised all the fresh young officers who had just been recruited into His Majesty's Navy for the war and would run away again as soon as peace came. Pearson had been a navyman all his life. Sean enjoyed listening to his stories of sea-battles and sinkings. He had been shipwrecked once in the Atlantic and spent a full day in the sea before he was picked up. His big laugh filled the kitchen as he told them about the raw young sailors who had started to swim and were never heard of again. He attributed his own survival to the high 'blubber percentage' of his body and to his laziness in not trying to swim the Atlantic to safety. He was quite content to wait for the Royal Navy to find him – which they did eventually. Another enormous laugh shook his whole body, quivering all the layers of fat: tears streamed from eyes that were half-closed by the puffy flesh of his cheeks.

Christmas came and Pearson spent it with them. He brought extra goodies from the ship – things they hadn't seen since the start of rationing. Sean was suffering from a surfeit of chocolate and fruit-cake by the time his mother switched on the BBC to hear the King's speech at three o'clock. She had already warned them all to be quiet and respectful while the King was speaking. Sean found it all a bit boring: the monarch had a bad speech impediment and would keep them waiting for what seemed minutes on end, before completing a single word or phrase. But the family knew better than to say anything about it in the presence of an English naval officer. As the monarch struggled to pass greetings to his loyal subjects around the world, this Chief Petty Officer in the King's Navy turned towards the wireless and addressed his

191

sovereign with an unexpected familiarity: 'Cough it up then, Georgie – cough it up, boy.'

Eamonn and Sean were keen on fishing, but the recent closing of the dry-dock area behind the Swilly station took away one of their best spots. It was in there they had caught two flat-fish once. His mother wouldn't have anything to do with them when she heard they had come from the Foyle, but Sean cleaned them out himself and then fried them in the scullery when she had gone up the town shopping. You'd often get eels in there as well, but they'd leave your hooks and line all tangled up in a slimy mess. It might be ages before you'd realise they were on the line, as they didn't give the quick jerk of a hooked fish but would begin a slow series of twists and turns in their efforts to free themselves. But there was no longer any point in thinking about sitting happily at the end of the dry-dock. Their quiet fishing spot had become a hive of activity and top security, as carpenters, welders and riveters worked night and day to keep the British fleet in command of the North-West Approaches. Sean had often heard them talking about the 'Approaches'. He had no clear idea what they were, but he did know they had put an end to his hopes of more flat-fish.

His mother wanted to know why they wouldn't go fishing in a nice clean country river instead of in the filthy Foyle. That was when they decided to try the river Faughan out at Drumahoe. They were up early on a Saturday morning and digging worms in the far field before nine o'clock. When the cocoa tin was nearly full of good specimens, Sean threw some clay on top of them and grass, 'just to keep them alive'. They made a few holes in the lid with a nail, because they always did that: he wondered how worms managed for air when they were deep in the ground.

They took a bus to the Waterside and that gave them a great start on the journey. It seemed strange to be going beyond the bus terminus and taking the road marked 'Dungiven'. That was the way Mr McAdoo took them in his car last year when they went to Aunt Maggie's place in the country. But Drumahoe was only three miles out the road and the Faughan was supposed to be full of fish.

They fished and fished, but no fish came.

'It's too bright,' Eamonn said.

They moved to a darker spot beneath an overhanging tree.

'This is just right,' Eamonn said, giving the rod a big swing. The hook caught high in the branches and no amount of jerking would shift it. He cut the line and put on new gut and hooks.

'Are you hungry?' said Sean.

'Starvin'. Me belly thinks me throat's cut,' was the reply.

He took out the sandwiches while Eamonn set the lines, putting a big stone on each rod. He was clearly expecting a monster, thought Sean. It was a real pet of a day: they listened to the trout plopping in the river, only yards from the rods.

'Maybe the hooks are too big, Sean.'

'Aye. Maybe.'

The flies were collecting around them as they ate. Sean jumped up and shook himself to avoid them. Flies always gave him the shivers, particularly the big ones you'd find by the river.

'It might be better lower down,' he said.

Eamonn followed him towards the bridge. They could see an odd car passing on the Derry Road. An Army lorry went past and the soldiers waved to them.

'Them's salmon hooks,' said Sean, with an air of finality. 'You'll never catch trout with those big things.'

'Maybe we should get trout hooks and come back some other day,' Eamonn said hopefully.

They tidied up their gear and made their way along the bank until they reached the bridge. The evening rise was on and the fish were jumping furiously as he followed Eamonn over the barbed wire and on to the Derry Road. He heard the enormous splash of a salmon and was sure Eamonn had heard it too, but neither of them mentioned it.

They spent their last pennies on chewing-gum, so they had to walk all the way home. When they reached the Strand Road at last, they turned right to walk down the quay. It was always far more interesting than being on the main road. He'd be able to collect some grain for Gallan's pigeons too.

A dock policeman spoke to them. 'Are you naval officers?' he asked.

'No, we're not,' Sean answered. He couldn't help feeling a

certain elation that a dock 'horney' had mistaken them for officers. It was some compensation for the long walk.

'Don't you know that only naval personnel and authorised people are allowed on the quay now?'

It took some time for them to realise the awfulness of the new situation. As they turned to leave, Sean could feel the utter loneliness of a quay that wouldn't belong to them anymore.

They trudged down a very lonely Strand Road.

'Well, damn Hitler anyway,' Eamonn said.

Home to Derry, 1986

MICHAEL LONGLEY
b.1939

BELFAST, 1930s TO THE PRESENT

I began by loving the wrong woman.

In 1936 when she was seventeen Lena came from County Fermanagh to work for my parents as a maid. At approximately 4 p.m. on 27 July 1939 I was born, followed half an hour later by my twin, Peter. My sister Wendy was nine when we arrived. According to her we were cranky babies, victims of the now discredited Truby King method of feeding by strict regime rather than demand. We did not get enough milk and because we yelled day and night we were kept in separate rooms and prams – one at the back of the house, the other in the porch at the front. My mother concentrated on Peter, the slightly more difficult child. Lena looked after me and turned into my mother. She exchanged the uniform of a maid for that of a nurse, but this was for her much more than a promotion. She was a natural and devoted surrogate mother: the two of us became inseparable.

The Second World War began in September. My father who had survived the trenches enlisted again and was posted to England where he remained for two years. My mother, Lena and a succession of wayward maids looked after Wendy and The Twins (as we were called until puberty, when we changed to The Boys). The crying stopped as soon as we had graduated to solids; and some photographs show us peaceably sharing a large black pram. Because those years are mostly beyond my recall, I have to borrow Wendy's memories of the air-raids on Belfast, the search-lights, the hand-bells and whistles, the gas-masks into which Peter and I were inserted, the perspex visors through which we peered and tried to make sense of the huddle under the stairs. There survive in my mind the rough feel of khaki as I climbed over a soldier's knee,

195

the coolness of brass buttons, the kitchen light reflected in the polished toecap of an army boot. Had the maid been bringing her soldier boyfriend home?

Just down the road from our house the King's Hall, a huge Art Deco concrete and glass barn, was converted into a barracks for the troops. One of them, Bill Hardy, married Lena, and they left Belfast for Nottingham in 1941. I was inconsolable and for weeks afterwards toddled to the front door when the bell rang, expecting Lena to be there. The marriage was not a success. With her daughter Paddy, Lena returned in 1945 to live with us for a few more years. The three of us accepted Paddy as a sister and liked it when she called *our* father Daddy. As my love for Lena deepened, my relationship with my mother grew more tense and complicated.

I last met Lena in 1967 when, on her way to visit relations in Fermanagh, she called briefly to meet my wife and our first child. My arms melted around her in acceptance and surrender. She was (and, so far as I know, still is) working as a priest's housekeeper in New York. A few years ago Paul Muldoon and I gave a reading there in the Public Theatre. I had thought of contacting Lena, but was anxious that no audience would turn up and that she would be upset and embarrassed on our behalf. The evening turned out to be a considerable success. Lena should have been sitting in the middle of the front row.

My parents came from Clapham Common to live in Belfast in 1927. My father was a commercial traveller for an English firm of furniture manufacturers, Harris Lebus. Before the war his territory was the whole of Ireland, and the family album is full of his photographs – Antrim, Donegal, Kerry: he seems quickly to have fallen in love with the island. Business did not resume until well into the fifties; so on leaving the army my father for several years scraped a living as a professional fundraiser – for the Ulster Hospital for Women and Children and, when the introduction of the National Health Scheme rendered him redundant, for the War Memorial Rebuilding Fund. The inventiveness and panache of his schemes were a minor talking-point in the community. Photographs of him receiving cheques and smiling at Ulster's grandees appeared regularly in the local press. He was always referred to as Major R.C. Longley, MC, a billing he disliked. The war was over, he used to insist. But Ulstermen adore military titles and my father's, with its aura of courage as well as authority, endured stubbornly. To this day when certain people hear my surname, which is unusual in Northern Ireland, they ask 'Any relation to the Major?'

As a commercial traveller my father did as little travelling as possible. In no time at all he had sewn up the smaller territory of the Six Counties. Rising late and after a breakfast of tea and Woodbines, he would accumulate the day's orders over the telephone. 'I've got a lovely little number here, Mr Gillespie. Only £200. No, you won't be disappointed.' He was that rare thing, an Englishman accepted and trusted by Ulstermen. Handsome, charming, deft with people, he could have gone far in public life, I believe. He had enjoyed his charismatic fundraising days, but now preferred to stay at home, in retreat. I picture him chainsmoking in his dressing-gown and giving the fire a last poke before strolling to the telephone with his bundle of catalogues.

Having lived through so much by the time he was thirty, perhaps my father deserved his early partial retirement. At the age of seventeen he had enlisted in 1914, one of thousands queuing up outside Buckingham Palace. He joined the London-Scottish by mistake and went into battle wearing an unwarranted kilt. A Lady from Hell. Like so many survivors he seldom talked about his experiences, reluctant to relive the nightmare. But not long before he died, we sat up late one night and he reminisced. He had won the Military Cross for knocking out single-handed a German machine-gun post and, later, the Royal Humane Society's medal for gallantry: he had saved two nurses from drowning. By the time he was twenty he had risen to the rank of Captain, in charge of a company known as Longley's Babies because many of them were not yet regular shavers. He recalled the lice, the rats, the mud, the tedium, the terror. Yes, he had bayoneted men and still dreamed about a tubby little German who 'couldn't run fast enough. He turned around to face me and burst into tears.' My father was

197

nicknamed Squib in the trenches. For the rest of his life no-one ever called him Richard.

After the war he travelled through Europe as part of an anti-German propaganda mission, which he found distasteful. ('Goebbels learnt a lot from us.') He also disliked the snobbery of the officers' mess where he was dismissed as a 'trench officer', his medals failing to outweigh the fact that he had not attended public school or Sandhurst. But for this he might have become a career soldier. Instead he vanished to West Africa and mined tin and gold there until he was thirty. In the photographs from Europe and Africa he is often accompanied by beautiful women. As I grew older, I noticed that he behaved most vitally in women's company, and most peacefully as well. For him a sense of unexpected bonus pervaded all the ordinary aspects of life: he would not take being alive for granted. He once showed me the gas-burns like birth-marks on his shoulder, the scars on his legs. Running away from a successful German offensive, he had been wounded by shrapnel without feeling any pain. Back in his dug-out he discovered that he had been shot through his scrotum, that the top of his penis had been severed. His children owe their existence to skilled medical orderlies. We were three further bonuses whom he enjoyed deeply and with as little fuss as possible.

To use a geological metaphor, my father's personality was sedimentary, my mother's volcanic. She had been born with a congenital hip malformation and walked with a severe limp. My grandmother, a beautiful Jewess called Jessica Brahams, died at the age of twenty when my mother was still a baby. My Grandpa George, a man of limited sensibility, then married his housekeeper Maud who was insanely jealous of her step-child. My mother's childhood was an unrelieved misery: daily humiliations, mental and physical cruelty. My heart goes out to the little girl cowering in a corner, sobbing at the top of the dark stairs. My father told me of the first time he visited his future in-laws. Maud rushed at the young couple sitting nervously on the sofa, scrabbed her nails down my mother's face and then ran out of the room screaming. When my parents had departed on their honeymoon, Maud took

198

the wedding guests up to my mother's bedroom to show them the mess she had left it in (after working overtime the night before at her job in a record shop). My father's mother, by all accounts a saintly woman, said to the embarrassed assembly, 'You know the trouble with Maud? She's jealous!' Every time I remember that story I savour the release of vengeance.

When they married, my mother was not yet twenty and my father thirty. She told me several times of their first meeting. 'He was just back from Nigeria, tanned, a bit overweight but terribly dashing. I stopped to admire his red setter and he invited me to meet him in a tearoom the following week. He was something of a local hero in Clapham. Could have had any girl he wanted. Why did he choose me with my dot-and-carry walk? I still wonder. In the tearoom he said, bold as brass, "We're going to have wall-paper like that when we get married."' Soon they were living in Belfast, and Clapham shrank to a yearly phone-call to Grandpa George on Christmas Day, birthday cards from Auntie Daisy. I visited Daisy and two of my father's brothers, Maurice and Charlie, when I was sixteen and on holiday in London. I never met Uncle Hugh, nor my paternal grandparents (he a journeyman carpenter, she the possessor of second sight). Because my mother's retarded brother had molested her, Grandpa George threw him out of the house. He was last heard of following the stretcher parties across No Man's Land with a sack into which he was putting bits and pieces of soldiers.

So there was no hinterland of aunts, uncles and cousins to which Wendy, Peter and I could escape and still feel at home. Perhaps because of my father's passivity, her children became the main outlet of my mother's emotions. Her moods changed unpredictably. It has taken me a long time to forgive her that atmosphere of uncertainty, its anxieties, even fears. I appreciate now that somewhere inside her intelligent humorous personality crouched the tormented child. Perhaps I was responding to this even as a boy when I would bring her sticky little bags of sweets as peace-offerings. My father sat quietly until the storm clouds passed. If this was taking too long, he would venture, 'A little gin and orange, Connie?' Out of sight in the kitchen he would take a long swig of neat gin before presenting the drinks with ostentatious ceremony. 'There we are, dear.' Occasionally, if he realised Peter and I had been really disturbed by the climactic changes, he would say, 'Your Mum may walk a little bit funny, but she's a marvellous woman all the same.' A well-meant but patronising simplification.

I remember her solving crosswords swiftly in ink. She was a first-class bridge player. My parents did not engage in any regular social intercourse except for bridge parties. Where were their close friends? My mother's good moods could be a firework display of wit and surreal invention. She would laugh for minutes at a time, her eyes watering, so that even when Peter and I were too young to understand the joke, we would join in. Though her bad moods meant perhaps that the child in her was competing with us, her generosities as a mother could be bottomless. During the war she limped down many streets to buy us second-hand tricycles and other toys. Despite rationing, powdered eggs, Oxo cubes, parsnip disguised as banana, we looked forward to her carefully prepared meals. Like my father she was depressive, and the latter part of Peter's and my childhood probably coincided with her menopause. By that time she would have been well into her forties, my father in his mid-fifties. They withdrew into themselves still further, and Wendy, a maturing teenager who at sixteen had already fallen in love with her future husband, Ernie Clegg, started to fill in the emotional gaps. She became my second surrogate mother.

Grandpa George was the only relative who crossed the water to visit us. He took the train to Stranraer, then the boat to Larne – an ordeal for a man in his eighties. On arrival he would claim that his journey had been 'in the lap of the gods', a phrase I pretended to understand. Grandpa had been a teacher of ballroom dancing in Clapham. Top hat and tails, sequins and swirling tulle. He liked to dress up and hold centre stage, a natural master of ceremonies. His chief ambition, to be Mayor of Battersea, was never realised, despite his masonic connections (he had risen as high as Worshipful Master). I realise now that he could be vulgar and pompous, but at the time I found his Cockney accent with its genteel adjustments, his taste for polysyllables and periphrases, really exotic. A good meal was always 'a highly satisfactory repast'. Inclined to choke at the dinner table, he would declare, 'A particle of food would appear to have lodged itself against my uvula.' Every morning he would give us a full account of his 'motions' (I guessed what that word meant). Laxatives, All-Bran, elastic stockings, Vic, Thermogene, long johns: these were among his obsessions. At the seaside he would roll up his trousers and rub seaweed on his white shins. 'Iodine, Michael. Good for the pores.' On a calm day he would lie down at the water's edge and siphon the sea through his long nose. Legs astride, bending over, he would then snort out a stream of snot. 'Salt water, Michael. Very good for the tubes.'

Grandpa taught me cribbage, a card game not much played in Ireland. I was happy to listen to his endless monologues and fantasies as we pegged up and down the board: he needed an audience. Rickets had left him with bow-legs. 'Got those riding horses. The cavalry. Tipperary, 1916.' Sometimes it was the Boer War (he was jealous of my father's military record). He never mentioned his retarded son, and found it impossible to accept that he had fathered a physically imperfect daughter. 'A nurse dropped little Connie on the floor after she was delivered.' He referred once or twice, tearfully, to Jessica Brahams and seemed after all those years to be in love with her still. He also passed on to me an interest in good food and drink about which he knew a great deal. I owe to him my first taste of pheasant, hare, smoked salmon, tripe and onions, lambs' kidneys. He allowed me to sip his Guinness.

Towards the end of his life I visited Grandpa George and Maud in London. They had rented out the rest of their house and were living in the ballroom in a maze of screens and curtains. Grandpa wept then, partly because I could not stay, partly because of the pain a catheter was causing him. 'The waterworks, Michael. The waterworks.' Maud burst out laughing. She may have been embarrassed, but I still hate those giggles. When he died in 1968 I was the only member of our family able to attend the funeral. A few of his old cronies turned up and went to the house afterwards. 'I need a whiskey,' Maud said. 'I've a bottle in the cabinet over there, but I'm not giving any of it to you lot.' This saddened rather than shocked me, because at the crematorium her tears had made on the linoleum circles the size of half-crowns. And she had sighed again and again, 'Poor George. Poor George. Poor George.'

Being a twin meant that until I was sixteen I hardly ever slept alone. My father had painted our names in red on the cream bed-heads and covered one wall with Disney characters. The Boys' Room. We fought a lot, our differences so freely expressed that it is only recently that Peter and I have recognised how much we have in common as personalities. Beneath the tussles, tangles, power struggles an affection developed, natural, quotidian, in-expressible, so deep and lasting that to comprehend it would be a madness. I was a withdrawn watcher, Peter a rebel. If he was chastised, I would shed tears of sympathy. When he was ten Wendy and I visited Peter in hospital where he was recovering from an eye-operation. Bandages covered both his eyes, but I knew he was crying as we prepared to leave. No surge of passion or compassion in later life has quite equalled the wracking of my whole being that I experienced then. His eyes were still in bandages when he returned home. I remember reading to him at night from *The Water Babies* and *The Snow Queen* and feeling completely fulfilled – fraternal, paternal, maternal. Being a lover, a husband, a father has since enabled me to draw parallel lines only.

Because of our reduced circumstances my parents could not afford to send Peter and me to one of the posher preparatory schools. (They were both old-fashioned Tories.) We attended the local Public Elementary School where, out of a large class of nearly forty pupils, we were almost the only middle-class children. Most of the others lived on 'the wrong side' of the Lisburn Road. Their clothes were different from ours – woollen bala-clavas, laced boots with studs in the soles. Alongside them Peter and I must have appeared chubby and well-scrubbed. I noticed at

202

once the skinny knees and snotty noses, but most of all the accent, abrasive and raucous as a football rattle. This I soon acquired in order to make myself less unacceptable. 'Len' us a mey-ek' – 'Lend me a make' (a ha'penny). At home I would try to remember to ask for 'a slice of cake' and not 'a slice a' cey-ek', to refer to the 'door' and the 'floor' rather than 'doo-er' and 'floo-er'. By the age of six or seven I was beginning to lead a double life, learning how to recreate myself twice daily.

I made friends with the other pupils and started to explore the Lisburn Road. Belfast's more prosperous citizens have usually been careful to separate themselves safely from the ghettoes of the bellicose working classes. An odd exception is the Lisburn Road which runs south from the city centre. Intermittently for about three miles workers' tiny two-up-and-two-down houses squint across the road at the drawing-rooms of dentists, doctors, solicitors: on the right, as you drive towards Lisburn gardenless shadowy streets, on the left rhododendrons and rose bushes. Belfast laid bare, an exposed artery.

I spent much of my childhood drifting from one side to the other, visiting the homes of my new friends: the lavatory outside in the yard, stairs ascending steeply as you entered, low ceilings and no elbow-room at all. My first tea at Herbie Smith's was fried bread sprinkled with salt. Herbie came to our house and gasped when he saw the size of our back garden. For the first time I felt ashamed of our relative affluence. Our separate drawing and dining-rooms, the hall with its wooden panelling, the lavatory upstairs were all novelties to Herbie. He seemed curious rather than envious. Every corner of the home I had taken for granted was illuminated by his gaze as by wintry sunlight.

Another pupil John McCluskey was often caned for being late. He delivered papers for Younger the newsagent. If the *Belfast News-Letter* was delayed, John without complaint or explanation would be standing at 9.30 in front of the class, his hand presented to the whistling cane and then hugged under his armpit as he stumbled over schoolbags to his desk. Should I have told the teacher that he delivered papers to *our* house? Sometimes, as though to drown his sorrows, John would swig the blue-grey sludge from one of the small white inkwells. Every December my father gave me a half-crown as a Christmas box for the paper boy, as he called him. I never told my father that the paper boy was in my class. On the doorstep John McCluskey and I behaved like strangers and avoided each other's eyes as the half-crown changed hands. Later in class the transaction would not be mentioned.

John and Herbie shared with me their mythology which was mostly concerned with Roman Catholics. Did I know why Taigs crossed themselves? What dark practices lurked behind confession and Mass? Didn't the nuns kidnap little girls and imprison them behind the suspiciously high walls of the big convent at the top of the Ormeau Road? The Orange Order and the B Specials marched through our conversations. The son of English parents, I was, at nine, less politically aware than my classmates. A photograph at home of Grandpa George lording it in his Mason's apron prompted me once to speak with snooty disparagement of the less dignified Orangemen. I was sent to Coventry until I apologised. To secure the conversion two friends smuggled to me under the desks pamphlets which purported to describe Catholic atrocities from the twenties and thirties. Every page carried blurred photographs of victims who, it was claimed, had been tortured and mutilated, their brains or hearts cut out, their genitals chopped off. Forgeries? Adaptations of photographs of road accidents from forensic files? Or real victims? This vitriolic propaganda burned deep into my mind, and I perused those grim pages with the same obsessiveness that I was later to devote to *The Red Light* and nudist magazines. I craved the bond of shared fears and superstitions.

At primary school (and later at grammar school) there was little on the curriculum to suggest that we were living in Ireland: no Irish history except when it impinged on the grand parade of English monarchs; no Irish literature; no Irish art; no Irish music. When we sang in music classes we mouthed English songs. One inspector criticised our accents and forced us to sing, 'Each with his bonny lawss/a-dawncing on the grawss.' Our teacher in Form Three, an affable man who coaxed us through the Three Rs with care and skill, became tense when for one term we were joined by

204

a boy from Dublin – a Protestant but still a focus for our suspicions. Having flirted for a while with the unfortunate nine-year-old's political ignorance and his own paranoia, the teacher eventually decided to confront this embodiment of menace and treachery. It was a crude question.

'Niall, who owns Belfast?'

'Dublin, sir.'

'Who? Who?' This was much more than he had hoped for. 'To the front of the class, boy.'

'Who owns Belfast?'

'Dublin, sir.' A slap in the face.

'Who told you that?' Another slap. A spittly crescendo of hatred.

'My granny, sir.' More slaps. And Niall in tears.

We were invited to correct the error, to put down the rebellion. We did so and felt frightened and exhilarated.

With its dozens of little shops and the Regal Cinema where entrance to the front stalls cost threepence, the Lisburn Road became my hinterland. The cinema was demolished not so long ago, and many of the shops have now been transformed into Chinese restaurants and fast food take-aways. But the rows of back-to-back houses remain, the homes of Herbie Smith, John McCluskey, Norman Hamilton, Sally Patterson, John Boland, Alan Gray, Helen Ferguson, Norma Gamble.

I went on to specialise in classics at grammar school and university. Peter left home at sixteen to take up an apprenticeship. He is now Chief Engineer on a Shell tanker and lives in Newcastle upon Tyne. Wendy and her family live in Toronto. My father died in 1960 when I was twenty and too young to appreciate his strengths or understand his weaknesses. My mother died in April 1979. For about a year beforehand we both knew that she was going to die. I wanted to feel free to embrace her as I had embraced Lena, and agreed to call with her every day for five minutes or five hours – for as long as both of us could stand it. Over several tumultuous months we lived out her childhood and mine. She gave me X-ray pictures in which the shadowy shapes of Peter and me curl up and tangle about five months after conception. ('Tu'penny stung for a penny bung,' my father had said.) She confessed that in the early days of the pregnancy she had attempted in an amateurish way to abort us – or 'it' as we then were. I registered neither shock nor pain. Somehow this knowledge made it easier for me to hug her dying lopsided body. It was like a courtship, and I accompanied her on my arm to death's door.

Since April 1979 I have been promising myself that some day I shall phone New York and talk across the Atlantic with Lena.

'Tu'penny Stung', *Poetry Review*, vol. 74, no. 4, January 1985

POLLY DEVLIN
b.1944

COUNTY TYRONE, 1940s–1950s

The doctors and researchers who still speculate whether Catholicism is directly connected to the extraordinary prevalence of schizophrenia and mental illness in Ireland have surely not been reared in the ways and practices of Irish Catholicism that obtained until recently, in which everything was coiled in on itself, and religion, history and social conditions were entwined in a mesh that entangled one further the more one struggled to get free. The Catholic faith in Ireland, although it has fanatical adherence to Rome and the Pope as its visible head on earth, is a religion on its own. Its history of social ostracism, the legal persecution that drove it underground where it had to nourish itself on itself, has nurtured it into something more obsessive than the Catholic faiths of other countries that have continued to grow in the light.

Reading Tocqueville's *Letters from Ireland* many years after I had ceased to breathe that old unchronological air I came across a sentence spoken by a priest to Tocqueville in 1832. 'The Protestants hold that we love the dark; they will soon see that we do not fear the light.' But over a hundred years later we still lived in the dark. Geographical isolation, persecution, the extraordinary courage and tenacity of its practitioners, the prevalence of terror, the threat of punishment gave Catholicism a profound sentimental and patriotic appeal. For the decades when the Penal Laws were in force it was, after all, the only thing that Irish Catholics could call their own, although to do so was to risk persecution. And when with the passage of time and the swing of events it became the established religion of Ireland it retained elements of fanaticism as part of its creed – an absolute belief in its own

207

rightness, a refusal to compromise or to see another person's point of view, a belief that anyone outside its tenets was an enemy or a betrayer. It also acquired a woeful capacity for dispensing not grace (although it professed to do that), but guilt.

Jesus, the kingpin of our religion, was fed into our imagination from the earliest age as a victim rather than a teacher. 'But a glorious victim, girls –' Father Lappin is exultant – 'a glorious victim, and it is his triumph that he has been assailed in a most brutal manner.' That bloody assault, his slow death on the Cross, is ceaselessly described with pious and loving relish, its gruesome details lingered over, not that we may appreciate love, but that we may apprehend the full extent of our sins and the enormity of the sacrifice needed to redeem them. Each one of us has inflicted a lash, driven in a thorn, a nail. The words seem to tumble from the priest's throat as he builds up the word-pictures for our delectation and to stir us to remorse.

There is visual evidence in plenty too – at school and in chapel we are surrounded by religious pornography, explicit images, lavish, potent and sexual, showing in sadistic detail the progress of the Passion of Our Lord. Spears enter flesh, thorns pierce the bowed head, muscular soldiers whip the acquiescent red-robed man who forever stumbles under the weight of an enormous cross. Almost all the statues in church depict saints holding open garments to reveal a bleeding heart, benignly clasping the instrument of their torture with peerless resignation. And these images have more power and impact in our lives than they could ever have in other cultures where there is a tradition of visual images and paintings and decoration. There is no such tradition in our part of Ireland: how things look is of little account. The only coloured pictures on most people's walls are a picture of Our Lady of Perpetual Succour, a grisly picture of Jesus as a doe-eyed, long-haired man with his heart exposed and surrounded by flame, and a romantic impression of the men of the 1916 Rising defending the General Post Office in Dublin, which is regarded in much the same religious light as the other two.

Perhaps the most vivid of all our religious icons are the fourteen Stations of the Cross, three-dimensional panels hanging at intervals around the inside walls of the church and depicting the crucial episodes in Christ's journey from Golgotha to Calvary. To 'do the Stations' is to follow the symbolic path of the Passion, and is both a way of gaining indulgences and a vivid and moving aid to contemplation and contrition.

One of the Stations shows Simon of Cyrene helping Jesus to carry the Cross. I once found, in an old magazine at the bottom of a bookcase in our sitting-room, a story about this man – an imaginative human account of a simple man, an onlooker, on his way to market, suddenly caught up in extraordinary events as the soldiers forced him to help Jesus, a convicted criminal staggering under the Cross, lest he die before he reached his destination. The story ended with the moment when Jesus, feeling the weight suddenly lightened, looked back at the ashamed and resentful Simon and smiled in gratitude; and Simon, his life changed by that gratitude, tried to shoulder all the burden.

The story moved me very much; it gave a kind of redemption to the whole bloody scene of the Passion that had been so deeply embedded in our lives, like the coins in the Pin Tree, that we grew around it. We lived with guilt, yet were unable to do much to redeem the guilt, except by not actually doing much. With this Simon one got a chance to feel that humanity was not all wicked, that somewhere there was always one who could help, if only reluctantly, and who might be me or a sister. Until then there had been no leavening in the blackness of humanity. When I had finished reading it, quite laboriously, for I was no more than six or seven, I found that it had been written by my mother.

The Stations of the Cross can be a private devotion, but once a year they constitute a kind of Pilgrim's Progress for the whole district; these services, held each night in October, are attended by great numbers who go as much for the spectacle as for piety, for the Devotions are a theatrical event. The church is lit with candles and a few oil-lamps so that it is full of shadows. The smell and haze of incense floats out from the vestry where one can see the shadowy figures of the priests and altar-boys robing but they are always just out of eyeshot here, as they are at the lough shore cere-mony. The schoolmaster who plays the old harmonium tests it for

209

wheeze, and the men and women push in through the swing doors, still crossing themselves with the holy water from the font in the little outside porch, and still shivering from the night air.

The chapel is strictly divided inside, with all the women to the left of the main aisle and the men on the right and we, the choir, an arbitrary band of children chosen not for voice but availability, upstairs above the women's side. There are no other women in the gallery although the men's gallery opposite is full; it has been known for the priest to stop the service below and bellow up to the younger men and boys to be quiet and 'to quet wrecking' it.

When it is time for the service to begin, the priest and altar-boys come out in a procession from the vestry, genuflect in front of the altar and come through the little carved wooden gate in the railings that separate the aisle from the body of the church. Two boys each carry a candelabrum, another carries a censer from which the incense is already smoking up and out and which he swings with considerable flourish: at each Station he reluctantly yields this trophy to the priest who genuflects and swings it. The priest reads out a description of each scene – 'Veronica wipes the face of Jesus', 'Jesus falls the first time', 'Jesus falls the second time'.

It is a magical and mysterious ritual for us children, but I do not feel it is holy, as I feel Benediction is holy, when the Host is revealed on the altar and I hardly dare look. When I read later about how Incas could not look at the face of their king I knew how easily such thaumatolatry could arise, for I never sidled a glance from behind my clasped hands at that white Host held aloft in its sun-burst monstrance without feeling that I would be blinded. It would have been the sin of presumption made manifest, and presumption was a word much used by our teachers – not about our earthly manner and stances, but about our eternal expectations. Those who were presumptuous, by simply relying on God's good graces to see them right, as it were, would certainly be damned.

Anyone happening on our ceremony of the Stations of the Cross from the outside world might have thought they were in Plato's cave or had stumbled on occult, forbidden ceremonies, calling up the darkness in men's hearts rather than celebrating the good: the long flames of candles flickering their light across the priest's face, and the white lace on his vestments highlighting the gold cope and chasuble; the acolyte's censer gleaming as it swung, with each swing a puff of incense drifting up and out like the flies by the lough shore. As the little group of celebrants intone the prayers and responses they move in a sparkling cluster from Station to Station and the congregation turn their bodies to follow. Above the ceremony we chant the hymns that are more like ballads than sacred music, filled with death-wish, expressed with a melancholy energy:

> Our fathers chained in prison dark,
> Were full of hope and conscience free,
> How sweet would be our children's fate
> If we like them, could die for you.
> Faith of our fathers living still
> We will be true to thee till death.

No-one would have questioned the sentiment. The priests were constantly exhorting us to fight to the death for our faith, and the continuing process of keeping us enclosed in that faith, barricading us into our moral place, was an obsessional job for priests and educators. In every sermon the outside world was presented as a sinister amphitheatre of evil, of lewd dances and films that were occasions of mortal sin, peopled by determined proselytisers stealthily, inexorably advancing to try to separate us from our faith.

'Ah, children,' Father Lappin says, raking us with his wild pale eyes, 'if any one of you would fight Communism with even only half the energy and dedication that each and every Communist brings to his evil desire to lead you to Lucifer, we would defeat it. But we do not, my children, we do not.'

I resolved to fight Communism with my bare hands if necessary, or die nobly like the new young saint Maria Goretti who had resisted to death the clumsy attempts of a young man to seduce her. Not that we knew why he had killed her. There was no dissembling, no holding back on the number of blows she had

211

been struck or on the details of her death agony, but as to why the young man had battered her to death in a frenzy was a dark mystery only hinted at. 'She would not do what he wished, the vile thing that he wished. She remained pure, pure in the midst of filth and evil, she resisted all attempts on her purity even when struck and struck again.' There were tears in Miss Rogers's eyes as she read out the account from the book on modern martyrs. There were tears in ours; but there were no Communists around waiting to vent their ideological lust and batter us in their frenzy.

Communists had no corporeal shape; they just existed, elementary and awful, and when I tried to visualise them I saw them as not unlike the massed hierarchies of Heaven, waiting and watchful behind the sky. Communists waited, watchful, from behind the Iron Curtain, that heavy barrier suspended God knows how across the map of Europe; one day at some cosmic cue that curtain would rise and then it would be a wailing and gnashing of teeth, especially for us, their truest enemies, whom they would know instinctively at any distance. None of that seemed unreasonable: after all, any one of us knew instinctively when we went outside our territory to Cookstown who was a Protestant and who was a Catholic. And we knew that it worked the other way round. There was nothing magical about it; we operated on tribal signals. But for the moment it was the devil we knew whom we had to fight, and we must never rest in the twenty-four-hour battle that the creatures of darkness waged for our souls.

Lucifer, as we all knew too well, had been God's favourite acolyte and most powerful angel, and there had been an infinitesimal moment when he and God had teetered for ascendancy in the battle of the Firmaments that had ended in the creation of Heaven and Chaos, and the establishment of Pandemonium, the high capital of Satan and his peers; but the battle was continuous, Good and Bad were for ever warring, and there remained always that teetering moment when Bad might win. Each one of us could tip its balance and I still believe it.

There was nothing general and distant about this battle between Lucifer and God, or the Holy Trinity, as God was always spoken of in our theology. It was a most particular struggle waged for each of us, for since Lucifer was perpetually consumed by the twin searing pains of the perpetual loss of love and jealousy of those who still had love, or could have it, we knew that if we tried especially hard to draw near to that good source Lucifer's appetite to have us would be vastly whetted. Lucifer desired us, Miss Rogers explained, to add to his legions so that the battle could always continue; but more, because our loss would cause such anguish to God. I felt that if I could tread the thin line between being moderately good, so that I wasn't a favourite, and moderately bad, so that Lucifer couldn't quite claim me, I would be safer; but I inclined towards being a saint, and moderation, I knew, was lukewarm and I would be vomited out of his mouth. I felt considerable panic at the idea of my cosmic importance in the heavenly scheme, especially as it was so out of kilter with my earthly perceptions of our place and importance.

The sin that most exercised our consciences and imaginations was the sin against the sixth commandment, which was the greatest sin except for the one against the Holy Ghost which we didn't know how to commit either. Not that we wanted to, but you could never be quite sure over which brink of mortal sin you might be teetering, and although we were supposed to be comforted by the knowledge that you had knowingly to commit sin in order for it to gain the status of sin, again, like Bad Thoughts, one never knew where culpability began.

The sixth commandment – 'Thou shalt not covet thy neighbour's wife' – was so astonishingly irrelevant that at first I could not believe it was such a dreadful sin; it seemed to exclude the possibility that any of us, or our mothers or aunts – or indeed any woman – could commit it. Miss Rogers never expounded on it; then Father Lappin explained it as Bad Thoughts, Immodest Touching, Indecent Behaviour and Sins against Chastity. Bad Thoughts was the thing we had most to guard against. The phrase was run together as one word with a special narrow definition, meaning speculations and fantasies and curiosity about sex. What such injunctions, interdicts and strictures did was to make divisions within the confines of our heads, to teach us that there were forbidden territories in our minds, places to be kept at bay.

And although thoughts that were labelled 'bad' were supposed to be vanquished or banished by prayer or by the rite of confession, they skulked in a depth of the mind, under a trapdoor, hunkered and hideously shapely, waiting for any weak moment to come pushing up to the surface. Those famous Bad Thoughts which we were so ceaselessly exhorted to resist tumescently haunt many an Irish life.

The Holy Family was our shining example of what the perfect life should be: the ideal woman was the Virgin Mary; the ideal form of fertilisation, the Immaculate Conception; the ideal husband, Joseph – a shadowy figure in the interior of his carpenter's shop dressed in flowing garments and looking, in my imagination and indeed in pictorial representations, not unlike the priests as they robed for Mass in the vestry. We girls were representatives of the Blessed Virgin and should at all times try to emulate her behaviour. But there was a built-in failure factor – if we became mothers, we would have to leave her behind as an ideal since we could never achieve a Virgin Birth. Our fairy-stories were of Lazarus dragging his decomposing body from the tomb; the ungrateful lepers, who never returned to say thank you for their deliverance; the woman who had haemorrhaged for twelve years, and Mary and Martha, especially Mary, who by letting her sister do all the work chose the better part and won all the praise, which seemed manifestly unfair.

Mary, the Holy Mother and Blessed Virgin, standing in utter resignation at the foot of the Cross waiting to receive the battered body of her son, was presented as the perfect role-model; her passivity, her lack of protest, was the only way to greet adversity and evil. Perhaps such absolutes did help women to accept with resignation and humility the many crosses that religion and life laid on them, and certainly there were many truly devout people in the parish who gained comfort from religion, and not just disturbance of their spirit and terrorism and fear. But those two last stalked our childhood in a horrid linkage with righteousness and Christ, and they stalk Northern Ireland still.

And yet many Irish women, for all that they have laboured under such burdens, or perhaps because they have, often possess a goodness and a kind of purity that is rare. In the novel *Langrishe Go Down* by Aidan Higgins, which I believe bears all the hallmarks of truth, the German hero Otto, who has come to live in Ireland, says with fervour: 'Irish women. . . they are so pure and clean. So pure, and that's not to be found any more in Germany, that great purity. But here you have it. And also that look in the face, the eyes, and one knows that such women are not corrupted. . . a man might sometimes have filthy thoughts about girls. That's natural enough. But when I meet Irish girls and can recognise at once their essential purity then I am touched, incapable of a base thought.'

The reverse of this has been that when Irish girls leave Ireland their purity is given another interpretation; it is seen as a pathological condition and becomes merely the expression of a repressed sexuality; just as innocence, viewed in the same light, becomes ignorance. There was for years a tradition and belief, doubtless with a certain foundation, that convent-bred Irish girls were sexually voracious once they were liberated from the restraints of their society.

We were from the earliest age so steeped in the idea that chastity was the highest virtue and that being in a nunnery was a greater vocation than a worldly or sensual life that it was hard to resolve the ambivalences, or to perceive the denial of our selves that this *modus vivendi* entailed. It was a way of life based on a dark and frightful ambiguity; women were viewed both as powerful creatures, stained with Pauline and liturgical descriptions of them as darkling female stews, potent potential occasions of sin, and as inferior beings, domestic creatures, with no effective life apart from motherhood and wifehood. The fear of sex, the forbiddenness of any pleasure in sex, was deeply interwoven with our teachings. The same priests and nuns who read out, 'There is no fear in love: but perfect love casteth out fear because fear hath torment. He that feareth is not made perfect in love,' presented the whole issue of human love to us as something darkly morbid, so covered in moral pitch that even to think of it was to risk being besmirched.

We were taught that we were fashioned in the image of God and thus were fit vessels to receive Him, alive and well in the form of the sanctified Host at Communion; yet in the same lesson we were taught that these same bodies were tabernacles of sin, the source of unspeakable passions and uncleanliness. We never openly questioned such discrepancies or mysteries since we were also taught that by doing so we were questioning the very edifice of our faith. Mysteries are an absolute part of our faith, inexplicable and irrational and lying heavy and morose at the heart of our religion.

'What do you mean by a mystery?' Father O'Hare, the curate who has come into our classroom to examine us, to see if we are fit to receive our First Communion, flings the question from the front of the class to the back. Miss Rogers tries to divert it by sheer force of will towards those she thinks may be able to answer him. Those of us who know the answer (although we have no idea of its meaning) chant it in confident unison: 'Please Father, by a mystery I mean a truth which is above reason but revealed by God.'

'Is the Holy Mass one and the same sacrifice?' We knew about sacrifice and its meaning and its reality. From earliest childhood we had been taught to offer up our sufferings as sacrifices. Any thwarting of desire, any frustrations, any unfairnesses, any hardships or disappointments could be made all to the good, if we would but offer them silently to God. And we contrived sacrifices too, giving up sweets in Lent, walking when we wanted to run and remembering St Brendan who, it was reputed, abandoned the letter 'O' in mid-stroke when he heard his superior calling him, so perfect was his obedience. We rather thought that if any of us laid down our pens with such a nice obedience we might be accused of clock-watching or lack of enthusiasm for the job in hand. And with every sacrifice we remembered the ultimate one, held up before us night and day – the lacerated, tortured, naked Jesus on the Cross.

'Yes, the Holy Mass is one and the same sacrifice with that of the Cross, inasmuch as Christ, who offered himself a bleeding victim on the Cross, continues to offer himself in an unbloody manner on the altar through the ministry of his priests.'

'What is the Holy Eucharist?' Father O'Hare moves nearer to the front row of desks.

'The sacrament of the Holy Eucharist is the true Body and Blood

216

of Jesus Christ together with his Soul and Divinity under the appearance of bread and wine.'

Priest and teacher beam. We have passed the test and can certainly receive First Communion. Thirty years later I looked up the meaning of that word 'Eucharist', embedded so deeply in my word-store that I had never thought of it as having a meaning at all. It means the giving of thanks, gratitude.

Eiram, Morgan and I made our First Communion, or we 'received the Sacrament', as it is called, on the same day. In the commemorative photograph we are all three wearing short white net veils attached under our chins by elastic, and look like fairly unwilling participants in a parody of bridal ritual. The Catholic church knows all there is to know about ceremony and magic initiation rites, and their central function in our human lives.

Eiram's knuckles are clenched. Morgan's hands are clasped across her silk sash. Our dresses are white, with long sleeves, and all three of us are very conscious of the fact that Jesus has just entered us. Not for nothing are we attired as brides. I feel that an aura of holiness, a bodily halo must surround us; I, who could never look at the Exposition of the Host at Benediction in case something shattered, was very put about to have to receive the same Host on my tongue. I feared that in trying to swallow it, I would choke.

Of all the sisters Morgan seemed the most affected by the ritual and outward forms of religion. Indeed at times she appeared to be afflicted by that psychological ailment that nuns and student priests are heir to and are warned against, an over-scrupulousness of conscience in which the slightest deviation from some pre-scribed course of action appears to be a major breach of the rules. Those who suffer from this encroachment of scruple seem increasingly to need to introduce rules and limits and patterns into their lives, to keep the chaos of life at bay.

Each night she knelt at the side of her bed in the little room behind my parents' room where she and Sinclare and I slept. Sinclare had to go to bed earlier, being younger, and she lay boring a hole through the wall with a finger whose nail was worn down and permanently white-tipped by the small silent scrapings

217

through mortar and plaster. Like a creature in a fairy story or a fable she scratched towards the other side where Ellen lay, and every night the little conical hole got deeper. Sinclare's eyes were so large and round that they reminded people of kittens' eyes; they gave her face a startled look and her voice had the same quality, rising higher as she talked or told a story, so that even common-place things appeared astounding since they invariably ended up on high 'C'.

There was always an oil-lamp on the dressing-table, and on winter nights it was kept lit and turned down low. One night I climbed on to the table, turned the wick up and burned a book by holding each page across the small glass globe. Sinclare watched me, her eyes expanding even more and her voice becoming a squeak that only incited me further. When my mother found the charred pages the next morning she stood very still and it was through this unexpected silence – for she was normally voluble – that I realised what I might have done.

Each night Morgan pressed her hands together – the most beautiful hands in the family, pale and smooth (indeed everything about her is shapely and smooth, her hair, her face, her body and the little white gleaming half-moons at the bottom of her nails) – and anxiously began her prayers. If anyone interrupted her at any point she had to start all over again and, since her prayers seemed endless, and our patience was none too long, we nearly always did interrupt. We were fundamentally sympathetic and understood the talismanic significance of reaching the end of the long inter-cessions with God without interruption. But we each had our own rituals, our own way of conducting life and imposing order on it, and we never expected sisterly co-operation. Indeed most of us anticipated the opposite, and were as rough in our justice towards Morgan.

Every night each one of us prayed silently the prayer that we had been taught in school: the Act of Contrition. 'Oh my God I am heartily sorry for having offended thee and I detest sin above every other evil, because it offends thee my God Who Art worthy of all my love and I firmly resolve by Thy Holy Grace never more to offend thee and to amend my life. Amen.' Then we prayed the prayer that guaranteed we would never die in our sleep, or die unawares, and climbed into bed and crossed our arms over our chest as a surefire way of gaining an indulgence. We did not seek indulgences for ourselves, but for all those who had had the misfortune to be born outside the Catholic fold. We were taught daily to thank God for the inestimable privilege of being born a Catholic, a blessing and privilege that the rest of the world would give its eye-teeth for. 'The luck, the gift, girls, the blessing of being born into the only one true faith,' Miss Rogers marvelled. 'Whatever else happens to you, no matter what you do or don't do, remember that *more* will always be expected of you since you started out with more, and must account for it at the end.' Stones under the saddle, as it were, before the race of life.

It was granted non-Catholics, as they were always termed, might be saved if they had led as good a life as possible in view of their benighted circumstances. We were extremely relieved by this caveat, since it meant our cousin Maurice, who lived in Warrenpoint and whom I loved with a passion that persisted, and whom the fishermen with their predilection for nicknames called 'Whiteskull' as soon as they saw his silver-blond hair, would not be banished to burn in Hell for all eternity, but would only be temporarily incarcerated, although burning, in Purgatory.

'Do you remember,' Morgan asked me once, 'when we were very small, how you found me crying behind the hayshed in the haggart? I told you it was because of my Bad Thoughts and I didn't know what to do?' It was at the end of a long conversation about the coil that sisters are tied in; from her tone I knew that the hour was vivid in her mind, the quality of the day, her despair, my presence. From my shaky vantage-point of a year older, the world seemed always to have been shouting of sin and morality at Morgan and I was fearful for her, but fearful of her too. I minded this more than I let myself know, because of that law in the hierarchy of sisters that the older must always inspire awe or fear – never the other way around.

So although I do not remember that afternoon in the haggart behind the hayshed when stars were shining out of sight and Morgan told me of her fear of her thought-sins, I can too easily relive others when I was crying myself, lying in the silver lichened branches of a fallen tree in a small triangle of land hidden by ditches, which was the secret place, where no-one would find me. The truth was that no-one was looking, and eventually I would rise up from the crook of the tree, and the moss, and the beetles which had begun to roam over me, and resentful of the lack of alarums over my disappearance go back into life, plotting revenge or seeking succour, or both.

It is odd that I do not remember Morgan's attempt to get help with her religious pain, since given our habitual defences it must have been a rare appeal on her part; but she had cause to believe that I could help her as I had tried to turn myself into her guardian. If I had not done so I would have tried to destroy her. One of the salient things about Morgan was the enchanting effulgence of her face, incandescent with goodwill. When she smiled her face switched on. After Barry-Paul was born when she was three her expression changed subtly and a stricken look entered her face. The significance of the arrival of a male had percolated to her; she approached our mother feeding her newborn son and asked, 'Am I still your little girl?' Our mother, perhaps locked into a moment of pain of her own, or simply harassed, answered, 'Oh give my head peace.'

We all choose our moments to ask such questions and we choose our answers, even in heat and tiredness, so that they will reverberate in a certain way: as my mother ruefully recognised. For it is she who tells the story years later and who recognises, dearly enough, what happened that day and who in telling the story hopes perhaps to drain that sump, to draw the poison, to gain redemption for her response.

'A child doesn't ask a question like that twice,' she said wearily to Nell, her youngest daughter, who holds her own daughter the tighter.

All of Us There, 1983

BERNADETTE DEVLIN
b.1947

COOKSTOWN, COUNTY TYRONE, LATE 1940s—EARLY 1960s

If it hadn't been for the fact that I had an essentially Christian background from my mother, poverty would have made me bitter rather than socialist, and what I knew of politics would have made me mad republican. This is the common situation in Northern Ireland: if you don't have basic Christianity, rather than merely religion, all you get out of the experience of living is bitterness. My mother was, from my point of view, despairingly Christian. You could have kicked her fifty times a day and she would still have turned the other cheek – and not just in a passive way: if you had tripped in the action of kicking her she would have lifted you up, knowing that as soon as you got on your own two feet you were going to kick her again. Her life – the conflicts with her family; the loss of my father; the struggle to bring up six children on welfare benefits – gave her two choices: she could either become bitter and reject everything; or she could accept that none of this really mattered because the world, after all, was only a stopping-place. She chose the second. She had a kind of martyr complex which to some extent has rubbed off on me. She had plenty of moral courage. Her attitude all the time was, if in your own conscience you know you are right, it doesn't matter how many people think you are wrong. Just plough on. Nobody will appreciate it, but you're not doing it for anybody's appreciation. You do it because it's right, and if it's right it's worth doing, and if it's worth doing it's worth doing properly.

She was full of these sayings from popular wisdom: a thing worth doing is worth doing well. If you objected, 'But I can't do it', she would say, 'If there's a will, there's a way: the fact that you can't do it and give up means that you don't really want to do it hard enough.' My father's philosophy of life was less reducible to proverbs, but I do remember two sayings he had. One was: 'Your teeth are for keeping your tongue behind', and the other: 'If you put your foot in dirt, it spreads. Just walk round it.' And there was one observation which my parents shared, which was: 'There'll be days when you're dead.' When that phrase was used it meant we were going to do something rash, something we either couldn't afford to do or didn't have the time to do, but which we were going to go ahead and do, anyway.

On the days-when-you're-dead principle we used to spend two weeks at the seaside every summer – at Portrush, scene of my mother's early romance. When my father, being politically suspect, was obliged to work in England we saw him only at Christmas and Easter and occasional weekends in between – he blamed and hated the English for that, and so did we all. But the big reunion of the year was the holiday at Portrush. As soon as Christmas was over and paid for, we started saving up. Tins of food to be taken on the holiday began to fill the top shelf of the larder. My father started cutting down on his weekends at home – these were expensive, not only because of the fares but because to make the journey worth while he had to travel on working days, and so lost money. As well as coming home fewer weekends, he would send home slightly less money, and save it up in England instead. My mother's one failing was that she couldn't save money: if she had some spare cash and someone came to the door collecting for charity, or begging, she would give it away; if we had run up against our relatives and needed a morale-booster she would blow the housekeeping on something like strawberries and ice-cream. And we would be poverty-stricken for a week!

So my father did the saving, and when Portrush-time came round we all set off with enough food to last the family for a fortnight. Hardly any of the money was spent on food. It paid the rent of a house for two weeks, and it paid for extravagances and pleasures. Not that we did anything very exciting. The older half of the family got up at seven o'clock to go to Mass with my mother, and on the way back called at the harbour and bought fish, and at the home bakery for bread; then home to make breakfast. After this, all the swimming costumes and towels and so forth were piled on to the push-chair – there was always a push-chair in use in our family, because there was always one of us of push-chair age – and we all set off together for the day, to spend the family savings on shows and candy-floss.

Because he died when I was young, my memories of my father are idealised. He didn't live long enough for me to start appreciating him critically, and I still have the impression that he knew an awful lot. It seems to me – and evidence from photographs bears me out here – that he was quite a handsome man. He was fairly tall, well-built, athletic: not at all the sort of person you expect to die, as he did, of thrombosis. He had dark hair and a very firm jaw-structure, which would have given him a stern face, but the effect was ruined by a large dimple in his chin – and by his eyes. My parents both had the same sort of eyes, but my father's were more beautiful. They were pale blue, very calm, and honest – the sort of eyes which stopped him telling lies, because they always gave him away. My mother, however, had eyes that made other people tell the truth: they were grey-blue and, like my own, rather round and staring. They were mystic eyes, looking through you rather than at you and dragging the truth out of you.

In her teens and twenties my mother was a slight person. She must have had a large bone structure, but in those days she looked very thin and frail. Probably because she had six children she became in her thirties big and stout, and later she got very fat. She was in the end a great big moving bus of a woman. She was never healthy: her heart was weak and she suffered from angina in her later years, so that she was obliged to walk slowly. But she didn't look as if she was struggling along under the burdens of her weight and a weak heart: she looked as if she was walking serenely because life was much too good to be enjoyed at any quicker pace. When she got to the top of a hill, she would stop – simply because she *had* to stop to get the strength to walk on – but even then she looked as if she was pausing at the top of every urban hill to view the beauty of the surrounding smoke and chimneys.

In spite of working in England, my father played a part in the family which was unusual for an Irish father – or at least wasn't common in the circle we lived in. Other people's fathers' role was, it appeared, to earn the money, punish the children –'You wait till your father comes home!' – and let the wife get on with the housework. My father was a better cook than my mother and, in fact, taught her to cook all the things worth cooking, like fudge and toffee apples and pancakes. She had learned a mundane, square-meal kind of cookery when she lived with my grand-mother, so when it came to Shrove Tuesday, it was my father who made the pancakes; at Hallowe'en, he made the apple tarts and apple fritters and all sorts of sticky, gooey stuff for putting apples in. But he didn't just keep his talents for special occasions. If my mother had been pretty busy during the day he would cook the supper – and we preferred it when he did, for he served us weird things that it was bad to send children to bed on. He thought nothing of doing the housework on a Saturday, if he wasn't working, and was totally unashamed of hanging washing on the line – a thing most men in Cookstown wouldn't be seen dead doing. Cookstown in general thought he was round the bend: he had no masculine self-respect at all, and was quite happy going shopping, or pushing the baby's pram, or buying clothes for his children. Other men waited for their wives outside the shop, looked uncomfortable, and carried the parcels. But Cookstown learned to admire my father because although he was from the bottom he walked with his head up.

My father was essentially a very gentle person. When he was working on the airstrip at Ardboe he noticed that the fellow beside him never brought any lunch, so my father used to bring double rations, share it out, and complain that his wife always gave him more than he wanted. After my father died, I remember this fellow coming to the house and telling us what a gentle person he had been. But along with his gentleness, he had authority. At work he was always the one chosen by the men to talk to the management, and he was much more keen on discipline than my mother. He wasn't hard, but he believed very firmly that right and wrong existed: you should do the right thing for the right reasons, but until such time as you were prepared to accept the right reasons, you would have to do the right thing because you were told. He had a fondness for the civilities of life which was perhaps surprising in a working-class man. Since my mother came from the middle class, she could have been expected to insist on formalities, but instead she reacted against them. She didn't care whether we washed our hands or not before we came to the table, because she had been made to do it as a child. My father cared very much, and he cared about how we treated the food we were given.

Once when I was seven or eight I came in late to tea, to discover that my sisters had eaten up all but one of the square ends of the slices of bread, which I – and they – preferred to the round ends. The one remaining square end was at the bottom of the plate, and I began flicking through the bread like the pages of a book in search of the piece I wanted. Whereupon my father slapped my hand from the table, looked at me, and said, 'What have you done?'

'Nothing,' I said, big tears standing in my eyes.

'Do you expect any other human being to eat the food you have rejected as not fit for your consumption?'

'But, Daddy,' I said, horror dawning, 'I can't eat five slices of bread – not with my tea as well.'

My father removed my meal, set down one empty plate, put the five slices of bread on it, and said, 'You can have butter on them. You can have jam on them. You can have anything you like on them. But nobody is going to eat that bread but you. And if you can't eat it tonight – don't make yourself sick! – it will be there for your breakfast tomorrow.' And I ate every one of those slices of bread. My father didn't put on this performance just to impress on me that one did what one was told: the important point was that I had not shown consideration for others, expecting them to eat what I had cast aside.

He was very strict about basic civil behaviour. He was much stricter than my mother about people who raised their voices. Shouting, kicking, and biting were forms of combat not to be tolerated. We very seldom fought among ourselves, but neither of my parents minded if we did – so long as we fought it out and ended up as friends. But when a fight developed into a kicking and

225

biting match, whoever was involved got the wooden spoon. The wooden spoon – an ordinary kitchen spoon – was my mother's punishment tool and the terror of our lives. It was kept in the knife-drawer, and once you heard the drawer open, you knew you were in danger. I don't ever remember my mother beating any one of us in a temper. She would sit there quite serenely, while things were getting out of hand, and say, 'I'm warning you once – stop it! I'm warning you twice – stop it, or you will get the wooden spoon!' The third time the knife-drawer opened and the wooden spoon actually made its appearance, and my mother stood over the culprit: 'Now, do you actually want me to use this, for this is your last warning?' Usually we were smart enough to stop whatever we were doing at that point. If we were not, she very calmly took us off by the ear and spanked our backsides with the wooden spoon.

When we got slapped it was always on the bottom, except for kicking, which merited a slap on the legs. But once I got a more unusual sort of punishment. In our kitchen we had a long couch, like a bench, which we sat along for meals in order of age: Mary, Marie, Bernadette, Elizabeth, Paddy, John – our place at table matched our place in the family. One day a fight developed on the bench, during which Paddy took a great bite out of Biff (the family's name for Elizabeth), unnoticed by anyone but me. Ever valiant in the cause of justice, I came to Biff's defence and bit Paddy. And I was seen. Calmly my mother called me out from the table and said, 'Roll up your sleeve.' I looked at her, wondering where on earth the wooden spoon was going to fall, but I rolled up my sleeve. Calmly my mother lifted my arm and calmly she bit me as hard as she could – amid screams and roars and 'No, Mummy, that hurts!' 'Now you know what it feels like,' she said, 'you'll not do it again in a hurry, will you?' It was against all the family traditions that I should say, 'But Paddy bit Elizabeth first.' Sneaky tales were forbidden: sisters should stand loyally by each other. If my mother caught someone doing wrong she punished the male-factor, but if one of the others came in whining 'Mummy, do you know what she did. . .?' it was the tale-teller who got the punishment: not only had she failed to prevent her sister from erring, but she had maliciously come telling tales as well. It was this curious discipline that made us all the peculiar characters we are.

Although like me, my mother was careless of her own appearance, she made a point of dressing us well, and she dressed us all alike. Partly this was for economy. She was very handy with the sewing-machine, and she used to buy material in vast quantities and make half a dozen dresses, identical in every respect except that each was a size smaller than the next one. So there we were growing up, and the frocks just moved along the line. But we were dressed alike for another reason as well: my mother had once seen this American Easter Parade photograph of an idiotic-looking family of about a dozen boys and a dozen girls – perhaps that's an exaggeration, but there was a massive row of children, and they were all dressed exactly alike. My mother fell for this photograph. I do believe she cherished at the back of her mind the idea that one day she would have five daughters and five sons, all dressed in uniform. It was an idea to horrify my poor father. 'Just one boy will do me, honestly,' he would say; 'If we had that number of kids, we'd have nothing to put on them, never mind dress them all alike!' Occasionally, my father would bring five frocks from England. The ones I remember best were blue and white with big, detachable, white collars. Because they were prim and proper, they were English, and because of the collars, they were sailor; so we called them our 'English sailor frocks', and we thought they were great. I can't think of another father who would have had the courage to go into a shop and buy five identical dresses, but it never cost my father a thought.

My parents' marriage was, I believe, more or less ideal: no-one was boss; everything they did was worked out between the two of them, though I would say my father's word would have been final. There was a peculiar mental sympathy between them that let each know what the other was doing and thinking and feeling, even when one was in England and one at home. My mother used to ride a bicycle in those days, and she was always falling off it. Once she had a worse fall than usual, and that night when she telephoned my father – she used to ring him up about every other evening, just for three minutes – he said as soon as he lifted the phone, 'I've *told* you to stay off that bicycle!'

Our family was a very democratic assembly: we were not a family in which there was a father who did a job, a mother who did a job, and the kids who did what they were told. As each one of us came to the use of reason, as it were, we were included in the family decisions. Once we knew how to count, we were involved in the family expenditure. We never had regular pocket-money as children, but if we needed money for something, we got it. As long as the money was there, we could have it, even for frivolous and unnecessary purchases. But we were brought up to reflect that since we could get what we asked for, we ought to be pretty responsible about asking. If you wanted something only because someone else had it you were forced to think, 'Well, that's not much of a reason. I don't really need it', and reconcile yourself to doing without it. After my father died, this training paid dividends. We all took sick that winter – this was another thing where family solidarity showed itself: we all fell sick together; once any sort of germ got into the house, we all went down with it at two-weekly intervals – and the only two people left on their feet were Elizabeth and myself. Paddy, fretting for her father, had developed pneumonia; everybody else had the measles; Asian flu was hovering about; and the budgerigar died. And this house of mourning and sickness was run by seven-year-old Elizabeth and myself aged nine. I couldn't cook – still can't – but she could, so I did the shopping, peeled the potatoes, and did the humble unskilled work, and she cooked the dinner. 'Well, she's got a good family,' neighbours said of my mother, but they didn't interfere. We had lived independently of the entire town – not in isolation, exactly, but in a sort of unforthcoming friendliness. Now, instead of staying away from us because they didn't wish to offend the Establishment, people stayed away and hesitated to offer their assistance because they were afraid they might offend us.

We were brought up to ignore Cookstown, on the principle that it didn't care about us and we didn't care about it. Of course there was contact with our relatives. Sunday was walking and visiting day, and after Sunday dinner we used to set off in one direction to visit our wealthy grandmother, Mrs Heaney; then five or six miles in another direction to visit our poor grandmother; then back home for tea. (My father used to turn these walks into educational sessions, teaching us about the rhythm of the farming year and to identify birds and trees. We weren't aware we were learning 'natural history': it was just part of Sunday afternoons.) My rich grandmother helped us financially all our lives, but in a stern moral fashion that made it difficult to be grateful. She would send us a box of groceries, and make sure we knew how much hard-earned money it represented, or she would give my mother money to buy us shoes, with the comment, 'Don't say I didn't warn you!' But the contact with relatives didn't extend to their visiting us. Very few people came to our house, and I particularly remember one fellow who came for the first time after my father's death. He looked round at the books and the piano and the general air of comfort and civilised activity, and said, 'My God, you wouldn't think this was a working man's home!' Remarks like that made me a socialist.

Because we were more or less related to half Cookstown, we had simply dozens of cousins, and they all hated us. It could be pretty nasty in school. When they were feeling particularly spiteful they would roar insults across the street at us, but on the whole we didn't carry our wounded spirits home. For one thing, we weren't really bothered, and for another, we didn't want to upset my mother more than necessary. Mary, my eldest sister, and I – the two most precocious members of the family – would select and edit the version of the day's happenings to be told to my mother. However, if some stupid busybody of an adult had over-heard the exchange of insults and could be expected to pass it on at home, then we had to tell.

There is no doubt that I owe the dawn of political feeling to my father. One way in which he was more involved in family life than most Irish fathers was in telling us bedtime stories. When I was quite little and he was working in Northern Ireland, and later, on his brief visits from England, he would put us to bed while my mother washed up the supper dishes. The stories he told us then were not about fairies and pixies but the whole parade of Irish history from its beginnings with the Firbolgs and the Tuatha de

229

Danain, the supposedly magical people of Irish mythology. He told us bedtime stories from recorded history as well – the battles and invasions, the English oppression and the risings, the English-Irish trade agreement which crippled the country's economy. Naturally, he didn't attempt to be objective about all this: this was Ireland's story, told by an Irishman, with an Irishman's feelings. It wasn't until I went to grammar school that it occurred to me there were people who believed the Act of Union, making Ireland part of England in 1801, had not been brought about by perjury. To me it was accepted fact that Pitt and Castlereagh had conspired together and by every treacherous means under the sun had fooled everybody into signing the Act of Union. For that matter, I was surprised when I went to school that you had to learn about the Battle of Vinegar Hill or the decline of the Irish linen industry in formal history lessons. I hadn't realised this was history: it was something I had always known, from hearing it over and over again as a bedtime story.

Perhaps children do begin to develop a social consciousness from listening to stories about bad children being tortured by bad fairies and good children getting birthday cakes. In our family we developed an unconscious political consciousness from listening to the story of our country. The first nursery rhyme I remember learning was:

> Where is the flag of England?
> Where is she to be found?
> Where there's blood and plunder
> They're under the British ground.

My father taught me that jingle, and I used to say it as another child would say 'Jack and Jill went up the hill', not relating it to England or feeling frustration or bitterness, but all the same acquiring a partisan outlook. 'Don't say things like that,' my mother used to protest, but my father would intervene: 'Ah, it's good for them,' he would say. And it *was* good for us. The songs we practised to sing at children's concerts were never the 'I had a bonnet tied with blue' variety, but 'All around my hat I'll wear the tricoloured ribbon.' When I was about seven I could sing 'The

Croppie Boy' right through, and it has something like fifteen verses, each containing ten lines. At that age I suffered badly from asthma, and it was a battle of willpower and a challenge to my physical failings just to get through fifteen verses, for I had to stop to draw breath half-way through each line. 'The Croppie Boy' is about a young lad who goes to the priest's house for confession, but after he has made his confession the 'priest' jumps up, announces that he is a Yeoman guard in disguise, and that he holds the house for his lord, the king. The priest has been beheaded and is floating down the river. The guard then kills the young boy. I don't remember singing this song with any feeling of bitterness: I was taught it for its beauty, and because it was part of Irish culture, and it came naturally to me.

But such political lessons as I learned as a child came in indirect ways, through poetry and history, until I went at the age of ten to a madly republican grammar school. If my father had any real involvement in politics, I never knew about it, but one circumstance suggests that maybe he had. He died in August 1956, just at the beginning of what the Unionists called 'the IRA terrorist campaign', which lasted five or six years, with sporadic outbursts of violence and attempts at sabotage and so forth. At that time it was quite common to hear the sirens beginning to wail at night, up and down, up and down, as it must have been for air-raid alerts during the war. As soon as the sirens started, doors in our neighbourhood would open and our neighbours would appear, pulling on their heavy coats and shouldering their sten guns. Most of the Protestant men in our district were B men, or Specials – members of the civilian militia in Northern Ireland which was formed to fight the IRA. So while some of my friends' daddies were disappearing into their houses to lie low, other people's daddies were setting out armed after them. At times like those the tragic division in Northern Ireland split even wider to set the Protestant working class against the Catholic working class, while the church and the middle-class nationalists threw up their hands in horror at the freedom fighters, and stood solidly behind the Government. The B men were pretty busy in those days: not in Cookstown itself but beyond it on the way towards south Derry, where the land is poorer and the people, naturally enough, more republican.

Just outside Cookstown, and lying between it and Omagh, there is an expanse of useless bog land known as the Black Bog. Invariably the IRA seemed to head for it, and none of them was ever caught there. Yet there was no cover: the Black Bog is like heath. If a man were to run across it he could easily be seen. Perhaps they had a dug-out in it, or perhaps they lay flat in the bog for a whole day; but for whatever reason, though the authorities put searchlights on it by night and sent helicopters over it by day, the Black Bog never gave up an IRA man. From our front bedroom window you could see, between two houses opposite, the beam of the searchlights travelling over the bog, and my mother used to stand there on alarm nights, looking across at the bog, and she would say, 'At least they'll never get your father now.' And even if we didn't know quite what she meant, we could guess. . .

At the age of twelve I made my first political protest. I decided to enter a talent competition which for some reason or another was being organised in Cookstown. Most of my family are quite talented. My eldest sister, Mary, now a nun, paints a little but her main gift is for making something out of nothing. When she was a child our house was coming down with Japanese gardens: there would be clay all over the place, and bits of twig, and an old biscuit tin, and suddenly there was a Japanese garden. I'm useless at that sort of thing. She used to write what I, as a younger sister, thought was excellent poetry, but unfortunately she took it all off with her to the convent. Marie is talented in an entirely different way: she does the ordinary things that everybody does, like sewing and knitting and embroidery, but in half the time and twice as well as anybody else, and she cooks brilliantly. Elizabeth is musically talented, she's a very good pianist. Elizabeth, Paddy, and myself all sing, and I'm considered the best singer because I've got the loudest voice. As children we often used to perform either for visitors or at children's concerts, but we were not encouraged to consider ourselves talented children: my mother squashed any tendencies to conceit.

232

When I was in my first year at grammar school, I had a long-playing record, 'The Rebel', on which the actor Michael Mac Liammoir recited the works of Padraig Pearse, one of the martyrs of 1916. I thought it was great stuff, and played it over and over again, and the more I listened to it the more convinced I became that although Mac Liammoir had put it over as a work of art, he had failed to convey the true emotion of a patriot saying what he felt. Anyway, I learned three pieces from the record for the three heats of the talent competition, and they were all very militant. 'The Rebel' ends:

> I say to the master of my people, 'Beware the risen people who will take what you would not give!'

Another piece I chose was 'The Fool', which has this passage:

> But the fools, the fools! They have left us our Fenian dead!
> While Ireland holds these graves, Ireland unfree will never be at rest.

And my third and final choice was Robert Emmett's speech from the dock before his execution in 1804.

Well, off I went and recited this fighting stuff at the talent competition, and I recited it well, went through the three heats, and won the first prize. Cookstown was outraged. During the three weeks of the competition, the horror grew. 'Imagine a daughter of Lizzie Devlin having the cheek to go down there and say a thing like that! That comes from her father's side of the family.' I believe I won on merit, but the general townspeople said I had blackmailed the judges, who were local businessmen and so forth, into awarding me first prize because I could have accused them of bigotry if they hadn't. Feeling got very high and on the last day I had to have a police escort home to protect me from the people who would otherwise have given me a cuff on the ear for my impudence. My mother was delighted; she was somewhat embarrassed, but secretly glad and proud that at least I had enough of my father in me to go somewhere I was hated and look people straight in the face. This was a gift both my parents had: they never shied away uncomfortably from company they knew

233

rejected them. As well as showing courage and defiance, I had won £10 and this too was welcome at home. To me it was like £100. I'd got the average weekly wage of a man in Northern Ireland just for standing up and saying a wee bit of prose. A year or two later, from the same feeling of defiance, I wore a tricolour pin in my coat, precisely because the Northern Ireland Flags and Emblems Act forbade it. Only once did a policeman ask me to remove it. 'You remove it,' I said, but as his hand came out to take the badge, I added: 'If you touch me without a warrant, I'll have you in court for assault!' He just laughed and said, 'Go on there, you trouble-maker!' I trotted on, feeling very proud I had won, but once I'd discovered I could get away with it, I lost interest in the badge. . .

St Patrick's Academy, Dungannon. . . was a militantly republican school, and it owed its fiery partisan slant to. . . Mother Benignus, whom we called Reverend Mother, and who is, among the people who have influenced me, one of those I most respect. To Mother Benignus everything English was bad. She *hated* the English – and with good reason: her entire family had suffered at the hands of the British forces. Everything we did in school was Irish-orientated. She was a fanatic about Irish culture, which was all right for people like me who were also fanatical about it, but which did drive lots of people away from it who couldn't take Irish culture for breakfast, dinner and tea. She didn't hate Protestants, but her view was that you couldn't very well put up with them, they weren't Irish, and that clinched the argument. When I was a senior, the school produced a netball team which could have beaten any netball team in the North of Ireland, but Mother Benignus wouldn't let it play Protestant schools on the argument that we might have to stand for the national anthem and it would be embarrassing. We told her, 'Mother, it wouldn't be embarrassing at all: we would stand. Then we'd invite them over here, and play "The Soldier's Song" and they would stand too. It would be just a matter of politeness.' But she wasn't to be persuaded.

We learned Irish history. People who went to Protestant schools learned British history. We were all learning the same things, the same events, the same period of time, but the interpretations we were given were very different. At the state school they teach that the Act of Union was brought about to help strengthen the trade agreements between England and Ireland. We were taught that it was a malicious attempt to bleed Ireland dry of her linen industry which was affecting English cotton. We learned our Irish history from *Fallon's Irish History Aids*, Fallon's being a publishing firm in southern Ireland. Now the Ministry of Education had issued a memorandum saying that *Fallon's Irish History Aids* were not to be used in schools, because they were no more than sedition and treason in the name of history. On a point of principle, *all* our books were published by Fallon's. When the Ministry wrote to complain, Mother Benignus wrote back in Irish, just to make another point clear.

We were a very voluntary voluntary school, under the minimum control of the Government, and occasionally offers would come of more financial help in exchange for a greater government say in the school. Officers would come from the Ministry of Education, and argue, 'Look, if you come under government control, you'll get another twenty per cent grant.' And they would be chased off the premises. Immediately, a mass movement would start to raise enough money to produce the necessary facility before the Ministry inspector came back. All our days were spent organising concerts or raffles or draws or competitions to raise the money to get more equipment for the lab, or a new cooker in the kitchen, or for resurfacing the tennis court. This is where it was a good school. It had a good academic reputation, though socially it wasn't a good school: it did not attract the better class of citizen. There was very little discipline and it didn't produce people who took an active part in the community; but at least in our struggle to do without government help and interference, we ended up appreciating things much better than if they had been forced on us.

I knew no Irish when I went to grammar school, but the class I joined was a class of crude political rebels: we knew nothing about politics except what we were for and against, and we were for Ireland and Mother Benignus was our heroine. In addition to our passion for Ireland we had a very good teacher of Gaelic, with an enthusiastic approach to the subject, so that at the end of my first year the whole class was way above the standard of Irish-speaking expected of eleven-year-olds. Each year the Gael Linn, an organisation which exists to preserve the Irish language, sponsors a schools competition in Northern Ireland, awards a shield to the school with the best Irish-conversation standard, and a scholarship to the best individual pupil. At the end of my first year, our school won the shield and I won the scholarship, and when the shield was presented, special mention was made of my class who had been partly responsible for the award. Since I was the best of the best who had helped to win the shield, I became the darling of Mother Benignus's life and a protégée to be sent to the stars ever afterwards. I got away with murder in that school on the basis of my heart being in the right place. Each year an Irish drama festival was held in the locality and other things being equal we were allowed to go to it on Wednesday afternoon. One particular year the programme looked very good: it was getting away from the old Irish kitchen-sink drama and presenting plays in translation, such as the plays of Chekhov. So three of us organised a large-scale truancy and about twenty pupils sat watching plays for three whole days. With twenty of us missing school, Mother Benignus knew perfectly well where we were. She also knew who was responsible. But when the festival was over and we turned up in school once more, she merely said, 'I hope you benefited greatly, and that you will keep your enthusiasm in *reasonable* bounds in the future.'

When I first joined St Patrick's Academy, I was a very timid, terrified person. The other girls all seemed to be independent toughies. Their general attitude was: 'We know you have to wear your berets coming to school in the morning: that's why we carry them in our pockets.' I was so scared of them that I asked to leave the room when the teacher left, so I could get away from them. But my success in Irish and the prominence this gave me in the school cured me of that. The combined effect of Mother Benignus and my fellow-students turned me into a convinced republican, and a year of absorbing the lesson 'We are Irish. We are proud of our history, our dead, our culture, and our language' groomed me for the talent competition.

Mother Benignus was a very kind-hearted woman. Financially, the school was never what it should have been because when it came to the paying of fees, if you didn't have the money, you didn't pay. It was written off, or held over, and she would just say, 'Well, we'll work a bit harder and make up for it.' She was a good kind of socialist. She imposed a capital fee to cover the school's expenses on all qualified pupils, the ones getting scholarships from the State, that is; it came to one guinea a term, which of course everybody could afford, and so she collected one guinea a term from all the people who didn't have to pay to make up the deficit of the children who had neither scholarships nor the money for fees. When we got into unreasonable debt, we just held another competition.

But she was narrow-minded. She couldn't bear, for instance, to see women in masculine attire: wearing jeans was disgusting. And knocking around with the scruffy boys in the boys' academy next door was just a total disgrace. This was amusing enough when you were young, but as you got older it became tiresome to feel her eagle eye upon you when you wanted to walk to the bus-stop with some reasonably handsome male. She never missed anything, and you would be hauled over the coals next morning: 'You were seen eating crisps out of a bag in the street! Have you no self-respect?' Sucking lollipops in the street was the depths of degradation, and the punishment for these things was quite severe. They merited lengthy tellings-off, but if you knocked somebody half-way down the stairs, you wouldn't get a blessing on your work; it was very un-Christian; you had better apologise, and that was that.

When I was a senior pupil we resented the fact that we didn't have a common room to ourselves, so we took over a small library where we studied and made ourselves at home in it. We smuggled in a kettle, and a jar of instant coffee and some cups and hid them in the library cupboard. When the bell rang for break and everybody was supposed to go outside for fresh air, we locked the library door and made coffee. And talked. We didn't gossip about other girls in the school or make cynical remarks about the teachers. Instead we analysed the situation in Northern Ireland and discussed why most of us were going to leave it. I was one of the few who didn't plan to leave Northern Ireland. But the only possible future the others could see was either to get a university education and leave Northern Ireland, or go to Catholic training colleges and become Catholic teachers in Catholic schools. None of us wanted to be Catholic teachers – and none of us wanted to be nuns. This was a big drama in the school: for something like fifteen years they hadn't produced a nun from the school, until my sister went and broke the record – and was I disgraced! They wanted about six of us to enter the convent, and we had to fight them off tooth and nail.

Anyway, one day when we were dissecting Northern Ireland behind the locked doors of the library, a general assembly was called. I was head girl at that time, and should have called it, but when we got to the assembly hall things were already in progress. It was a uniform inspection – one of many – held this time because girls' gym tunics were getting disgracefully shorter with every passing day. So there was a crisis on, and we had missed it. When we made our appearance, Mother Benignus demanded: 'Where have you been? And what have you been discussing?' One of my friends, Bernadette O'Neill, who was about the most militant person I knew at school, roared from the back of the hall: 'Politics, Mother. We have been discussing politics!'

'And if,' said Mother Benignus, standing up, 'the senior girls of this school have nothing better to discuss than politics, I suggest they should be working. Politics is a waste of time.' And she the most political person in the school!

I was head girl at that time by popular acclaim, and the next year I was elected head girl by the prefects. Mother Benignus didn't want me to be head girl the second year: she thought it was making me big-headed and that I was taking over the school from under her feet. In fact, there were three of us – Aideen Mallon, Sheila O'Farrell, and myself. For two years we made ourselves responsible for behaviour in the school and in that time took it from the brink of chaos and made of it a reasonably civilised society. The nuns weren't prepared to cane anybody: their attitude was we should behave ourselves for the greater honour and glory of God. But delinquent juveniles don't work on those assumptions, and there was very little discipline or respect for one's betters in the school. Aideen, Sheila and I created our own detention period. We used to make children stay in after school and anyone who broke the silence merely prolonged the detention period by another three minutes. The extra three minutes were totted up on the blackboard, and sometimes we were there for an hour and a half. Another complaint was that girls didn't change from their heavy outdoor shoes into their indoor shoes, and they were damaging the school floors. We put a guard on the cloakroom: any girl who forgot to bring indoor shoes was made to go in her stocking feet. After about three days of that, people generally discovered that it wasn't hard to remember their indoor shoes. So we built up our little syndicate of Stalinism, which only lasted a few weeks, for all that was necessary was to impose discipline in the first place. We made the school something more than an academic machine by producing a debating society and a netball team, and we widened its interests from exclusively Irish culture to English-speaking drama and debates.

Because it was the kind of school it was, the history teacher, Mrs Bradley, was Stalin in disguise. Outside the classroom, she was a very friendly, enthusiastic kind of person, but inside the classroom her system of teaching was to thump everything down your throat. 'That's it! Learn it! Or out against the wall!' You had to stand up without moving until such time as your brain registered that which it should have registered; or, if you hadn't learned it in the first place, until you gave in and admitted it. But anything she taught you, you never forgot. She came to us in the library one day for help. She had a particularly stupid class, and even her thump-on-the-head-with-a-book-out-against-the-wall-and-stand-till-you-drop tactics had failed to get anything into these kids' brains. So she decided a bit of the education touch wouldn't do any harm; she would produce a wall chart, and she asked us to make it for her. It was to cover the junior history course, which

239

included most of British history from the Stuarts to the Battle of Waterloo.

We got the junior class working to bring us in pictures of all the important British kings and heroes and generals they could find, and gathered up old encyclopaedias and history books, and with all the material made a good, colourful, lucid chart, showing who was who and what they had done in the fewest words possible. To head it off we took a page from an educational magazine which showed a picture of Nelson under the caption 'They fought for their country'. The chart was put on the wall, Mrs Bradley was very grateful, the children were most impressed and started reading the facts and learning something.

Mother Benignus walked into the classroom one day and read on the wall at the back of the room: 'They fought for their country'. Her eyes lit up with their favourite patriotic glow. As she walked down the room, she said, 'Who did this?'

'Oh, Bernadette Devlin and Sheila O'Farrell and the girls in the library did it,' said Mrs Bradley.

'Very good – I'm glad to see the seniors helping the juniors.'

By which time she had got to the back of the room and old Horatio Nelson caught her eye. In one blinding flash she realised that her patriotic Fenian wall was decorated with British generals and British heroes, and she just tore the chart, from one end to the other, right off the wall. She crumpled it up, stamped on it, and stormed out of the room, threatening to fire Mrs Bradley on the spot and demanding that Bernadette Devlin be brought to her immediately. A terrified junior came up to the library: 'M-M-Mother Benignus wants B-B-Bernadette Devlin, and she's in an awful temper.' So off I trotted to pacify her, and found her back in the classroom. She was white.

'Are you really responsible for this?' she said.

I looked down and saw our weeks of work lying crumpled on the floor, all the kids sitting around shaking, and Mrs Bradley on the point of exploding in the background. 'I'm not responsible, Mother,' I said, thinking she wanted to know who had torn it down. 'Mrs Bradley knows we made that chart. I don't know who tore it off the wall.'

It was the wrong thing to say.

'*I* tore it off the wall! And I want it in the wastebin immediately!' Whereupon two or three children scuffled down to put it in the wastebin.

'Don't touch that!' roared Mrs Bradley, 'it's going back on the wall the minute it's cleaned up properly.'

And a dialogue ensued on the lines of:

'Not on *my* wall!'

'Then I'm not teaching in your school!'

I was called in to referee. Mother Benignus said, 'You agree with me, Bernadette, don't you?'

'No, Mother,' I said. 'I did most of the work on that chart, and it's not my fault, nor Mrs Bradley's fault that British history is taught in this school. If you don't like it being taught you should take it up with the Ministry of Education. But as long as it is taught, we have to pass exams. And it doesn't do any harm to learn about those people. They did fight, very bravely, for their country, and have as much right to be considered patriots as Pearse or Connolly or anybody else.'

That finished it. 'They have *no* right to be considered patriots.' And she went over the litany of all the British people who had tortured the Irish for five hundred years.

'But, Mother,' I said, 'those people didn't torture the Irish. They have nothing to do with the Irish Question. They fought mostly on the Continent.'

'They are British!'

So I said, 'Mother, you are a bigot,' and left her, shutting the classroom door behind me.

'Come back here! I'll not be called a bigot by a pupil of mine.'

I opened the door again, stuck my head round it, and said, 'Mother, you *are* a bigot. I'm very sorry you're a bigot. But you *are* a bigot.' I went back up the stairs with Mother Benignus storming up after me. At the top of the stairs we stopped and the argument began again, with Mother Benignus claiming she wasn't a bigot, but a patriot. My favourite habit then was waving my finger, so I waved my finger at her and said, 'Mother, you are one of the greatest bigots I have ever met!' She had a ruler in her hand and she practically took my finger off with it. She was beaten. She just said, 'Don't wave your finger at the principal of this school!'

I had called her a bigot, I had walked out without being dismissed, I had closed the door in her face, I had forced her to walk up the stairs after me. But she knew I was right, and all she said was, 'Don't wave your finger at me.' The chart went back up. Mrs Bradley stayed, and there has been a love-hate relationship between Mother Benignus and myself ever since. Although I have outgrown her politics, Mother Benignus will always have my admiration and affection because she is the most truly charitable person I have known. Her heart is in the right place.

The Price of My Soul, 1969

ROBERT JOHNSTONE
b.1951

BELFAST, 1950s—1960s

My earliest memory is an impression of colours, brown above green. They shone with that incredible vividness which adults cannot recapture in ordinary consciousness: rich soft chestnut glowing with vitality, deep dark greens glistening in a bright light. I deduce that a horse was looking over a hedge into my pram on a sunny day. If you are too young to understand it, the world is full of marvels.

I know roughly the place where this happened, although the image belongs to a Belfast that rapidly disappeared. My mother must have wheeled my pram from our flat at the Crossroads up Finaghy Road North, in the direction of the mountains. In the early 1950s a short walk would have taken us to where horses might graze, though now it would only lead to more houses and another busy junction at Andersonstown. In thirty years my playgrounds and places of escape have been torn up and built over, and much that is fundamental about the city has changed, often for the worse.

But if the past is a doubly foreign country, in some way Belfast remains a mysterious place. Its dark hearts lie unexplored in my cognitive map like old charts of Africa. Terrible and dramatic crimes occur obscurely in places one has no reason to visit and often every reason to avoid; civilised and measured lives carry on in unremarkable streets. Belfast is an incorrigible extra parent or shady uncle, who shaped one's life but whose doings only filter through in news reports or rumours. If asked, large numbers of its citizens will profess to love the place. They do so with such alacrity that you begin to suspect they don't think you believe them. The city remains a member of the family, from whom you might at times want desperately to escape, but with whom there is an unbreakable bond.

Finaghy is a junction on the Lisburn Road, between Upper Malone and Andersonstown. When I was born it was an outpost of the suburbs, and in fact my mother could have wheeled my pram in any three directions to reach 'the country' in minutes. Walking south east you were quickly into the gentle landscape of the Lagan Valley. The cars along the Malone Road provided a diversion rather than an irritant, and you could measure your walk by turning at the cottage on the corner of Dunmurry Lane. Its garden always seemed to be overflowing with the colours of flowers. Walking north west towards the mountains – hills really, but they were always called mountains – you crossed over a rustic railway bridge which the trains would blast black on both sides, leaving a smoke-ring enveloping the road. There was a little station, complete with ticket office and waiting-room. The houses grew more sparse from there until you got into the more severe upland scenery, where there were the wilds of Colin Glen and all the promise of what lay over the other side. In the third direction, down the Lisburn Road towards Dunmurry and Lambeg, there were thick woods and low marshy fields.

In some ways it was better just to look at the mountains from our kitchen window and think of their names: Black Mountain, Divis, Cave Hill. They had an infinite variety of colour and in-cident, innumerable subtle shades of blue and purple, grey, a hint of green. The buildings were laid in a carpet before you, petering out as the slope grew. At night car headlights would mark romantic journeys across their face. There was excitement as the BBC and ITV television masts were erected, with their little ladders of red lights and one lamp at the top of each, winking for the planes coming in and out of Nutts Corner. Sometimes the mountains would smoulder like Sertsey when farmers burned gorse, and swathes of steely smoke would sweep across their tops. And the quarries – there was an active quarry where the moun-tains dipped at the southern end, its huge machinery silhouetted against the skyline. Blasting at the quarries could be heard dis-tinctly where I lived, and I think you could hear the rock tumbling and see the smoke of the dynamite and the stone dust billowing. I remember that just beyond that quarry, in a niche of the horizon, was the shape of a single tree. Sunsets could be dramatic affairs, as the disc sank behind the mountains or lit up vivid clouds like a vast theatre, golden light transforming the ordinary roofs of our neighbours. I would not like to live in a place without mountains.

Ignorance has its advantages. For what now seems an indecently long time, I did not understand that I lived in what we like to call a divided society. My parents were Protestant and I have no doubt, although they refused to say how they voted, that they added their support to the tens of thousands who reliably gave the Unionist candidate in South Antrim his monotonously huge majority. I was being brought up and was being treated by the rest of the world as a Prod, although I didn't know it. I detected prejudices as a child, but these seemed to stem more from class snobberies and notions of respectability than from an argument about the meaning of the Eucharist. I had no clear concepts of 'Protestant' and 'Catholic' (something that's easier, they say, for a Protestant child), so that if sectarianism was getting to work, it had no tools for my less-than-subtle mind to work with. Seamus Heaney identifies an Ulster attitude in his poem 'Whatever You Say Say Nothing', but such indirectness can be self-defeating. Besides, Heaney is a south Derry man and, although we townees like to think we are sophisticated, I was certainly not as sly as my co-religionists expected me to be.

In any case it did not occur to my childish mind that Finaghy offered a geographical symbol, as an interface of Protestant and Catholic, only that the rich nobs lived on the Malone Road, and down Finaghy Road North were poorer people, while we were in the middle. I have still not been able to work out exactly what class my family belonged to, certainly not with the accuracy of Orwell's 'lower-upper-middle class', and suspect that this is true of many people in Belfast. My parents, like so many others, came to settle there from the country, my father from a farming background in Tyrone, to start a shop in what was then the growing village of Finaghy. Because of the rural origins of many Belfast people, because of sectarian distinctions, and also because of how the dissenting Protestants saw themselves, with their tinge of radicalism and their tangled roots, the more usual definitions of class do not apply. Manners may make classes as much as money, and one gets the impression that, because of manners or whatever, society in Ulster is not stratified in quite the same way as in England. My family would present a headache for any student of social class and religion: in three generations we have farmers, a commercial traveller, a shipyard worker, a soldier, a teacher, an air-traffic controller, lukewarm Anglicans, Methodists, Presbyterians, an atheist, a Baptist lay preacher and a band of missionaries scattered across the globe. I don't think any of us turned to 'dig with the other foot', but I probably wouldn't have heard about it if they had. No wonder I was confused.

In a small stretch of the Lisburn Road, on either side of the Crossroads, was a cornucopia of denominations: Church of Ireland, Presbyterian, Methodist, the more exotic Plymouth Brethren and, up the road a bit, Baptists and a Catholic convent. Mormons took over a large house up towards Malone, and clean-limbed young American lads in raincoats and trilbies could be seen doing their rounds with a message about fiery chariots coming to end the world on a certain, though postponable date. We'd hear every so often of a new convert – it always seemed to be a middle-aged woman in the gossip – to the strange sect that operated behind the blank face of that big house. By the time I left the area in the late seventies there was even a colony of followers of Sri Guru Maharaj Ji. But nothing could be more colourful than our home-bred sects, one of which took over the old scout hall behind our flat and carried on charismatic lectures in the evenings. The lecturer regularly exhorted his teenage audience to shout ever louder their responses, so that 'Hallelujah!', 'Praise God!' and more mundane catchphrases would rend the air with all the fervour – and decibels – of a rock concert. We are a passionate people, but our passions take odd forms.

There were plenty of churches and shops, but there wasn't a single pub, and although an off-licence did eventually open up, it was only despite petitions signed against it after Sunday services. The other controversy at our Church of Ireland services that stays in my mind concerns a young assistant minister who provided a strong contrast with the elderly and well-respected, if occasionally prolix, canon. This must have been in 1964, five years after Lady Dixon presented a large park on the Malone Road to the City Council, with the proviso that its facilities should be open on Sundays. The young firebrand preached a sermon in which he argued that, all things considered, God might not be offended if children's swings were not locked up in the playgrounds on Sundays. Not quite everyone, after all, was a Sabbatarian. The effect was extraordinary, with the usual somnolent congregation arguing the fine points of doctrine all the way home and no doubt right through *Two-Way Family Favourites* as well. According to Charles Brett, its chairman in 1963, the Northern Ireland Labour Party's confused stance on the Sunday swings issue destroyed its credibility as a non-sectarian party.

There were other more arcane organisations represented at the Crossroads. A Masonic hall, distinguished by a moulded device of protractors set into the brickwork, sat over the Milk Bar, and dinner-jacketed men could be seen of an evening brushing past the teddy boys to go to their secret ceremonies. There was also a little old building that looked like a cross between an ancient school and a midget church. It had a plaque saying 'Orange Hall', but I only ever remember it being used for that purpose around the twelfth of July, when bandsmen in outlandish tartan would gather there for practice with their gleaming instruments. It served as a kindergarten and as a library, and the local pigeon club kept its hampers under the stage.

Finaghy was a happy place to grow up in, whether my ignorance was bliss or not. Finaghy Primary School was, as I later learned, one of the best equipped in Belfast, and I would run to school early in the mornings without a care in the world. Its classrooms were a mixture of three architectural periods, with wooden prefabs, an old stone building with BOYS' and GIRLS' entrances at either end (though we went in mixed) and modern pink corrugated metal classrooms with tall angled windows, full of light and air. We took schools broadcasts from the BBC and, apart from *Music and Movement*, during which we would

247

impersonate trees or flowers or act out the drama of *Peter and the Wolf,* I remember particularly the local programmes about such aspects of Ulster endeavour as the building of the Antrim Coast Road or the inauguration of the Enterprise Express to Dublin. We were taught about St Patrick, the Siege of Derry, and Prince William's defeat of King James in 1690. Our geography lessons preserved the medieval conceit that the sun revolved around Ulster, with the rest of Ireland as remote as England or Scotland. We also seemed to have a lot of religious lessons, although in the upper classes our teacher was painstaking in his open and scientific interpretations of the miraculous. If I could define the effect of this education on a contented and uncritical child, it seems to have been to promote an interest and pride in my native city and country. While I learned a lot about Christianity there and at Sunday school, it was by no means a dogmatic instruction: Jesus was a good, gentle person and Lazarus may have been dead or merely comatose. The fact that my country relations knew about people being healed and miracles performed on a regular basis did not tend to reinforce credulity.

I had still learned nothing about the Catholics up the road, and little about the rest of Ireland. Indeed, no-one seemed sure even what to call it – 'Eire' and 'the Free State' were the most popular names. It existed as a vague dreamland, foreign and intriguing in the way that imaginary islands are in storybooks, full of leprechauns, thatched cottages and picturesque donkeys. We had a souvenir cigarette lighter, shilling-sized, decorated with shamrocks. Yet there was an ambivalence in attitudes to Dublin. My parents were born before Ireland was partitioned, and I detected, in the way they looked at what was once the capital of their country, a different perspective from people born within the lifetime of the Northern state. Belfast was our town, but Dublin, in the way it was referred to, seemed big and important, more like a real city.

The fifties were a placid and optimistic time from my point of view. I had learnt that Belfast had the largest ropeworks in the world (now no more – its 25-acre site has been hived off, and the largest sign outside is now for Citroën cars); the biggest shipyard in the world; Shorts, which made the most beautiful aircraft of them all, the Short Sunderland; a great linen industry (no longer the case by then); the world's largest gasometer; and so on. Belfast had suffered like London in a just and victorious war, and evidence remained of that. I remember a small bomb-like object lay for years on our kitchen window-sill. It may have been a souvenir collected elsewhere, but I liked to think it had been dropped by a German Stuka and accounted for the small crack at the bottom of the window-pane. Swastikas were the signs of revolt my schoolfriends chalked up on the telegraph poles. The received wisdom seemed accurate: Belfast was a centre of industry and enterprise, the hardworking capital of a modern, efficient little state.

I went on an expedition one day on an old bicycle my father had reclaimed for me. It seemed terribly exciting and adventurous as I passed the old iron marker of the city boundary at Balmoral Golf Club and rode on into town to the City Hall, so grand in its white stone, with its great dome of green copper. It was like pictures of London, Rome or Washington. Inside, every surface shone in cool polished marble and up at the very top, inside the dome, was a little disc of salmon pink. John Luke's bright mural summed up all I had been taught about the city: the mountains, the wondrous paraphernalia of industry, the historical figures hinting at English or misty Celtic connections.

But my cosy little corner was changing before my eyes. A big new housing estate was started on Finaghy Road South – brick semis – and two 'skyscrapers' (fourteen-storey blocks of flats) were erected in the Benmore estate behind our school. In a class project we marvelled at an old map of 'Ballyfinaghy', drawn before the estates were built: it looked so white, an empty space with a little stream running through it, such a contrast to the mazes that represented the cream pebble-dashed terraces of Benmore with its narrow roads (planned for residents who could not afford cars). It is something of a shock to realise now that my parents, immigrants themselves, were probably among the early arrivals.

Building was also creeping up the Andersonstown Road from the Falls, but there were still plenty of fields and woods where the

Wolf Cubs could practise tracking each other and concealing themselves in piles of leaves. I could play cowboys and Indians on vacant lots and get into trouble when I didn't come home after Sunday matinees at the Tivoli. I had a comprehensive selection of six-shooters for the purpose, but I remember clearly my shock on first noticing the huge black revolver carried by a policeman standing at the Crossroads. In the 1950s the IRA carried on an abortive bombing campaign on the border, but I was unaware of that. My terrors were less tangible, provoked one night on a trolleybus trip to Castlereagh, where I saw a policeman with a sub-machine-gun guarding an electricity switching station; by my uncle from east Belfast, who had a repertoire of stories about unsolved local murders (the most vivid being 'The Headless Turk'); or by the escaped convict Hinds, who was thought to be hiding in Ireland, and whom one suspected – and hoped – was really innocent. Many commentators have noticed the relish with which the Irish recount bloody incidents, and Belfast people are no different.

I persevered in my vagueness about what country I lived in and what was happening to it. Perhaps this is not so surprising. The films we saw at the Tivoli were American, my reading matter was D.C. Thomson's best (which included Desperate Dan, a cowboy, and Little Plum, an Indian), war stories about the British fighting the Nazis or the Bosche, and Batman, Green Lantern and Superman. We don't hear much of it now, but in those days people were worrying publicly about 'the invasion of American culture'. The war would still have been vivid in adult minds and Belfast must have greeted the American servicemen with the customary fascination with which it regards foreigners. We were just emerging from the drab postwar years and indeed there was still rationing when I was born in 1951 (my mother occasionally threatened to make a 'wartime banana' with food flavouring and a parsnip). America, which has more people of Scots-Irish than of Irish Catholic descent, was the centre of energy and modernity. I was all for the American invasion, as it seemed more fun. People used to stick things on their Ford Consuls to make them look like Cadillacs (someone at Finaghy had a white convertible with a great golden eagle on the bumper) and those lads who weren't teddy boys were donning leather jackets and trying to look as dangerous as Elvis Presley. I remember the arrival of Pepsi Cola at Mr Scott's sweet shop, a taste with which the mineral factory down Diamond Gardens could not compete. My sister was buying Chris Barber records on which Ottilie Patterson sang like Bessie Smith.

I sometimes suspect that my vagueness was the result of a conspiracy of silence to make us good little loyal Ulstermen. My exposure to 'local culture' was extremely limited, confined to John McCormack records or my father's feat of being able to sing all the words of 'Phil the Fluter's Ball'. In the cinema he would note with pleasure that Victor McLaglen, Barry Fitzgerald and even John Wayne were Irish, but I don't suppose that counts. Quite a contrast with my country relations, who had a more definite view of things, like an uncle who would recite 'The Ould Orange Flute'. I once asked my father what the capital was, and he told me London. Now, I knew that Dublin was the capital of Ireland, and that Ulster was a part of Ireland, and I also knew that Belfast was the capital of Northern Ireland, but then half the map of the world was coloured red, including our small part, and London was the capital of it all, so it made some sort of sense. When an uncle arrived from Canada, one of the biggest red bits, he came from a continent across which many family friends and relations had settled. On the television, Mr Eden and Mr Macmillan were invading Suez, exploding atom bombs, pacifying Aden and Malaya, and conferring with President Eisenhower on the future of the rest of the world. Our horizons were not narrow. Perhaps, like England's they were too broad for us to be able to see ourselves clearly.

I stayed in my real world, of course, my immediate surroundings in Finaghy, where I could construct elaborate fantasies of battle, pursuit and exploration. Revisiting it now, I am frightened by the fact that there just don't seem to be any wild spaces left for a child to play in. There is a park and a community centre, but where do the kids go to be free? The city has crept up on them. In my day a trip into 'town' was a weekly affair, for my mother's shopping or to see a Western at one of the many cinemas. It was always seething with people. We would often visit my cousin at Cregagh, which even then was urban, with large factories like British Oxygen and the Hughes Tool Company, but where there were plenty of unorganised green spaces to play commandos in.

There were also special trips, as when our school was transported down the Lisburn Road and lined up along Bradbury Place. We were told to cheer as a black shiny car swept past, with a waving figure in white sitting in the back. I remember of this incident only that, and the toy shop we were standing outside. It must have been some princess. Perhaps she visited the shipyard to launch a ship. One of my trips was to see the *Bonaventure*, a Canadian aircraft carrier. Despite its naval grey paint it was full of romance, promising happy adventures to far-off lands, very possibly Vancouver, a place I intended to visit because of the name and because we got calendars from a relative there. In 1960 the TV had a programme about the building of the *Canberra*, another name full of possibilities. I took a great interest in it because of its beautiful shape and the many advanced and unusual features of its design. My uncle at the shipyard gave me a plastic kit for a model of its sister ship, the *Oriana*, which had electric motors to turn its twin propellers. It later turned out that the *Canberra* was the last large passenger ship to be made at Queen's Island.

On another trip my mother took me away from her usual beat of Royal Avenue and Woolworths. There were odd little shops selling peculiar wares – nightlights with red candles, tiny bowls of water to hang on the wall (for budgies when they leave their cages?), strings of beads with crosses, statuettes of the Virgin Mary, and weird paintings of Jesus with a bleeding heart exposed, or rather looking as if it had been stuck on as a badge. Clearly some of the items were religious, for religious shops in my experience sold black Bibles, or perhaps white hymnals for brides, and occasionally, for the more daring, improving comic books about the life of Jesus. Nor could I understand how the proprietor had made a mistake in his depiction of Jesus: the Roman's spear had pierced his side, not ripped open his chest like an Inca sacrifice. Besides, there was something sickly about his spaniel expression and something unhealthily prurient about the artist's decoration of rays around the pop-out heart. I imagined the shop-keeper was doing so badly out of his strange religious articles that he had to supplement his business by selling jewellery and bric-à-brac.

We went into a little brown church, unlike any church I knew. St Polycarp's at Finaghy was tall and light, with plain wooden pews and white stone pillars. This church was small and smoky, as dark and exciting as the cinema. It felt crowded, for apart from several people – surely unusual in the middle of a weekday – there were various unfamiliar items of furniture and unnecessary decoration, like a little booth with curtains and an array of candles before another statue of the Virgin Mary. It was like Aladdin's cave, rich in mysteries, like what lay behind the tiny door in a story like *Alice*. We went to a courtyard where people walked around a cliff of what I thought was living rock. There were hollows in the rock, and more statues set into them – I remember Mary, wearing a crown, always the same expression, the same robes, the colours blue and white. It was almost as good as Santa's cave in the Co-op at Christmas, except that I knew there was something more serious to it: adult people were as intent as I was. And the words were equally intriguing: *niche, grotto, madonna*. I understood in a dim way that this was also some kind of religion – alien, dark and attractive, more 'religious' than St Polycarp's, but a perplexing mixture of the frivolous and the intense, the tawdry and the mystical.

Do I remember correctly? Perhaps the church wasn't so cramped and cloudy with incense. Some day I can go back to see, for the little brown church, the grotto and the religious emporia are still there on the edge of Smithfield. Such things can assume a shape in our heads through all the theories we devise and the prejudices we unwittingly absorb later on. Perhaps my childhood games were not played in acres of free ground and big woods – places shrink alarmingly when we grow up – and the hills are green more often than purple. Like Alice, we find we can't get through that tiny door into the past. But in Belfast what you think you remember has its own importance as well as what actually happens. . .

My father bought supplies for his shop – fruit, vegetables, flowers, fish – several times a week from the old markets near the Law Courts and close to the docks. I often went with him, relishing the chance to enter an adult world of expertise and specialisation where, ostensibly, a huge casual structure of relationships and customs had evolved around the process of buying and selling perishable goods.

The very names of the merchants were sonorous. There was Jack Horner, a small quick man with black-framed spectacles, selling flowers; for fish, Owen O'Hagan, relaxed and friendly; Devine's, the big fruit and vegetable firm.

The flowers in all their colours, pristine as the blocks in a new paintbox, were set out in tubs, bordering a narrow pathway to Jack Horner's little office. Like a daily spring in the tundra they arrived and left rapidly, and appeared in such abundance, yet each bloom was precious and delicate. Professionals often handle their tools, even their animals, with rough familiarity. Sometimes they appear to take pride in doing so. But no one treats flowers with less than respect. You cradle a bloom in cupped hand as you test its perfume. The dandy lifts his carnation from the bunch with a flourish, but delicately, holding the stem between finger and thumb, twirling it perhaps, snapping the stem with efficiency, and looking down to admire the effect once it is threaded through his buttonhole.

There might be tulips from Holland, flown in like news of life or death, as if it were vital that supplies get through to Belfast. Some flowers came not in bunches but in long cardboard boxes, wrapped in tissue paper and separated with cardboard struts. Lifting out the long flowers was like finding an expensive new dress that had just arrived from a swanky store in a presentation package. Once or twice there would be an orchid – a single orchid – to remind us how impossibly extravagant nature could be. My father had some glass phials with pierced rubber stoppers, so that the orchids could be preserved like strangely living specimens.

How ephemeral it was. The huge chrysanthemums, big as the globe lights at school, dropped their petals in showers at the slightest touch. It was hard to believe there would be anything left of them by the time they reached the customers. We would usually come in the early morning when the place was crowded with colour. By late morning it was almost bare. The flowers were like ice that had melted away to every shop in Belfast.

The fruit and vegetables were piled high on either side of the narrow roadways that ran through the markets. There would be walls of oranges a couple of stories high and big red lorries would nose in between them to load or unload. The drivers decorated their trucks with white heather or photos of busty girls, or fixed elaborate chromium hubcaps on their radiator grilles. One would tell you how his potato lorry had burned off a private motorist who had fancied himself.

I remembered from school how the port of Belfast both exported and imported spuds – we grew the seed potatoes, sent them to Cyprus and Egypt, then bought them back when they were grown. Potatoes came from Cyprus not in plastic bags but in boxes full of soft black humus, the potatoes clean like white pebbles in the spongy soil, wrapped in crinkly brown paper. Potatoes in colours like jewels or varieties of gold – white, blue, purple, brown and subtle red.

Sometimes I would try to count the countries that sent their food to us. There were all the different sorts of oranges, from Israel, South Africa, Morocco, Spain, oriental names. They might be big and pale or small and oily, with skin like coloured, polished hide. The apples came in cardboard boxes from the four corners of the globe, and with the most frivolous names – Mac Red, Golden Delicious. Those from Canada were packed in cells of impregnated cardboard, each waxy scarlet apple all the way from Canada in its individual cube of air. The Dayglo green apples from France arrived in refrigerated trailers that had driven all the way from Avignon. Then there were the lemons from Famagusta, each one wrapped in tissue paper, each wrapper with a gold motif of the Venus de Milo.

Grapes would come in barrels full of cork. You split the lid with a crowbar and lifted out a bunch like a dripping, dusty chandelier. Melons came in flat wooden crates, wrapped in woodwool. Lying cushioned there, they were like a drawer from a giant's collection of blown eggs. The peaches lay in dimpled polystyrene trays covered with cellophane, downy as a girl's neck, coloured as richly as amethysts or opals. Onions were in sacks of red netting tied with hemp, their loose skins crackling like dry paper, thin as gold leaf. So much trouble had been taken to pack these things, to keep them in perfect condition on their long journeys, it was difficult to look upon them as mere items of commerce. They were more like presents from abroad. In a crate holding twelve melons, there might be nine pieces of wood, two or three metal bands, and at least thirty-six nails, as well as the bed of woodwool.

Deals would be done at the side of the produce. Buyer and seller would discuss the quality of the goods, the price would be mentioned, a quantity noted down on a clipboard, as casually as if they were discussing the weather. My father might taste a plum with the critical air of a wine-taster, or weigh a melon in his hands, probing it like a doctor for ripeness.

The market was airy and open, its gates were never closed during the day, and there were always lorries edging in and out and people rushing to and fro. The aromas of every continent hung about – the acid tang of citrus, the musty smell of apples, the winy bouquet of grapes in cork – and even the faint odours of decay, from a pile of fallen cabbage leaves or a rotten lemon, purply-white, squashed like a cushion at the corner of its box, were intriguing.

It was almost as if the sea reached into the fish market, for it was always wet and cold, salt, seminal-smelling. I shared my father's romantic fascination with the life of the sea – fish were the only food Western men still went out to hunt in the wild. They went in their little trawlers to win their living from the oceans off Iceland, the Faeroes, the North Sea, and sent their catches to us. Filletted on board or at the dockside in Aberdeen, they would arrive in little wooden boxes lined with a single sheet of white paper and stuffed with snow. Or there would be white polystyrene boxes or big aluminium trays. A man in rubber boots and an oilskin apron, bare-armed, would stir a huge sink of herring, oily, their scales encrusting everything like transparent sequins. We would be shown any oddities: a couple of stray dogfish like miniature

256

sharks, or the biggest cod, too long to fit any of the trays, which I preferred to think had been captured on the Grand Banks. Occasionally there would be lobsters, monstrous living things that waved their pincers in a tired gesture of dismissal when you lifted them up.

Since this was Belfast, I have to mention that our fish merchants were Catholic. Most fish was sold on Fridays because of the Catholic custom of refraining from meat on that day. Many Protestants had the same habit, though I think it has declined latterly. When the present troubles started, the Catholic fish merchants painted out their name on their vans, whether for their own safety or to avoid embarrassing their Protestant clients I am not sure.

The old wholesale markets were mainly about business, and Belfast had nothing as picturesque as Billingsgate or Covent Garden, but I felt that there was some sort of communal liveliness there. It had its own characters: tramps who might wander in looking for rotten fruit or maybe just a piece of cardboard to make a bed; old women looking for bargains; the labourer with the long blond hair who was known to everyone as Gloria; the flower sellers from outside the City Hall, a contrast with the solid small shopkeepers. The markets might have been awkwardly situated, causing problems as you dodged the heavy traffic with your head buried in bunches of flowers to get to your car, but they were busy and part of the city's texture. Now, in common with Covent Garden and Les Halles, they have been moved out of town, to Boucher Road beside the motorway. That was after my father's time, but I doubt if the new markets, in their modern advanced factory-style home, are as much fun, however efficient they are.

The fish and livestock markets remain across the road, but the City Council has promoted a Variety Market on Tuesdays and Fridays in the old St George's Market. The vast halls are filled with stalls: where once the lorry-loads of crates, boxes and sacks were piled high, small retailers operate within their corrals of fruit and veg. Signs advertise Ballynahinch eggs (is that good?) and fish fresh from Portavogie. On one long row of stalls is a communal grave of ghostly white chickens, gutted and dressed. An old-fashioned caravan dispenses old-fashioned hot sweet tea in old-fashioned white mugs.

The stallholders each have a style appropriate to their métier. Those selling vegetables are the most lively. A man with a woollen cap studded with metal badges calls out to the contemplative throng, 'Who's next, ladies?' more in encouragement than inter-rogation. Neighbours shout their competing claims: 'Fresh red tomatoes only thirty pee a pound', 'Spanish onions ten pence a pound' and so on. (Do the onion-advertiser's tomatoes cost more than 30p?) They flick open their brown paper bags with a flourish, check the desired weight, which they have guessed with uncanny accuracy, and thrust the bag at the customer in a fluid movement.

Much of the market is taken up with second-hand clothes. So much that one imagines that all the clothing in Belfast must sooner or later come here to die, or rather to be reincarnated. These stallholders sit patiently behind their wares, beside huge piles of old shoes – can you find a matching pair? – that remind me of a photograph from a prison camp.

Those selling the cheap new clothes walk up and down their stalls rearranging trousers and cardigans, folding them neatly flat. An old woman sells attractive patterned pullovers. 'These are quality garments you're looking at, girls, all at half price!' The 'girls' are mostly elderly women. The Sikh looks like a man dedicated to his calling. From the neck down he might be anyone, except that he wears so many clothes: a blue nylon anorak over the jacket from a light summer suit, a heavy pullover and a loud shirt. But his face has a full beard and magnificent mustachios, and his turban is a riotously printed length of fabric, quite in keeping with his cheap but cheerful goods.

A row of flat glass-topped cabinets hold jewellery and digital watches. This stall looks overmanned: what must be a family of stallholders discussing with every customer the intricacies of the digital alarm chronograph or the carats of the red and yellow gold bracelet. Disturbingly a sign announces 'Ears Pierced'. While-you-wait, no doubt. I do not witness this gory public spectacle being performed.

A large proportion of the shoppers are elderly ladies, hunting with the fascination I remember my mother had in the fifties for bargains. The white plastic bags rustle like grass as they thread their way through the throng. Young mothers cause bottlenecks as pram and push-chair meet in the narrow spaces. One woman, who must be in her sixties and doesn't look like a football supporter, stuffs items into a bag with the legend 'Northern Ireland – Spain 1982'. A superb young girl – pink glasses, hair bleached and dyed in contrasting colours and pointing in several directions – examines the racks of second-hand clothes for additions to her exotic wardrobe.

On the way back from the Variety Market it is *de rigueur* to call in to Dowds Aquatics in Victoria Street. Unfortunately for me and the schoolboys who were there, we were five minutes late for the feeding of the piranha – rather inoffensive in his gentle colours – and the bird-eating spider was skulking halfway under a bit of wood, ignoring the doomed but cheerful grasshopper in his tank. Equally impassive were the tangle of yellow rat snakes ('Do not tap on the glass: these animals are wild and easily alarmed' – an irresistible temptation to my browsing companions). But I did make acquaintance with the hordes of red-eared terrapins and the snapping turtle, who lolled among the shreds of a hasty meal. And with the blue triggerfish and the golden angels and the black moors, more like bug-eyed spaceships decorated with feathers, the goldfish vibrating in their tiny voids: all so extravagant and outlandish it required an effort of imagination to remember they were part of the animal kingdom like ourselves.

Outside again in the unextravagant Belfast streets with their familiar concerns, ordinary life seems more colourful rather than less. We are amazed that natural wonders should exist at all, while the strangest constructs of the human mind are taken for granted.

Images of Belfast, 1983

BIOGRAPHICAL NOTES

SAM HANNA BELL
b. 1909 in Glasgow of Ulster parentage. Brought to Co. Down in 1918. Worked as features producer for BBC Northern Ireland region, 1945–69. His books include *Summer Loanen and Other Stories*, 1943; the novels, *December Bride*, 1951, *The Hollow Ball*, 1961, *A Man Flourishing*, 1973; *Erin's Orange Lily*, 1956, on Ulster customs and folklore; *The Theatre in Ulster*, 1972, and a prose anthology, *Within Our Province*, 1972.

JOHN BOYD
b. 1912 in Belfast, the son of a locomotive engine driver. Educated at Mountpottinger National School, the Royal Belfast Academical Institution, Queen's University, Belfast, and Trinity College, Dublin. Worked as teacher, lecturer and producer for BBC radio and television. Honorary director of the Lyric Theatre, Belfast, and editor of the literary magazine *Threshold*. His *Collected Plays*, vols I and II were published in 1981 and 1982.

GEORGE BUCHANAN
b. 1904 at Kilwaughter, Larne, Co. Antrim. Educated at Larne Grammar School and Campbell College, Belfast. Worked as journalist on various Irish and English newspapers. Joined RAF in 1940. Has published two journals, two volumes of autobiography, six novels and a book of essays, and has had a number of plays produced. His collections of poems are *Bodily Responses*, 1958, *Conversation with Strangers*, 1961, *Annotations*, 1970, *Minute Book of a City*, 1972, *Inside Traffic*, 1976, *Possible Being*, 1980, and *Adjacent Columns*, 1982.

SHAN F. BULLOCK
b. 1865 in Crom, Co. Fermanagh, where his father was a bailiff on the Earl of Erne's estate. Worked on father's farm for two years, then joined Civil Service in London. His novels and collections of stories include *The Awkward Squads*, 1893, *By Thrasna River*, 1895, *The Squireen*, 1903, *The Red Leaguers*, 1904, *Dan the Dollar*, 1905, and *The Loughsiders*, 1924. Died 1935.

WILLIAM CARLETON
b. 1794 at Prillisk, near Clogher, Co. Tyrone. Son of a small farmer who spoke both English and Irish. Attended a hedge school. His many novels and collections of stories include *Traits and Stories of the Irish Peasantry*,

1830, *Tales of Ireland,* 1834, *Fardourougha the Miser,* 1839, *The Black Prophet,* 1847, *The Tithe Proctor,* 1849, *Willy Reilly and his Dear Colleen Bawn,* 1855, and *Redmond Count O'Hanlon, the Irish Rapparee,* 1862. Died 1869.

BERNADETTE DEVLIN
b. 1947 in Co. Tyrone. Educated at St Patrick's Girls' Academy, Dungannon. Studied psychology at Queen's University, Belfast. Elected MP for Mid-Ulster at the age of twenty-one. Founder member of the Irish Repulican Socialist Party in 1974.

POLLY DEVLIN
b. 1944 in Co. Tyrone. Broadcaster and journalist. Author of *The Vogue Book of Fashion Photography,* 1979. Her children's book, *The Far Side of the Lough,* was published in 1983.

ROBERT GREACEN
b. 1920 in Derry and brought up in Belfast. Educated at Methodist College, Belfast, and Trinity College, Dublin. With Valentin Iremonger, he co-edited the *Faber Book of Contemporary Irish Poetry* in 1949. His own collections of poems are *One Recent Evening,* 1944, *The Undying Day,* 1948, *A Garland for Captain Fox,* 1975, *I, Brother Stephen,* 1978, *Young Mr. Gibbon,* 1979, and *A Bright Mask: New and Selected Poems,* 1985.

ROBERT HARBINSON
b. 1928 in Belfast. Worked for a time in the Belfast shipyard, later as a trapper and teacher in Canada. Under the name Robin Bryans he has written a number of travel books, including *Summer Saga,* 1960, *Danish Episode,* 1961, *Fanfare for Brazil,* 1962, *Morocco,* 1965, *Trinidad and Tobago,* 1967. Among his other publications are *Tattoo Lily and Other Ulster Stories,* 1961, the novel, *Lucio,* 1964, and the poems, *Songs Out of Oriel,* 1974.

DENIS IRELAND
b. 1894 in Belfast. Educated at the Royal Belfast Academical Institution and Queen's University, Belfast. Served with the Royal Irish Fusiliers in France and Macedonia. Invalided home with rank of captain. Travelled for the family linen firm in Britain, Canada and the USA. Freelance writer and broadcaster. First resident of Northern Ireland to become a member of the Irish Senate. His publications include *Patriot Adventurer,* 1936, the biography of Wolfe Tone, and *Six Counties in Search of a Nation,* 1974.

From the Jungle of Belfast, 1973, contains reprints and reworkings of pieces from his two earlier volumes of autobiography, as well as some new material. Died 1974.

ROBERT JOHNSTONE

b. 1951 in Belfast. Educated at the Royal Belfast Academical Institution and the New University of Ulster. Serves on the editorial committee of *Fortnight* magazine and is joint-editor of *The Honest Ulsterman.* His collection of poems, *Breakfast in a Bright Room,* was published in 1983. *Images of Belfast,* with photographs by Bill Kirk, appeared in the same year. He has also edited *All Shy Wildness,* 1984, an anthology of Irish animal poetry.

PATRICK KAVANAGH

b. 1904 in Co. Monaghan, son of a country shoemaker. Left school at thirteen and worked on the land. Entered the Dublin literary world in the 1930s. His main collections of poems are *Ploughman and Other Poems,* 1936, *The Great Hunger,* 1942, *A Soul for Sale,* 1947, *Come Dance with Kitty Stobling,* 1960, *Collected Poems,* 1964, and *Complete Poems,* 1972. Edited *Kavanagh's Weekly,* which ran for thirteen issues between April and July, 1952. His autobiographical novel, *Tarry Flynn,* was published in 1948 and his *Collected Pruse* in 1967. Died 1967.

C. S. LEWIS

b. 1898 in Belfast. Educated at Malvern College and University College, Oxford. Served with the Somerset Light Infantry in the First World War. Fellow of Magdalen College, Oxford, then Professor of Medieval and Renaissance English at Cambridge. Among his critical and religious writings are *The Allegory of Love,* 1936, *The Problem of Pain,* 1940, *The Screwtape Letters,* 1942, *Beyond Personality: the Christian Idea of God,* 1944, *Studies in Words,* 1960, and *The Discarded Image,* 1964. Author of the 'Narnia' books for children. Died 1963.

MICHAEL LONGLEY

b. 1939 in Belfast. Educated at the Royal Belfast Academical Institution and Trinity College, Dublin, where he read classics. Taught for some years in Dublin, London and Belfast, then joined the Arts Council of Northern Ireland, where he is at present Combined Arts Director. His collections of poems are *No Continuing City,* 1969, *An Exploded View,* 1973, *Man Lying on a Wall,* 1976, *The Echo Gate,* 1979, *Selected Poems,* 1981, and *Poems 1963–1983,* 1985.

SAM McAUGHTRY

b. 1921 in Belfast. Joined RAF in 1940 as aircraft rigger and later became flying officer. Worked in London after war, then entered the Ministry of Agriculture in Belfast, 1947. Retired in 1980 to become a full-time writer, journalist and broadcaster. His books include *The Sinking of the Kenbane Head*, 1977, *Play It Again, Sam*, 1978, *Blind Spot and Other Stories*, 1979, *Belfast No. 1*, 1981, and *McAughtry's War*, 1985.

FLORENCE MARY McDOWELL

b. 1888 in Doagh, Co. Antrim. Spent all her working life as a teacher in Cogry Mills National School (later known as Cogry Memorial Public Elementary School, then Kilbride Central Primary School). She was in her seventies when she began work on *Other Days Around Me*, published in 1966. Died in Doagh in 1977. *Roses and Rainbows* was published posthumously in 1986.

CHARLES McGLINCHEY

b. 1861 in Co. Donegal. Weaver and tailor on the Inishowen Peninsula. His memories were written down by a local schoolmaster, Patrick Kavanagh, in the late 1940s and early 1950s. Kavanagh's manuscript, edited and introduced by Brian Friel, was published under the title *The Last of the Name* in 1986. McGlinchey died in 1954.

LOUIS MacNEICE

b. 1907 in Belfast. Father became Rector of St Nicholas's Church, Carrickfergus in 1908. Mother died of tuberculosis in 1914. Educated at Sherborne Preparatory School, Marlborough College and Merton College, Oxford. First book of poems appeared in 1929. Joined BBC as scriptwriter and producer in 1941. Published works include poetry, radio plays, translations and criticism. *Collected Poems* appeared in 1966. Reprinted a number of times, most recently in 1986. Died 1963.

TOMÁS Ó CANAINN

b.1930 in Derry. Educated at the Christian Brothers School and St Columb's College, Derry, Queen's University, Belfast, and Liverpool University. Lecturer in electrical engineering at University College, Cork. Member of Irish traditional music trio Na Filí. Has lectured on music, taught the uilleann pipes and worked as a radio presenter with RTE. His *Traditional Music in Ireland* was published in 1978.

FORREST REID

b. 1875 in Belfast. Educated at the Royal Belfast Academical Institution and Christ's College, Cambridge. His many novels include *The Kingdom of Twilight*, 1904, *Following Darkness*, 1912, *Uncle Stephen*, 1931, *The Retreat*, 1936, *Peter Waring*, 1937, and *Young Tom*, 1944. Also published *Illustrators of the Sixties*, 1928, as well as critical studies of W.B. Yeats and Walter de la Mare. *Private Road*, 1940, was a sequel to *Apostate*, 1926. Died 1947.

PATRICK SHEA
b. 1908 in Co. Westmeath, son of a member of the Royal Irish Constabulary. Spent his childhood in Athlone, Rathfriland, Newry and other places. Joined the Northern Ireland Civil Service and became one of only two Catholics who attained the rank of Permanent Secretary. Died 1986.

BIBLIOGRAPHY

Bell, Sam Hanna. *Erin's Orange Lily,* London, Dennis Dobson, 1956

Boyd, John. *Out of My Class,* Belfast, Blackstaff Press, 1985

Buchanan, George. *Green Seacoast,* London, Gaberbocchus, 1959
  Morning Papers, London, Gaberbocchus, 1965

Bullock, Shan F. *After Sixty Years,* London, Sampson, Low and
  Marston, 1931

Carleton, William. *The Autobiography of William Carleton,* London,
  MacGibbon & Kee, 1968 (first published 1896)

Devlin, Bernadette. *The Price of My Soul,* London, Pan Books, 1969 (first
  published 1969)

Devlin, Polly. *All of Us There,* London, Pan Books, 1984 (first
  published 1983)

Greacen, Robert. *Even Without Irene,* Dublin, Dolmen Press, 1969

Harbinson, Robert. *No Surrender,* London, Faber & Faber, 1966 (first
  published 1960)

Ireland, Denis. *From the Irish Shore,* London, Rich & Cowan, 1936
  Statues Round the City Hall, London, Cresset Press, 1939

Johnstone, Robert. *Images of Belfast,* Belfast, Blackstaff Press, 1983

Kavanagh, Patrick. *The Green Fool,* London, Martin Brian &
  O'Keeffe, 1971 (first published 1938)

Lewis, C.S. *Surprised by Joy,* London, Fontana Books, 1966 (first
  published 1955)

Longley, Michael. 'Tu'penny Stung', *Poetry Review,* vol. 74, no. 4, 1985

McAughtry, Sam. *The Sinking of the Kenbane Head,* Belfast,
  Blackstaff Press, 1977

McDowell, Florence Mary. *Other Days Around Me,* Belfast,
  Blackstaff Press, 1972 (first published 1966)
  Roses and Rainbows, Belfast, Blackstaff Press, 1972

McGlinchey, Charles. *The Last of the Name,* Belfast,
  Blackstaff Press, 1986

MacNeice, Louis. *The Strings are False,* London, Faber & Faber,
  1982 (first published 1965)

Ó Canainn, Tomás. *Home to Derry,* Belfast, Appletree Press, 1986

Reid, Forrest. *Apostate,* London, Constable & Co., 1926

Shea, Patrick. *Voices and the Sound of Drums,* Belfast,
  Blackstaff Press, 1981

ACKNOWLEDGEMENTS

Grateful acknowledgement is made to:

The Appletree Press for permission to quote from *Home to Derry* by Tomás Ó Canainn;

Sam Hanna Bell for permission to quote from *Erin's Orange Lily*;

John Boyd for permission to quote from *Out of My Class*;

George Buchanan for permission to quote from *Green Seacoast* and *Morning Papers*;

Campbell Thomson & McLaughlin Ltd for permission to quote from *Other Days Around Me* and *Roses and Rainbows* by Florence Mary McDowell;

William Collins plc for permission to quote from *Surprised by Joy* by C.S. Lewis;

André Deutsch Ltd and Alfred A. Knopf for permission to quote from *The Price of My Soul* (1969) by Bernadette Devlin;

Robert Greacen for permission to quote from *Even Without Irene*;

Robert Harbinson for permission to quote from *No Surrender*;

David Higham Associates Ltd for permission to quote from *The Strings are False* by Louis MacNeice;

H.M. Ireland for permission to quote from *From the Irish Shore* and *Statues Round the City Hall* by Denis Ireland;

John Johnson Ltd on behalf of the Forrest Reid Estate for permission to quote from *Apostate* by Forrest Reid;

Robert Johnstone for permission to quote from *Images of Belfast*;

Des Kavanagh for permission to quote from *The Last of the Name* by Charles McGlinchey;

Katherine B. Kavanagh, c/o Peter Fallon, 19 Oakdown Road, Dublin 14, for permission to quote from *The Green Fool* by Patrick Kavanagh;

Michael Longley for permission to quote from 'Tu'penny Stung';

Sam McAughtry for permission to quote from *The Sinking of the Kenbane Head*;

Eithne Shea for permission to quote from *Voices and the Sound of Drums* by Patrick Shea;

Weidenfeld & Nicolson Ltd for permission to quote from *All of Us There* by Polly Devlin.

The publishers have made every effort to trace and acknowledge copyright holders. We apologise for any omissions in the above list and we will welcome additions or amendments to it for inclusion in any reprint edition.